Race Relations in America

Recent Titles in Contemporary Debates

RACE RELATIONS IN AMERICA

❖

Examining the Facts

Nikki Khanna and Noriko Matsumoto

Contemporary Debates

An Imprint of ABC-CLIO, LLC
Santa Barbara, California • Denver, Colorado

Library of Congress Cataloging-in-Publication Data

Names: Khanna, Nikki, 1974- author. | Matsumoto, Noriko, 1968- author.
Title: Race relations in America : examining the facts / Nikki Khanna, and
    Noriko Matsumoto.
Description: Santa Barbara, California : ABC-CLIO, An Imprint of ABC-CLIO,
    LLC, [2021] | Series: Contemporary debates | Includes bibliographical
    references and index.
Identifiers: LCCN 2020047767 (print) | LCCN 2020047768 (ebook) | ISBN
    9781440874000 (hardcover) | ISBN 9781440874017 (ebook)
Subjects: LCSH: United States—Race relations. | Racism—United States. |
    Minorities—United States—Social conditions.
Classification: LCC E184.A1 K4347 2021 (print) | LCC E184.A1 (ebook) |
    DDC 305.800973—dc23
LC record available at https://lccn.loc.gov/2020047767
LC ebook record available at https://lccn.loc.gov/2020047768

ISBN: 978-1-4408-7400-0 (print)
       978-1-4408-7401-7 (ebook)

25   24   23   22   21   1   2   3   4   5

This book is also available as an eBook.

ABC-CLIO
An Imprint of ABC-CLIO, LLC

ABC-CLIO, LLC
147 Castilian Drive
Santa Barbara, California 93117
www.abc-clio.com

This book is printed on acid-free paper ∞

Manufactured in the United States of America

Contents

How to Use This Book

Race Relations in America: Examining the Facts is part of ABC-CLIO's Contemporary Debates reference series. Each title in this series, which is intended for use by high school and undergraduate students as well as members of the general public, examines the veracity of controversial claims or beliefs surrounding a major political/cultural issue in the United States. The purpose of this series is to give readers a clear and unbiased understanding of current issues by informing them about falsehoods, half-truths, and misconceptions—and confirming the factual validity of other assertions—that have gained traction in America's political and cultural discourse. Ultimately, this series has been crafted to give readers the tools for a fuller understanding of controversial issues, policies, and laws that occupy center stage in American life and politics.

Each volume in this series identifies 30–40 questions swirling about the larger topic under discussion. These questions are examined in individualized entries, which are in turn arranged in broad subject chapters that cover certain aspects of the issue being examined, for example, history of concern about the issue, potential economic or social impact, or findings of latest scholarly research.

Each chapter features 2–10 individual entries. Each entry begins by stating an important and/or well-known question about the issue being studied—for example, "Are black people naturally better athletes than other racial groups?" and "Does racial bias negatively affect the health of Americans of color?"

The entry then provides a concise and objective one- or two-paragraph **Answer** to the featured question, followed by a more comprehensive, detailed explanation of **The Facts**. This latter portion of each entry uses quantifiable, evidence-based information from respected sources to fully address each question and provide readers with the information they need to be informed citizens. Importantly, entries will also acknowledge instances in which conflicting or incomplete data exists or legal judgments are contradictory. Finally, each entry concludes with a **Further Reading** section, providing users with information on other important and/or influential resources.

The ultimate purpose of every book in the Contemporary Debates series is to reject "false equivalence," in which demonstrably false beliefs or statements are given the same exposure and credence as the facts; to puncture myths that diminish our understanding of important policies and positions; to provide needed context for misleading statements and claims; and to confirm the factual accuracy of other assertions. In other words, volumes in this series are being crafted to clear the air surrounding some of the most contentious and misunderstood issues or our time—not just add another layer of obfuscation and uncertainty to the debate.

Preface

We live in racial smog. This is a world of racial smog. We can't help but breathe that smog. Everybody breathes it. But what's nice is that you can recognize that you are breathing that smog, and that's the first step.

—Alan Goodman, biological anthropologist

The United States of America is a relatively young nation, though one that has been beset with racial strife from its inception. As Europeans descended upon its shores in search of new lands, new beginnings, and new opportunities, they engaged in brutal conflict with Indigenous peoples already inhabiting those lands; they exploited Black labor for nearly 250 years of its history, building the nation's wealth as well as their personal fortunes on the backs of Africans, their descendants, and other people of color; and, as holders of power, they fashioned a society that, even in the twenty-first century, remains defined by systemic racism and racial inequality.

Many Americans are unaware of much of this nation's racial history and its lasting effect on contemporary race relations. Students typically learn about slavery, Jim Crow segregation, and the triumphs of the civil rights movement. However, schools tend to downplay many of the details, as well as other aspects of America's racist past, leaving many Americans ignorant to the nation's history of systemic violence and exclusion of people of color from many facets of American life. For example, students learn of the virtues of the Founding Fathers, such as Thomas Jefferson, who famously wrote that "All Men Are Created Equal" in the Declaration of Independence; they are far less likely to learn that at the time he penned these words, Jefferson was profiting handsomely from the enslavement of hundreds of people on his Virginia plantation.

Many learn about European conflict with Native Americans over land, but they often know few details, if any, about state- and federal-sponsored violence toward Indigenous people, the government sterilization of Indigenous women, or the decades-long effort by the federal government to forcibly assimilate their children. Many Americans are educated about the Civil War and the abolishment of slavery but they typically learn little about Black codes pressed into law in Southern states soon after the war ended that effectively denied newly freed Black people their basic constitutional rights (e.g., to vote, bear arms, own property, buy and lease land, and more). Even fewer Americans learn that because of these Black codes and similar restrictive laws, Black people were frequently arrested and imprisoned in the Jim Crow era for trivial offenses—such as for being unemployed, lacking a permanent residence, swearing, disrespecting a white employer, or keeping a "disorderly house" (offenses that were specifically criminalized for Black people). As prisoners, many were then forced to labor for planters and industrialists through a system of convict leasing; consequently, thousands of Black men found themselves essentially re-enslaved in the post-Civil War era and well into the 1930s.

Many Americans know something about lynching, but rarely do they learn that lynching was widely used by whites in the nineteenth and twentieth centuries as a tool of domestic terrorism to keep newly freed African Americans "in their place." Just as in the case for whites, Blacks were lynched for serious offenses such as alleged rape or murder, but many Americans are wholly unaware that Black people were also lynched for perceived transgressions of Jim Crow norms (e.g., for acting insolent or "uppity" to a white person or, if male, for engaging in a relationship or even socializing with a white woman). For example, in 1955, Emmett Till, a 14-year-old African American boy, was brutally beaten and murdered in Mississippi by two white men for allegedly whistling at a white woman. His "offense" left him disfigured and completely unrecognizable and, even though only a child, he and his family paid an unbearable price—his life. Thousands of other Black men and women met similar fates for trivial transgressions, and their deaths, often public spectacles, were flaunted as dire warnings to other Black people who might dare violate the perceived racial order of the era.

Many learn about race riots but not about race massacres. For example, many people are aware of the riots of the 1960s and the urban destruction associated with some of the Black Lives Matter protests in the twenty-first century. However, they often know little, if anything, about the massacres of people of color in the late nineteenth and early twentieth centuries that took place in Los Angeles, California (1871); Rock Springs, Wyoming (1885); Pine Ridge Indian Reservation, South Dakota (1890); East St. Louis, Illinois (1917); Chicago, Illinois (1919); Elaine, Arkansas (1919); Rosewood, Florida (1923); and other cities and towns across the nation. For instance, most Americans are unaware that white mobs massacred hundreds of Black Americans in Elaine, Arkansas in 1919 or that in Rosewood, Florida in 1923, whites killed 27 to 150 Black residents and incinerated every structure in the Black town (regarding the latter, no resident returned and the town ceased to exist). Most people also usually do not know that in Tulsa, Oklahoma in 1921, white mobs descended upon the wealthy Black district (then unofficially dubbed the "Black Wall Street"), burned all 35 city blocks to the ground, looted their homes, and killed dozens of Black people while permanently driving out hundreds more. Americans rarely learn that this was the first time in history that an American city was bombed from the air as white citizens dropped explosives from airplanes onto Black-owned homes and businesses.

Many Americans can recount stories of racially segregated lunch counters, buses, and schools in the Jim Crow South but they are often unaware of restrictive covenants and racial zoning laws that formally segregated American cities both within and beyond the South. They seldom learn of the thousands of towns, suburbs, and counties across the nation (most often outside Southern states) that explicitly barred people of color, especially African Americans, from residing within their limits, nor do they learn of the intimidation and violence widely used in the twentieth century to maintain white-only communities. Some Americans are also aware of the efforts by the U.S. government to make housing loans relatively affordable to working-class Americans after World War II—which, for the first time in U.S. history, made the dream of owning a home a reality for millions of families. However, many are unfamiliar with the decades-long practice by this same government to systematically deny these loans to people of color—simply because they were not white—consequently depriving them of a key instrument of wealth accumulation granted to their white counterparts. White families built equity over time while Black families were shut out of the housing market; the chilling effect of this government policy remains visible today and can be observed in the present-day disparity in wealth between Black and white Americans.

Because of these gaps in American education and collective memory, contemporary race relations remain baffling to some. Some Americans, no doubt frustrated with persistent interracial conflict in the United States, wonder, "Will we ever move beyond our racial problems and get along?" or they question why some racial groups cannot simply "get over the past" and "move on." Additionally, present-day social class disparities between racial groups are often rationalized not as a consequence of historical circumstance and centuries of systemic oppression but rather as the result of inherent racial and cultural differences. In other words, if a racial group is not doing well economically in twenty-first-century America, it must be their own fault (e.g., they must be intellectually challenged or lazy). Widespread ignorance of the nation's history and the social forces that have long shaped today's socioeconomic hierarchy have left many bereft of context, hampering the ability of many Americans to make sense of the racial inequality that they see around them.

Moreover, present-day racism as an explanatory factor of contemporary inequality in the United States is often downplayed, ignored, or simply denied altogether. In 2020, when asked by a reporter about the existence of systemic racism in the United States, then President Donald Trump flatly remarked, "I don't believe that." He is certainly not alone. Skepticism, or even disbelief, in systemic racism by politicians, pundits, and laymen alike is hardly surprising given that systemic racism is difficult to detect with the naked eye. If a person of color is denied a small business loan or passed over for a job, how would they know whether it was because of racism or something else? If living with hypertension or dying of lung cancer, how many Black people would consider systemic racism to be a contributing factor? If led to believe that "crime is largely a Black problem," how many Americans would recognize that systemic racism in the media and the criminal justice system contributed to that myth? A growing number of empirical studies, however, confirm that systemic racism in the United States is very real and that it lives and thrives across many American social institutions, including in housing, education, work, health care, banking, criminal justice, and the media, among others. Collectively, this research provides an unobstructed view into the different opportunities afforded to white Americans as compared to Americans of color—and the ways in which those differences shape how people of different races experience life in the United States.

This book provides historical context and draws on the growing body of scholarly research to answer frequently asked questions regarding race in the United States. In doing so, it addresses commonly held myths about the concept of race itself, power and privilege in American society, systemic racism, crime and criminal justice, social policy, immigration, and the belief in a post-racial America. America is a multiracial society, and race relations in America are complex. Rather than rely on one's own biases and limited personal experiences, attention to both historical circumstances and contemporary research provide an opportunity for Americans of all racial groups to take a step back to examine race in the United States with a more focused lens. That is the aim of this book.

1

❖❖❖

Race: Definitions and Realities

In 2018, *National Geographic* featured a story about Marcia and Millie Biggs, fraternal twins born in Birmingham, England, in 2006. From their birth, their parents noticed that their daughters looked very different from each other and, as they grew, those differences became even more evident: Marcia has light skin, blue eyes, and blondish-brown hair and favors her English-born white mother, and Millie has brown skin, brown eyes, and black hair, just like her Jamaican father. Their mother recalled the public's interest in the girls' very visible physical differences and countless questions from curious strangers when pushing them in their stroller:

"Are they twins?"
"Yes."
"But one's white, and one's Black."

People were taken aback, though intrigued. Proud of their unique differences, their mother often refers to them as her "one in a million" miracle. However, geneticists such as Alicia Martin of the Broad Institute say that it is not uncommon for interracial couples to birth children, even fraternal twins, who each favor one parent more than the other. In fact, a growing number of "Black and white twins" have attracted media attention through the years—for example, Cheryl and Karen Grant, born in 1983; Lucy and Maria Aylmer, 1997; Lauren and Hayleigh Durrant, 2001;

Kian and Remee Hodgson, 2005; Alicia and Jasmin Singl, 2006; Layton and Kaydon Wood, 2006; Orlando and Natalie Balasco, 2008; Ryan and Leo Grant, 2008; and Kalani and Jarani Dean, 2016.

Marcia and Millie and other Black and white twins are quite remarkable for how different they look, but more importantly, their stories raise questions about the ways in which people think about race: What is race? And what does it mean to say someone is Black or white—or even Asian or Native American? Though each set of twins shares the same biological parents and are full siblings, people likely perceive them very differently. If unaware of their familial ties, onlookers are likely to look at their different skin colors and conclude that they belong to different racial groups; hence, they may assume they are biologically different from each other. They may even ascribe stereotypes to each twin based on their presumed race, such as those regarding intellect, work ethic, athleticism, and more. Though most Americans see racial groups as biologically distinct categories and often attach a litany of stereotypes to each, Black and white twins upend these assumptions.

This introductory chapter unpacks frequently asked questions regarding the concept of race. Question 1 asks, "Is race biological?" and it specifically examines whether racial groups are biologically different from one another. People often assume that people of different races are genetically different from one another, but are they? Question 2 asks, "Is race a social concept?" Social scientists argue that race is not biological, but instead it is a man-made concept—a social construct—something created by society and people. But what does this mean? Included in this entry are concrete historical and present-day examples illustrating how race is socially constructed.

The final two questions examine persistent biological beliefs about race and perceived differences between racial groups: "Are Black people naturally better athletes than other racial groups?" (Question 3), and "Are racial disparities in health evidence that race is biological?" (Question 4). Data reveal that there are quantifiable differences between racial groups, and these entries examine whether this suggests that, indeed, race is biological.

Taken together, the questions in this chapter draw on a growing body of research by geneticists, biologists, epidemiologists, physiologists, anthropologists, historians, and social scientists to address widely held beliefs regarding the concept of race. Like Black and white twins, such as Marcia and Millie Biggs, who call into question the ways in which people think about race, a growing body of research challenges conventional beliefs about race.

Q1. IS RACE BIOLOGICAL?

Answer: According to decades of scientific evidence, no. Though some people assume that racial groups are biologically different from each other (in other words, that race is biological), this belief is false and, according to most scientists, a widely discredited myth. The vast majority of those who study human variation, including evolutionary biologists and geneticists, agree that biological races do not exist among humans and that humans, regardless of their racial classification, are remarkably similar in terms of their genetics.

The Facts: A widely held belief in Western societies (and perhaps elsewhere) is that racial categories represent natural biological divisions in the human population, though most scientists today agree that there is no biological basis to race. Many Americans believe that there are several subcategories of the human species (e.g., white, Black, Asian, and Native American); however, decades of anthropological, biological, and genetic evidence indicate otherwise.

In the 1970s, Harvard geneticist and evolutionary biologist Richard Lewontin found that there were practically no genetic differences between racial groups when he compared blood groups and protein genes. When describing genes, he noted the surprising similarities across races: "For almost every gene we know, either everybody in the world has the same form of the gene, in which case all human beings are the same, or if there's variation, the frequencies of the different variants are the same relatively speaking, close to the same, in Africans, Asians, North Americans, Austro-Asians, and so on" (Lewontin 2003).

The similarity of the human species was further confirmed in work in the late 1990s and early 2000s through the Human Genome Project (HGP), an international research program dedicated to the mapping of the human genome (also understood as the mapping of the complete set of DNA, including all genes, in humans). The HGP revealed that, genetically speaking, humans are nearly identical to each other. Regardless of one's so-called race or ancestry, humans share 99.9 percent of their DNA and have only a 0.1 percent difference, on average, from one person to the next. This 0.1 percent difference is what makes humans genetically unique from each other, though because this variation is remarkably small, it is not enough to sort the species into meaningful subgroups.

Furthermore, the small genetic variation observed in humans is not racially distributed. People belonging to different so-called racial groups may be more genetically alike than they are to others of the same race.

For instance, in a comparison of the full genomes of two American scientists of European ancestry, James Watson and Craig Venter, and that of Korean scientist Seong-Jin Kim, researchers found fewer genetic variations between Venter and Kim than between Venter and Watson (Gannon 2016). According to the American Anthropological Association, evidence indicates that most human genetic variation, about 94 percent (of the 0.1 percent genetic variation among humans), occurs *within* any purported racial group and that "there is greater variation within 'racial' groups than between them" (American Anthropological Association 1998). In other words, racial groups are more genetically similar than they are different. This is precisely because most human genetic variation has nothing to do with "race."

Microbiologist and bioethicist Pilar Ossorio further points out that it is impossible to locate any genetic markers "that are in everybody of a particular race and in nobody of some other race" (Ossorio 2003). There are no genes (or gene variants) unique to whites or Blacks or Asians—even genes that affect the color of one's skin, hair texture, or facial features, which are the visible phenotypic (or physical) traits often associated with race. In fact, similar traits can be found in different corners of the world and often transcend racial groups: for instance, dark skin can be found in Africa, Australia, and South Asia; tightly curled hair can be found in Africa, the Middle East, and southern India; slim noses can be found in Europe, Asia, and parts of Africa; and epicanthic eye folds can be found among East Asians, Indigenous peoples in the Americas, the Nilote and San of Africa, and some eastern European groups (e.g., Russians, Poles, Albanians, and Hungarians). Though people may make generalizations about the physical characteristics associated with particular racial groups, a closer look reveals a more complex picture.

Moreover, even if these outward physical traits *did* follow strict racial lines, this still would not be evidence that racial groups are biologically different from each other because these traits are genetically superficial. Scholar and social justice advocate Dorothy Roberts notes that genes contributing to the physical traits often associated with race, such as skin color, "represent a minute and relatively insignificant fraction" of all genes (Roberts 2011, 52). Two people, one dark and one light, may give the impression of having significant genetic differences because of their outwardly different appearances, yet their genetic differences are negligible when considering the entirety of human genome. For example, only a handful of our genes code for skin color. Though there are likely more skin color–influencing genes to be discovered as scientists continue to unravel the mysteries of our DNA, they point to 2 key gene variants

(SLC24A5 and MFSD12) that influence how our cells produce melanin (Zimmer 2017)—2 of more than 20,000 genes that make up the human genome. As a related example, two people, one with brown eyes and the other with blue, have some genetic differences; however, people do not claim that they belong to different biological groups. As with skin color, eye color is inherited and genetic, and also like skin color, genes affecting eye color represent a very small proportion of one's DNA.

As a species, humans have remarkably similar biology, likely for a few reasons. First, scientists today generally agree that the origin of modern humans can be traced to a single location—the continent of Africa, though there is debate over the precise location (whether Eastern or Southern Africa) (Briggs 2019). This theory is supported by a wealth of fossil evidence and by studies of mitochondrial DNA that can be traced to a common ancestor in Africa. According to evolutionary biologist Stephen Jay Gould, "We're all Africans . . . because that's where the species started. And that's pretty clear. I don't think there's much [scientific] debate about that" (Gould 2003). Evidence supports this "Out of Africa" hypothesis, as nearly all genetic studies reveal greater diversity in Africa than anywhere else in the world, suggesting that humans spent the majority of their time evolving there long before migrating to other continents (Campbell and Tishkoff 2010). In fact, evolutionary biologist Joseph Graves Jr. notes that most human genetic variability can be found among sub-Saharan Africans—about 93 percent—and he posits that "if there were a catastrophe which destroyed the rest of the world's population, 93% of the genetic variability in the world would still be present in Sub-Saharan Africans" (Graves 2003).

Studies also show that most genetic variation in non-African populations, such as those in Europe and Asia, are merely a "subset" of the variation found in African populations, further suggesting that our ancestors evolved in Africa first (Roberts 2011, 52). Gene variants for light skin commonly found in Europe and Asia, for instance, likely came from Africa and were carried from the continent by migrants out of Africa. Even today, the gene variant for light skin exists in parts of East Africa, such as in Tanzania (Zimmer 2017).

Second, humans may be genetically similar to each other because they are a relatively young species—likely less than 200,000 years old by most estimates—a mere blink of the eye in evolutionary terms. According to evolutionary biologist Stephen Jay Gould:

> There just hasn't been enough time for the development of much genetic variation except that which regulates some very superficial

features like skin color and hair form. For once the old cliché is true: under the skin, we are effectively the same. And we get fooled because some of the visual differences are quite noticeable. (Gould 2003)

Given that humans are very young, there has been comparatively less time for the development of genetic variability as compared to other species and hence less time to develop into subgroups with meaningful biological differences. For instance, older species, such as penguins and fruit flies, show far greater variability as compared to humans—two times and ten times, respectively. Even chimpanzees, our closest living relatives, are much older than humans; they have been around at least several million years, and according to one source, "There's more genetic diversity within a group of chimps on a single hillside in Gomba than in the entire human species" (California Newsreel 2003).

Third, and perhaps most important, humans may be biologically very similar to each other because different populations have shared genes throughout human history. Humans are, by nature, migratory and have a long history of movement around the globe. Biological anthropologist Alan Goodman proposes that "[it] might be useful to think of ancient peoples as nearly always being in motion" (Goodman 2001, 36), and as they moved and migrated, they mated and shared genes. As such, there are no pure races but, rather, people who may be best described as "mongrels"; this is because human populations have bred and crossbred for thousands of generations. Each human is the amalgamation of many groups.

In 2004, Francis Collins, then head of the National Human Genome Research Institute, called race a "flawed" and "weak" concept (Howard 2016), and he, along with many others, has called for a move beyond the problematic term. Given that race is not biological, some scientists have suggested that we replace the term *race* with *population* or *cline*, which may more accurately describe human variability. According to Graves,

The best way to understand the genetic differences that we find in human populations is that populations differ by distance. And so populations that are closer to each other geographically are more likely to share common gene variants, whereas populations that are further apart are going to share fewer genes. Human populations differ in gene frequencies relative to their geographic location. And it's a continuous change from one group to another. (Graves 2003)

Hence, it is incorrect to assume that human genetic variation can be clustered into a handful of discrete types or "races"; rather, it is gradual and perhaps better conceptualized as a gradient in which genetic variation is distributed in a continuous fashion from one population to the next (Jorde and Wooding 2004). For instance, skin color varies gradually around the globe from very dark people in the tropics to those with very light skin in places such as Scandinavia—though there exists a great deal of variation in between.

Regardless of the growing body of scientific data that show that race is not biological and despite the calls of many anthropologists, sociologists, geneticists, and biologists to abandon the term (or at the very least replace it with another), the belief that race is biological is stubborn and persistent. It is rooted in Western civilization and culture and shows little sign of disappearing anytime soon, as there appears to be disconnect between laymen views of race and scientific evidence. Robert Wald Sussman, a physical anthropologist and the author of *The Myth of Race: The Troubling Persistence of an Unscientific Idea*, writes that despite modern scientific views regarding human variation, "It seems that the belief in human races . . . is so embedded in our culture and has been an integral part of our worldview for so long that many of us assume that it just must be true" (Sussman 2014). To complicate the issue, there are some experts who still hold to the notion that race is biological, though they remain in the minority. One notable example is journalist Nicholas Wade, the author of *A Troublesome Inheritance*, who argued in 2014 that there are indeed genetic differences among racial groups. However, his book was heavily criticized and denounced by more than 140 biologists and geneticists, who, in an open letter to the *New York Times*, charged him with "misappropriation" of genetic research ("Letters" 2014).

Alan Goodman believes that to move away from the concept of race, human thinking about race requires a dramatic paradigm shift: "For me, it's like seeing what it must have been like to understand that the world isn't flat. The world looks flat to our eyes. And perhaps I can invite you to a mountaintop or to a plain, and you can look out the window at the horizon, and see, 'Oh, what I thought was flat I can see a curve in now'" (Goodman 2003). Race is not biological, though like the once-held belief of a flat Earth, our eyes certainly deceive us.

FURTHER READING

American Anthropological Association. 1998. "American Anthropological Association Statement on 'Race.'" Retrieved on February 18, 2019, at https://www.americananthro.org/ConnectWithAAA/Content.aspx ?ItemNumber=2583.

Briggs, Helen. 2019. "Origin of Modern Humans 'Traced to Botswana.'"
    BBC News, October 28.
California Newsreel. 2003. "Race: The Power of an Illusion: Background
    Readings: Human Diversity: Go Deeper." PBS. Retrieved on October
    23, 2020, at https://www.pbs.org/race/000_About/002_04-background
    -01-11.htm.
Campbell, Michael C., and Sarah A. Tishkoff. 2010. "The Evolution of
    Human Genetic and Phenotypic Variation in Africa." *Current Biology*
    20(4): 166–173.
Gannon, Megan. 2016. "Race Is a Social Construct, Scientists Argue."
    Scientific American. Retrieved on February 18, 2019, at https://www
    .scientificamerican.com/article/race-is-a-social-construct-scientists
    -argue/.
Goodman, Alan H. 2001. "Biological Diversity and Cultural Diversity:
    From Race to Radical Bioculturalism." Pp. 43–59 in *Cultural Diversity
    in the United States: A Critical Reader*, edited by Ida Susser and Thomas
    C. Patterson. New York: Blackwell.
Goodman, Alan H. 2003. "Race: The Power of an Illusion: Background
    Readings: Interview with Alan Goodman." California Newsreel.
    PBS. Retrieved on October 23, 2020, at https://www.pbs.org/race/000
    _About/002_04-background-01-07.htm.
Gould, Stephen Jay. 2003. "Race: The Power of an Illusion: Background
    Readings: Interview with Stephen Jay Gould." California Newsreel.
    PBS. Retrieved on October 23, 2020, at https://www.pbs.org/race/000
    _About/002_04-background-01-09.htm.
Graves, Joseph, Jr. 2003. "Race: The Power of an Illusion: Background
    Readings: Interview with Joseph Graves, Jr." California Newsreel.
    PBS. Retrieved on October 23, 2020, at https://www.pbs.org/race/000
    _About/002_04-background-01-06.htm.
Howard, Jacqueline. 2016. "What Scientists Mean When They Say
    'Race' Is Not Genetic." HuffPost. Retrieved on February 18, 2019,
    at   https://www.huffingtonpost.com/entry/race-is-not-biological_us
    _56b8db83e4b04f9b57da89ed.
Jorde, Lynn B., and Stephen P. Wooding. 2004. "Genetic Variation,
    Classification and 'Race.'" *Nature Genetics* 36(11): s28–33.
"Letters: 'A Troublesome Inheritance.'" 2014. *New York Times.* Retrieved
    on February 18, 2019, at https://www.nytimes.com/2014/08/10/books
    /review/letters-a-troublesome-inheritance.html?_r=0.
Lewontin, Richard. 2003. "Race: The Power of an Illusion: Background
    Readings: Interview with Richard Lewontin." California Reel. PBS.

Retrieved on October 23, 2020, at http://www.pbs.org/race/000_About/002_04-background-01-04.htm.

Ossorio, Pilar. 2003. "Race: The Power of an Illusion: Background Readings: Interview with Pilar Ossorio." California Newsreel. PBS. Retrieved on October 23, 2020, at https://www.pbs.org/race/000_About/002_04-background-01-03.htm.

Roberts, Dorothy. 2011. *Fatal Invention: How Science, Politics, and Big Business Re-Create Race in the Twenty-First Century.* New York: The New Press.

Sussman, Robert Wald. 2014. "There Is No Such Thing as Race." *Newsweek.* Retrieved on February 18, 2019, at https://www.newsweek.com/there-no-such-thing-race-283123.

Zimmer, Carl. 2017. "Genes for Skin Color Rebut Dated Notions of Race, Researchers Say." *New York Times*, October 12. Retrieved on February 18, 2019, at https://www.nytimes.com/2017/10/12/science/skin-color-race.html.

Q2. IS RACE A SOCIAL CONCEPT?

Answer: Yes. Race is not biological but rather a social concept—one that is created and maintained by people, groups, and societies. The social nature of race, for instance, is illustrated in its variability between nations and cultures, as well as in its fluidity over time.

The Facts: Race is commonly understood by many Americans as a "natural phenomenon" whose meaning is "fixed, as constant as a southern star" (Winant 1994, 13). In reality, however, race is a social construct; in short, it is a concept created and maintained by society. As such, race is flexible, as evidenced by its variability over place and time. For instance, racial categories (and even the concept of race itself) look remarkably different in different societies. Blackness, for example, has different meanings around the world. While Americans typically define *Blackness* as having African ancestry, the term *Black* in the United Kingdom has historically referred to anyone who is nonwhite—including those with African ancestry, as well as East Indians, Pakistanis, and other people of color (Zack 1993). In Brazil, *Blackness* is more narrowly defined; for example, having some degree of non-Black ancestry often means that one is not Black (a person may be classified in a number of other categories—none of which translate to Black) (Marger 2015). Nigerian-born novelist

Chimamanda Ngozi Adichie notes that when she was growing up, she never thought of herself as Black but rather in terms of religion, ethnicity, and nationality—as Christian, Catholic, Igbo, and Nigerian. She said, "I wasn't black until I came to America" (Reese 2018). Adichie's remarks suggest that Blackness has little, if any, meaning in Nigeria—and perhaps in Africa more broadly.

Brazil

A more in-depth comparison of the United States with Brazil further illustrates the socially constructed nature of race. Americans typically view race as based on ancestry, with humans divided into four or more discrete racial categories (e.g., white, Black, Asian, and Native American). In Brazil, however, race is not based on ancestry but on what a person looks like, and Brazilian categories are tied, literally speaking, to one's skin shade, hair texture, and facial features. Racial categories are carefully defined and based on even the most minute physical characteristics. Some racial categories in the United States, such as Black and white, are related to skin color, but not literally so, as they are in Brazil. Consider the following categories used by the people of Vila Reconcavo, Brazil, as reported by anthropologist Harry Hutchinson in the 1960s (Marger 2015, 431):

The *prêto* or *prêto retinto* (black) has black shiny skin, kinky, woolly hair, thick lips and a flat, broad nose.

The *cabra* (male) and *cabrocha* (female) are generally slightly lighter than the *prêto*, with hair growing somewhat longer, but still kinky and unmanageable, facial features somewhat less Negroid, although often with fairly thick lips and flat nose.

The *cabo verde* is slightly lighter than the *prêto*, but still very dark. The *cabo verde*, however, has long straight hair, and his facial features are apt to be very fine, with thin lips and a narrow straight nose. He is almost a "black white man."

The *escuro*, or simply "dark man," is darker than the usual run of mestiços, but the term is generally applied to a person who does not fit into one of the three types mentioned above. The escuro is almost a Negro with Caucasoid features.

The *mulato* is a category always divided into two types, the *mulato escuro* and *mulato claro* (dark and light mulattoes). The *mulato* has hair which grows perhaps to shoulder length, but which has a decided curl and even kink. . . . The *mulato's* facial features vary widely; thick lips with a narrow nose, or vice-versa.

The *sarará* . . . has very light skin, and hair which is reddish or blondish but kinky or curled. . . . His facial features are extremely varied, even more so than the mulato's.

The *moreno* . . . is light-skinned, but not white. He has dark hair, which is long and either wavy or curly. . . . His features are more Caucasoid than Negroid.

Brazilian categories are incredibly descriptive, though these are only the *major* categories according to Hutchinson; each can be further broken down into more detailed classifications (Marger 2015). Moreover, because race in Brazil centers on physical appearance rather than ancestry, as it is in the United States, family members—including full siblings—may be classified differently. This is an alien concept to most Americans given that full siblings are typically classified as the same race in the United States because they share the same ancestral lineage (Fish 2011).

Brazilians also employ many more categories than Americans. For example, one study found that when asked their race (or *cor*, "color"), Brazilians gave 134 different answers. Other studies have found even larger numbers, and the number of categories vary regionally, with fewer categories used in the southern region of Brazil than in other parts of the country (Fish 2011). The descriptions of racial categories also vary widely from region to region in Brazil, even community to community. Hence, categories found in the aforementioned town of Vila Reconcavo may greatly differ from those in other parts of the country, further revealing the socially constructed nature of race.

Moreover, racial divisions in Brazil are more porous than in the United States, making boundary crossing possible. A popular Brazilian saying, "Money whitens," for instance, suggests that wealth confers whiteness in Brazil. In other words, money (along with education or other indicators of social class) allows darker Brazilians to whiten or lighten their racial classification. As such, one's race can shift over their lifetime (such as with a change in social class), unlike in the United States where race is typically perceived as fixed. In Brazil, even a change in one's skin tone (perhaps because of tanning in summer months) can alter one's classification, given that Brazilian race categories literally describe skin color.

One's racial identity may also shift with context. According to anthropologist Livio Sansone, race can be quite fluid in Brazil: "[A Brazilian] can be *negro* (black) during Carnival and when playing or dancing samba, *escuro* (dark) for his work friends, *moreno* or *negão* (literally, big black man) with his drinking friends, *neguinho* (literally, literally little black man) for his girlfriend, *prêto* for the official statistics, and *pardo* in his birth certificate" (Sansone 2003; as cited in Marger 2015, 431).

The United States

American race categories, by contrast, look starkly different than those in Brazil. Americans conceptualize race as based on ancestry rather than physical appearance, utilize far fewer categories, and view race as stable. Comparing the two nations reveals that the categories of race and the concept of race itself can vary widely between societies, calling into question the presumption that race is natural and static. Furthermore, because conceptualizations of race vary between the two nations, one might be classified as one race in the United States but an entirely difference race in Brazil.

A closer look at the United States further illustrates how race has been socially constructed; in short, racial categories have changed dramatically over time. For instance, the federal government has collected information on the American population via the U.S. Census every decade since 1790, and the racial categories have changed *each* time a census has been taken (Wright 1993). These regular alterations suggest that these are not scientific categories but rather sociopolitical categories constructed by society at specific points in that society's history. For instance, the U.S. Census racially defined Asian Indians as "Hindu" from 1920 to 1940, even though this is a religious group not a racial classification and despite the fact that not all Indians are Hindu. They were then reclassified as "white" for three decades, only to be reclassified again in 1970 as "Asian" (Wright 1993).

Further, categories that once existed on the U.S. Census have long since vanished, including categories on the 1890 census, such as "mulatto" (someone who was between three-eighths and five-eighths Black), "quadroon" (one-fourth Black), and "octoroon" (one-eighth Black). These detailed categories were initially included to satisfy race scientists who were interested in proving the "physically, mentally, and morally degenerate" nature of mixed-race people and because white politicians wanted an accurate count of mixed-race people in the United States. Regarding the latter, they were particularly interested in knowing "whether the number of people blurring the line between the subordinated and the dominant races was increasing or decreasing, thriving or struggling, moving towards or away from whiteness" (Hochschild and Powell 2008, 69). By the next census, however, these categories were dropped altogether so as not to overburden census enumerators who went door-to-door collecting census data and because social scientists began to think that counting different types of mixed-race people was a "waste of time" after all (Hochschild and Powell 2008, 69). Thus, these fine-tuned racial classifications came and went, depending on the whims, prejudices, desires, and goals of men—specifically white men in positions of power. In each instance, these changes were socially constructed for the political purposes of the time.

Even today, federal race categories, like those found on the U.S. Census, are socially constructed and, hence, for many Americans, confusing and counterintuitive. For example, people of Middle Eastern descent are currently classified as white, though arguably their day-to-day experiences suggest that they are not generally perceived as such by other Americans. There has been a push by some Arab American organizations, including the Arab American Institute and others, to get a new nonwhite category added to the U.S. Census to better reflect their lived reality; however, this proposed change was rejected for the 2020 census (Gedeon 2019)—perhaps because their exclusion would deflate white population numbers. People with North African ancestry, such as Egyptians and Algerians, are also classified as white, though this is baffling to many given that they (or their ancestors) originated in Africa. Alaska Natives and Native Americans constitute their own racial group, though they likely originated in Asia, and highly diverse groups (such as Indians and Japanese) are lumped together into a singular Asian category (Wright 1993). Author Lawrence Wright described American race categories as "arbitrary, confused, and hopelessly intermingled" (1993, 54), largely because of the role that politics play in their construction. For current federal classifications of race, see table 2.1.

The absurdity of the concept of race in the United States is further underscored by how the boundaries of whiteness have changed over time. The definition of *whiteness* has shifted substantially over the years, illustrating that whiteness itself has a long history of fluidity. Jews, Southern and Eastern Europeans, and Irish, all of whom were regarded as nonwhite by native-born white Anglo-Saxon Protestants in the nineteenth century, eventually found themselves absorbed into the category. In the mid to late 1800s, for example, the Irish in the United States were described as chimpanzees, dogs, subhuman, and nonwhite. Even the English regarded them as such, often calling them the "blacks of Europe." In a letter to his wife, English novelist Charles Kingsley wrote about his trip to Ireland: "I am haunted by the human chimpanzees I saw along that hundred miles of horrible country. . . . To see white chimpanzees is dreadful; if they were black, one would not feel it so much, but their skins except where tanned

Table 2.1 Racial Classifications of the U.S. Census Bureau, 2020

White	A person having origins in any of the original peoples of Europe, the Middle East, or North Africa.
Black or African American	A person having origins in any of the Black racial groups of Africa.
American Indian or Alaska Native	A person having origins in any of the original peoples of North and South America (including Central America) and who maintains tribal affiliation or community attachment.
Asian	A person having origins in any of the original peoples of the Far East, Southeast Asia, or the Indian subcontinent, including, for example, Cambodia, China, India, Japan, Korea, Malaysia, Pakistan, the Philippine Islands, Thailand, and Vietnam.
Native Hawaiian or Other Pacific Islander	A person having origins in any of the original peoples of Hawaii, Guam, Samoa, or other Pacific Islands.

Source: U.S. Census Bureau, https://www.census.gov/topics/population/race/about.html

by exposure, are as white as ours" (Davis 2007). By "white chimpanzees," Kingsley was referring to the Irish, though, of course, today people of Irish ancestry are considered white, illustrating that whiteness itself (like race more generally) is nothing more than a social construct.

Moreover, in the United States, seemingly arbitrary "rules" have been used to sort people into racial categories. Historically, these rules were purposely created for the social and material benefit of whites. One example is the one-drop rule—a rule only found in the United States and one that only applied to those of African descent (Davis 1991). This rule was originally an informal societal guideline, but it was codified into law in varying forms during the Jim Crow era. According to the rule, anyone having any "drop" of Black/African ancestry or any Black ancestor in their family tree (no matter how far back) was simply classified as Black. This rule stood regardless of physical appearance; this meant having light skin, blond hair, or blue eyes (traits often associated with those of

European ancestry) did not preclude a Black classification. During slavery, the one-drop rule provided an economic benefit to white slave owners who, through the rape of their Black female slaves, produced children who would be classified as Black and hence could be enslaved. Given that slaves were property and had monetary value, slave owners increased their personal net worth through interracial rape on Southern plantations. The rule further functioned to reconcile white-appearing slaves on plantations. Some multiracial slaves looked white which was likely discomforting to some white people, but the one-drop rule, effectively defined them as Black; as such the racial order of the day remained intact. Moreover, during the Jim Crow era, the one-drop rule provided a clear line between Blacks and whites in the segregated South. Those with any Black ancestry were socially defined as Black and, as such, were often prohibited from intermarrying with whites, denied entry into schools and other public spaces designated for whites, denied the vote, and generally subjugated in all aspects of society, even if they had more white ancestry than Black. Thus, though the one-drop rule may appear arbitrary, it was not. It served an important function for whites—namely, to maintain white supremacy in a multiracial society.

The State of Virginia, for example, formally defined *Blackness* as anyone who had any "ascertainable" Black blood; other states determined Blackness by fractions of blood: 1/32 Black, 1/16 Black, 1/4 Black, or 1/2 Black. Because definitions of *Blackness* varied state to state, individuals could simply cross state lines to change their race from Black to white, further illustrating the arbitrariness of American racial categories (Valdez and Valdez 1998). Some interracial couples also found ways to circumvent one-drop laws so they could marry. The State of Georgia banned marriages between Blacks and whites during the Jim Crow era, so when Dr. Fred Palmer, a white man, wanted to marry Carolyn Simms, a Black woman, he injected himself with a pint of so-called Black blood. He then testified before Georgia authorities that he no longer had pure Caucasian blood, thus legalizing his marriage to Carolyn. Authorities allowed the couple to marry in 1935 (Johnson 2005).

In rare cases, white legislators even circumvented their own one-drop laws when it suited them. Sarah Rector, a Black child, became a multimillionaire at the age of 11 after oil was discovered on a plot of land in her name. At age 12, the Oklahoma legislature declared Sarah white because they deemed her too rich to be Black. According to the *Chicago Defender*, "The white people have become so alarmed at the enormous wealth of this young girl that they do not like such wealth belonging to a girl of Afro American blood." After the state declared her white in 1914, she was able to bypass Jim Crow laws that banned Black people from first-class train cars" (Eleksie 2018).

South Africa

Another example of the social construction of race lies in South Africa during the Apartheid era. Unlike the United States, South Africa had no comparable one-drop rule or law. A white person was simply defined as "any person who in appearance obviously is or who is generally accepted as a white person" (Stone 2007, 75–76). This meant that anyone who looked white was classified as such, even if they had African ancestry. Because of the differing definitions of *whiteness* and *Blackness* in the two nations, one could be classified as white in South Africa (because of a white physical appearance) and be classified as Black in the United States (because they possessed some degree of Black ancestry).

Furthermore, during the Apartheid era, every citizen had to be racially classified by the South African government as white, Black, Indian, or colored (i.e., multiracial). Anyone whose race was in question had to appear before a Racial Classification Board; many even appealed to the board voluntarily in hopes of a racial reclassification (in particular, for a classification that was more beneficial in terms of access to civil rights, public spaces, economic opportunity, and social status). The board made final decisions on race, and because the Apartheid system granted privileges and rights based on one's racial classification, its final decision (one made by three or more white men who were typically civil servants with no special qualifications on the matter) had important consequences for the lives of those who appeared before it. Their racial assignments dictated where people could live, go to school, and work. Additionally, the board's decisions determined what public amenities were open to them, given that these social spaces were strictly segregated; this included public restrooms, restaurants, hotels, and even segregated public benches and pedestrian walks.

To make decisions regarding one's racial classification, the board relied on arbitrary pseudoscientific "tests," such as assessing the breadth and flatness of the nose, size of nostrils, and height of cheekbones; calling in a barber to analyze hair texture; comparing skin shade to a skin gradation chart; giving them the "pencil test" to see whether a pencil placed on the top of the head would fall if they bent forward (if their hair was straight and it slid out, they would likely be classified as white); examining the color of the testicular sac; checking eyelids, fingernails, and earlobes (whites held stereotypical beliefs about how each should look or feel based on race); and asking a litany of questions about their daily lives that were meant to help in determining their race (e.g., What did you eat for breakfast this morning? Do you sleep on a high or low bed? Do you play soccer or rugby?). Board members even pinched people to see what language they cried out in—whether in Afrikaans (the language of whites) or in an African language (Stone 2007).

These racial litmus tests were arbitrary and subjective in nature. As such, there was a case of identical twins who were granted different racial classifications, as well as cases in which individuals were racially reclassified multiple times throughout their lives. One infamous example is that of Sandra Laing, who was racially reclassified three times in her lifetime—from white to colored to white and then finally back to colored (Stone 2007). She was not alone; others similarly found themselves pushed back and forth over racial lines throughout the course of their lives. In another case, a Chinese merchant by the name of David Song presented the Racial Classification Board an affidavit signed by 350 white neighbors and colleagues who swore that they saw him as white; his classification was subsequently changed from colored to white (Stone 2007). Each year, hundreds of people were racially reclassified, and in 1984 alone, 611 people were reclassified in South Africa (BBC World Service n.d.). This fluidity begs the question: What does race even mean if it can so easily shift?

Furthermore, even the categories of race were conflicting and defied logic. For instance, Chinese people were typically classified as colored. Japanese people, however, were classified as white because, at the time, Japan was a valuable trading partner with South Africa. Black Africans were barred from most public spaces (especially those reserved for whites, such as restaurants and hotels), though visiting African Americans were considered "honorary whites" and hence allowed entry into segregated spaces simply because they were American (Stone 2007). These were political decisions, and the racial categories were merely social constructions created by those in positions of power at the time.

A look at Brazil, the United States, and South Africa reveals that race is not as clear-cut as some might believe. Though race is a social concept, this does not mean that race is not "real." Sociologist Howard Winant notes that even if race has no scientific significance, it "remains a fundamental organizing principle" and "a way of knowing and interpreting the social world" (1994, 2). Race, according to Winant, is "deeply embedded in every institution, every relation, every psyche" because we, as humans, make it real, and in doing so, allow race to take on a life of its own (1994, 2).

The experience of Jane-Anne Pepler of South Africa, a white child
born during the Apartheid era, illustrates this. After her diseased adrenal
gland was surgically removed, her white skin turned dark brown, and she
found herself, for the first time in her life, on the receiving end of racial
prejudice and discrimination. In 1970, her mother remarked that it was
"embarrassing" for her and her family that her daughter had been ostra-
cized by her friends and treated "just as though she were a real nonwhite"
(Stone 2007, 99). Though nothing had intrinsically changed about her
genetic makeup, Pepler's experiences living in South Africa during this
time certainly did. This is because though race may not be biologically
real, privilege, prejudice, discrimination, and racism are quite real. Pepler
and her family learned firsthand the social importance given to skin color
and, more specifically, the second-rate treatment given to people of color
in Apartheid South Africa.

FURTHER READING

BBC World Service. n.d. "The Story of Africa: Southern Africa."
    Retrieved on July 17, 2020, at http://www.bbc.co.uk/worldservice
    /africa/features/storyofafrica/12chapter7.shtml.
Davis, F. James. 1991. *Who Is Black? One Nation's Definition*. University
    Park: Pennsylvania State University Press.
Davis, Wes. 2007. "When Irish Eyes Are Smiling." *New York Times*, March
    11. Retrieved on April 19, 2019, at https://www.nytimes.com/2007/03
    /11/opinion/11davis-sub.html.
Eleksie. 2018. "Black History: Sarah Rector, Declared White because She
    Was Too Rich to Be Black." July 3. Retrieved on July 20, 2020, at
    https://www.eleksie.co.ke/black-history-sarah-rector-declared-white/.
Fish, Jefferson M. 2011. "What Does the Brazilian Census Tell Us about
    Race." *Psychology Today*, December 6. Retrieved on April 19, 2019,
    at   https://www.psychologytoday.com/us/blog/looking-in-the-cultural
    -mirror/201112/what-does-the-brazilian-census-tell-us-about-race.
Gedeon, Joseph. 2019. "As Census Approaches, Many Arab Americans
    Feel Left Out." AP News, April 13. Retrieved on April 19, 2019, at
    https://apnews.com/a25b5d977a5049d6a9038a536cc7129a.
Hochschild, Jennifer L., and Brenna Marea Powell. 2008. "Racial Reor-
    ganization and the United States Census 1850–1930: Mulattoes, Half-
    Breeds, Mixed Parentage, Hindoos, and the Mexican Race." *Studies in
    American Political Development* 22: 59–96.
Johnson, Stefanie. 2005. "Blocking Racial Intermarriage Laws in 1935
    and 1937." Seattle Civil Rights & Labor History Project. Retrieved on

July 22, 2020, at https://depts.washington.edu/civilr/antimiscegenation.htm.

Marger, Martin. 2015. *Race and Ethnic Relations: American and Global Perspectives*. 10th ed. Stamford, CT: Cengage Learning.

Reese, Hope. 2018. "Chimamanda Ngozi Adichie: I Became Black in America." *JStor Daily*, August 29. Retrieved on July 16, 2020, at https://daily.jstor.org/chimamanda-ngozi-adichie-i-became-black-in-america/.

Sansone, Livio. 2003. *Blackness without Ethnicity: Constructing Race in Brazil*. New York: Palgrave Macmillan.

Stone, Judith. 2007. *When She Was White: The True Story of a Family Divided by Race*. New York: Miramax Books.

Valdez, Norberto, and Janice Valdez. 1998. "The Pot That Called the Kettle White: Changing Racial Identities and U.S. Social Construction of Race." *Identities* 5: 379–413.

Winant, Howard. 1994. *Racial Conditions*. Minneapolis: University of Minnesota Press.

Wright, Lawrence. 1993. "One Drop of Blood." *The New Yorker*, July 25.

Zack, Naomi. 1993. *Race and Mixed Race*. Philadelphia: Temple University Press.

Q3. ARE BLACK PEOPLE NATURALLY BETTER ATHLETES THAN OTHER RACIAL GROUPS?

Answer: Though this is a popular stereotype, scientific evidence suggests that this is a myth. People of African descent dominate in only a handful of American sports (albeit some of the nation's most popular ones), and biological and genetic explanations are not sufficient to explain their overrepresentation in some sports and underrepresentation in others. Rather, socioenvironmental factors may better explain current trends in both American and international sports.

The Facts: A commonly held stereotype in American society (and perhaps worldwide) is that people of African descent possess innate and superior athletic ability that allows them to excel in sports, which leads many to argue that race is, in fact, biological. In the United States, for instance, African Americans are overrepresented in professional football and basketball when compared to their share of the overall population. Further, in endurance events such as long-distance running, East Africans tend to dominate on the world stage. Jon Entine, the author of the book *Taboo:*

Why Black Athletes Dominate Sports and Why We Are Afraid to Talk about It (2000), argues that the unique physicality of the Black body explains the athletic achievements of Black people including, for example, those of African American sprinters and Kenyan long-distance runners. In a television appearance on CNN in 2000, he argued that different groups "have different body types and different physiological structures that allow them to have advantages in one sport or another" (*TalkBack Live* 2000).

Like Entine, others have invoked physiognomy to explain Black domination in certain sports. In 1988, NFL sports commentator Jimmy Snyder falsely claimed on-air that Black athleticism is due to their superior bodies that were "bred" during generations of enslavement in the American South. According to Snyder,

> The black is a better athlete to begin with, because he's been bred to be that way. Because of his high thighs and big thighs that goes up into his back. And they can jump higher and run faster because of their bigger thighs, you see. . . . He's bred to be the better athlete because this goes back all the way to the Civil War, when, during the slave trading . . . the slave owner would breed his big woman so that he would have a big, uh big black kid. (Shapiro 1988)

Biological and genetic explanations have also been raised to explain the notable absence of African Americans in other sports. In 1994, three years before Tiger Woods won his first major PGA tournament, when asked why there were not more Black golfers, golfing legend Jack Nicklaus responded that Black people have "different muscles that react in different ways" (Shapiro 1994). His remarks were controversial (and false), but they arguably reflect commonly shared myths about Black bodies. In the 2003 documentary *Race: The Power of an Illusion*, high school athletes discussed race in sports, and one white student volunteered, "Well, I've heard some rumors [that] blacks have an extra muscle in their leg." She hastened to add that she did not believe the rumor to be true, but her words nonetheless reveal the widespread misinformation about so-called racial differences (California Newsreel 2003).

Though the stereotype persists that people of African descent are innately athletically advantaged, considerable evidence challenges this belief. First, some studies identify quantifiable physical differences between Black and white Americans. African American children, for example, have (on average) denser bones, narrower hips, larger thighs, lower body fat, and longer legs than their white counterparts, which hypothetically may advantage them in particular sports (Price 1997).

However, it is problematic to assume that these average group differences translate into significant differences between Blacks and whites more generally, and it is further problematic to assume that these physical traits translate into superior athleticism among African Americans. For instance, the described physical traits found in many American Blacks are not common in *all* people of African descent. Most African Americans trace their ancestry to a specific region of Africa (i.e., West Africa); hence, believing that these physical traits are prevalent in all descendants of Africa is simply false. In fact, there is great physical diversity in Africa and among people worldwide who trace their ancestry to the continent (i.e., traits common in one part of Africa, such as large thighs or narrow hips, are less common in other areas). As such, reducing physical traits to a simplified "Black versus white" argument makes little sense. In fact, *both* "races" (Black and white) show wide physical diversity worldwide.

Another problem is that while some theorize that the described traits translate into superior athletic prowess, there is no scientific evidence to support this assumption. David Hunter, an exercise physiologist who studies race and sports at Hampton University, emphasized that "if you test whether, independent of race, a narrower pelvic girdle is a predictor of speed . . . it doesn't hold true. Not everyone in the NBA, whether he's African-American or Caucasian, is 6'6, and not everyone has a certain percentage of fat. There's not a single characteristic that is unique and always present and responsible for the performance. If there were, I'd be able to predict at an early age who should go into certain [sports]. I'd be a billionaire" (Price 1997).

Moreover, genes theorized to be important in particular sports are not universal in top athletes. A 2003 study of sprinters, for instance, identified a gene that promotes "fast-twitch" muscles (a type of muscle fiber more powerful than "slow-twitch" muscles, but one also more prone to fatigue). Though believed to be important for success in sprinting, the gene was absent in two Jamaican track stars included in the study (Harris 2010).

Second, social scientists contend that attributing athletic ability to race ignores socioenvironmental explanations that are more useful predictors of who excels in what sports. Socioenvironmental factors include social class, region/geography, and culture, to name a few examples, all of which affect access and attraction to particular sports.

For instance, in 2012, African Americans made up approximately 66 percent of all professional football players and about 76 percent of all professional basketball players (Gates 2014). Though African Americans are overrepresented in these sports today, this was not always the case. In the early twentieth century, Jews dominated American basketball, and biological explanations were similarly called upon to explain their achievements in the sport. For instance, they were stereotyped as "artful dodger[s]," a trait once believed to be intrinsic in Jews and one that purportedly advantaged them on basketball courts (California Newsreel 2003). Evolutionary biologist Joseph Graves Jr., however, argues that "there are strong cultural aspects of what sports individuals choose to play. It has to do with the interaction of individual genetic background, of opportunities, and training. History shows us that as opportunities change in society, different groups get drawn into different [sports]" (Graves 2003).

A number of factors determine opportunity, including, for example, socioeconomic status. Sports that require few resources, such as basketball and football, arguably attract groups with few resources to commit. American basketball has traditionally been a "city game" that requires no gymnasium and almost no equipment (Entine 2000, 198). As such, it became an early favorite of blue-collar, inner-city immigrants (including Jews) and, later, working-class African Americans.

Conversely, sports that require money tend to attract the affluent—who historically have been much more likely to be white in the United States. Notably, African Americans are underrepresented in competitive skiing, golf, gymnastics, ice hockey, and figure skating—all sports that require expensive equipment or costly fees to access training facilities (also consider that these sports are typically absent in most public schools as compared to less costly sports such as basketball or big revenue-generating sports such as football). African Americans are also underrepresented in competitive swimming. The sport remains overwhelmingly white, and, according to a report by USA Swimming (the national governing body of competitive swimming in the United States), Black Americans made up less than 1 percent of all competitive swimmers in 2014 (Lloyd 2016). A common belief is that Black people cannot swim because of dense muscle mass (which theoretically compromises their buoyancy), but there is no scientific evidence to support that stereotype (Harris 2010). Matt Bridge, a professor at Birmingham University in the United Kingdom, points out that "thousands of black Americans have taken the US Marines' compulsory swimming test and none have failed" (as cited in Harris 2010).

Rather than rely on biological explanations, Black underrepresentation in competitive swimming can best be explained by the interplay of socioeconomic status, history, and visibility. Swimming is an expensive sport because one must pay for costly pool memberships; thus, swimming is cost prohibitive for children from low socioeconomic backgrounds.

Moreover, given the expense of pool facilities, most public schools cannot offer swimming as a sport as compared to sports that require less investment. Only schools with significant financial resources and community support can build and maintain such facilities (as such, they are more often found in private rather than public schools).

History also plays a prominent role. During the Jim Crow era, when racial segregation was legal and pervasive in American society, Black children were barred from most public pools, and, consequently, few learned to swim. Even after legal segregation ended in the 1960s, public pools still tended to be located in white communities, limiting swimming opportunities for African Americans (Lloyd 2016). Children with parents and grandparents who never learned to swim are less likely to be encouraged to do so themselves. Moreover, given the small number of Black competitive swimmers today, few Black children watching such events on television likely see swimming as a viable option as compared to sports where African Americans are more prevalent and visible.

Socioenvironmental factors can also include the physical environment where one lives as well as cultural norms unique to particular groups. Kenyan athletes dominate long-distance running, but not because of any known genetic advantage. In fact, Robert Scott and his colleagues at the University of Glasgow argue that scientists have identified no genes that can explain their successes that are not also present in other populations (Scott et al. 2004). Instead, some scientists theorize that adaptations to the physical environment (such as developing larger lung capacities in response to living in high altitudes) may play a role in their successes in endurance competitions. Scholar Ian B. Kerr (2010) takes this a step further by arguing that Kenyan achievements in long-distance events may also be attributed to Kenyan cultural norms. For instance, Kenyans consume a low-fat and high-protein diet, and Kenyan children typically walk and run daily to and from school, an average of 7.5 kilometers a day (Burfoot 2013). A feature story on elite Kenyan runners published in *The Guardian* noted, for example, that one elite athlete ran 18 kilometers to and from school each day as a child—all while barefoot and carrying his school bag on his back (Burke 2016). These factors, Kerr suggests, are "highly conducive to producing excellent long-distance runners" (Kerr 2010, 26). Meanwhile, most American children ride school buses (or other motorized transportation) to and from school and tend to live more sedentary lifestyles.

It is further worth noting that the identifier "Kenyan" is not a race nor a monolithic genetic population but rather a nationality—"a well-defined political and cultural group" (Kerr 2010, 25). Kenyans may excel in endurance running, but the same is not true for all Africans, challenging the generalized stereotype of African/Black superiority in the sport. Kenyan superiority in distance running cannot even be generalized to all Kenyans. Jon Entine, the author of *Taboo* (2000), admits that the majority of Kenyan winners come from a very specific region of Kenya—Eldoret—a town in western Kenya renowned for its year-round mild climate and high elevation. According to Kenyan coach John Velzian, "If you take a look at the Olympic medals that have been won in long distance running by Africans, they nearly all come from this region. It's a very, very small area, but there is an endless supply of world-class runners" (Entine 2000, 43–44). Further noting the distinctiveness of the town, one retired American track coach remarked, "If one were to circumscribe a radius of 60 miles around the town of Eldoret you would get about 90 percent of the top Kenyan athletes" (Entine 2000, 45).

Finally, while heightened media attention in America's sports-obsessed society may give the impression of Black superiority in athletics (especially on American basketball courts and football fields), scholar Henry Louis Gates Jr. observes that in 2012, "there were more black neurologists (411) and black cardiologists (690) by far than all of the black men playing in the NBA (350)!" (Gates 2014). He emphasized that the vast majority of Black Americans work in non-sports-related jobs and that a mere .0133 percent of the working Black population were professional athletes in 2012.

The one-dimensional stereotype of Black athletic superiority overshadows the myriad other contributions that African Americans make to American society. Moreover, the persistence of the stereotype gives too many Black children the impression that sports is their only viable career option. As Gates lamented, "Far too many [Black children] believe that it is, statistically, easier to make it into the NBA or the NFL than it is to make it into college and go onto professional school" (Gates 2014). Excessive media and societal attention given to Black athletes arguably advances the stereotype and perhaps creates a self-fulfilling prophesy for some Black children, who, in turn, prioritize athletics over academics. Black youth pursuing athletic careers further reinforces the racial stereotype and at a cost to the vast majority who will fall short of attaining careers in professional sports.

FURTHER READING

Burfoot, Amby. 2013. "Why Are Kenyan Distance Runners So Fast?" *Runner's World*, July 8. Retrieved on May 21, 2019, at https://www
.runnersworld.com/races-places/a20828246/why-are-kenyan-distance
-runners-so-fast/.

Burke, Jason. 2016. "Eldoret: The Kenyan Town Trying to 'Run away from Poverty.'" *The Guardian*, August 1. Retrieved on May 21, 2019, at https://www.theguardian.com/world/2016/aug/01/eldoret-the-kenyan -town-trying-to-run-away-from-poverty.

California Newsreel. 2003. "Race: The Power of an Illusion: Episode 1." PBS.

Entine, Jon. 2000. *Taboo: Why Black Athletes Dominate Sports and Why We Are Afraid to Talk about It.* New York: Public Affairs.

Gates, Henry Louis, Jr. 2014. "Why Are There So Many Black Athletes?" The Root, September 1. Retrieved on May 21, 2019, at https://www .theroot.com/why-are-there-so-many-black-athletes-1790876918.

Graves, Joseph, Jr. 2003. "Race: The Power of an Illusion: Background Readings: Interview with Joseph Graves Jr." California Newsreel. PBS. Retrieved on October 29, 2020, at https://www.pbs.org/race/000 _About/002_04-background-01-06.htm.

Harris, Tim. 2010. "Black Men CAN Swim." *Prospect*, July 21. Retrieved on May 21, 2019, at https://www.prospectmagazine.co.uk/magazine /black-men-can-swim.

Kerr, Ian B. 2010. "The Myth of Racial Superiority in Sports." *Hilltop Review* 4(1): 19–27.

Lloyd, Molly. 2016. "Exploring the Racial Disparities in Competitive Swimming." Swimming World, February 3. Retrieved on May 21, 2019, at https://www.swimmingworldmagazine.com/news/exploring -the-racial-disparities-in-competitive-swimming/.

Price, S. L. 1997. "Is It in the Genes? Studies Have Found Physical Differences That Might Help Explain Why Blacks Outperform Whites in Certain Sports—But Scientists Are Wary of Jumping to Conclusions." *Sports Illustrated*, December 8. Retrieved on May 21, 2019, at https:// www.si.com/vault/1997/12/08/8093395/is-it-in-the-genes-studies-have -found-physical-differences-that-might-help-explain-why-blacks-out perform-whites-in-certain-sportsbut-scientists-are-wary-of-jumping -to-conclusions.

Scott, Robert A., Colin Moran, Richard H. Wilson, and Will H. Goodwin. 2004. "Genetic Influence on East African Running Success." *Equine and Comparative Exercise Physiology* 1(4): 273–280.

Shapiro, Leonard. 1988. "'Jimmy the Greek' Says Blacks Are 'Bred' for Sports." *Washington Post*, January 16. Retrieved on May 21, 2019, at https://www.washingtonpost.com/archive/politics/1988/01/16/jimmy -the-greek-says-blacks-are-bred-for-sports/128a889e-83e2-44a3-b911 -851d5281ade4/.

Shapiro, Leonard. 1994. "Nicklaus Clarifies Remarks on Blacks." *Washington Post*, August 10. Retrieved on May 21, 2019, at https://www

.washingtonpost.com/archive/sports/1994/08/10/nicklaus-clarifies
-remarks-on-blacks/8be7f5f2-9672-49bd-a689-d3c8b6b7699e.

TalkBack Live. 2000. "How Important Are Genes in Determining Athletic Performance?" CNN, January 28. Transcript retrieved on May 28,
2019, at http://www.cnn.com/TRANSCRIPTS/0001/28/tl.00.html.

Q4. ARE RACIAL DISPARITIES IN HEALTH EVIDENCE THAT RACE IS BIOLOGICAL?

Answer: No. American racial groups do show disparate rates of disease
and health afflictions that have led many Americans, and even some
medical professionals, to assume that racial groups are biologically distinct
from one another. Evolutionary biologist Alan Goodman, however, challenges this assumption with two key arguments. When considering these
so-called racial patterns in disease and health afflictions, he says that (1)
environmental factors are rarely controlled for and (2) genetic variability
does not follow racial lines (Goodman 2001).

The Facts: Black women are more likely to die of breast cancer than
white women. Black children are more likely to be diagnosed with and die
of asthma as compared to white children. Black Americans have the highest rates of hypertension of any racial group in the United States. Native
Americans suffer from and die of alcoholism at higher rates than all other
racial groups. Aggregate statistics reveal clear disparities between races, suggesting that racial groups are perhaps inherently different from one another.

According to Dorothy Roberts, a professor of law and sociology at the
University of Pennsylvania, "the notion of 'racial diseases'—that people
of different races suffer from peculiar diseases and experience common
diseases differently—is centuries old" and rooted in beliefs of biological races (Roberts 2011, 82). Indeed, a visit to any doctor's office in the
United States typically requires patients to fill out forms inquiring about
their medical history, age, sex/gender, and, in many cases, their racial
background. Roberts notes that many doctors ask about race based on
the belief that they can provide better medical care to patients knowing
this information. In a 2002 cover story for *New York Times Magazine* titled
"I Am a Racially Profiling Doctor," one physician admits, "I always take
note of my patient's race. So do many of my colleagues. We do it because
certain diseases and treatment responses cluster by ethnicity. . . .When
it comes to practicing medicine, stereotyping often works" (as cited in
Roberts 2011, 92). These physicians are not alone. When it comes to

medicine, many health-care professionals believe that intrinsic differences exist between racial groups; therefore, knowing their patients' race is essential to their care. But is it? And most relevant here, if there are statistically identifiable differences, isn't this proof that meaningful biological differences exist between racial groups?

According to evolutionary biologist Alan Goodman (2001), at least two fundamental problems arise when assuming that measured race disparities in health are biological. First, Goodman argues that when considering racial differences in health, "the environment is rarely controlled for" (39). Environmental, or external, factors cannot be overlooked when explaining racial disparities in health. Second, genetic variability among humans, though real, does not follow racial lines. In other words, there are populations of people who may be more susceptible to certain diseases than others, though this is not true of races.

External Factors Are Often Overlooked

The environment can include any number of external factors that affect one's health, including (but not limited to) wealth and poverty, education, access to medical care, quality of health care, environmental stressors, pollution, and culture (several of these factors may also influence personal lifestyle choices, such as diet and exercise). For example, breast cancer rates are roughly equal for Black and white women (CDC 2018), but Black women are about 40 percent more likely to die from the disease. Though this may imply something biologically different about Black Americans, a 2017 study found that lack of insurance explained more than a third of the Black-white gap in breast cancer deaths (Rubin 2017). Variability across U.S. states in the Black-white gap also suggests that external factors play a key role; Massachusetts and Connecticut, for example, show similar death rates among Black and white breast cancer patients, which according to the authors "likely reflect achievements in equitable access to health care in these states" (as cited in Rubin 2017).

Disparate asthma rates by race also illustrate the importance of external factors on health. Black children are twice as likely to be diagnosed with asthma and are six times more likely to die from the respiratory condition than their white counterparts (McClurg 2016; Preidt 2017). As some researchers search for possible biological explanations for these discrepancies (McClurg 2016), others point to external factors. For example, air quality plays an important role in the prevalence of asthma, and several studies find that pollution in the United States is disproportionately inhaled by Black and Hispanic minorities as compared to white Americans

(Tessum et al. 2019; for more on the uneven effects of pollution, see Q16). (Note: The term Hispanic is used interchangeably with the term Latinx throughout this book; the term Latinx is a gender-neutral replacement for the traditional gendered labels Latino and Latina.) Moreover, external factors such as poverty, lack of patient education, inadequate medical care, misuse of medications, and lack of available resources in the communities where some Americans live increase their risk of dying from the disease (Preidt 2017; see also http://asthma.nmanet.org/members1.htm).

Even the effects of daily racism, another social factor, may be observed in differential rates of hypertension (i.e., high blood pressure). African Americans have higher rates of hypertension than white Americans, and they have among the highest rates in the world. Hypertension in African Americans was long assumed to be genetic, though scientists have found that people in West Africa, from whom many African Americans descend, have among the *lowest* hypertension rates in the world (Adelman 2003). Another popular theory asserts that African Americans have high rates of hypertension because their ancestors were those who survived the journey from Africa during the transatlantic slave trade. They were able to overcome brutal conditions on slave ships, such as water deprivation and dehydration, because they had the ability to retain sodium; this theory, however, has been widely debunked in recent decades (Roberts 2011). One study, for example, found that Black people in other former slave societies, such as the West Indies, do not have the same high hypertension rate of African Americans (Roberts 2011).

Larry Adelman, the executive producer of the 2003 documentary *Race: The Power of an Illusion*, notes that a "focus on race as innate biology, as genetic difference, would lead health professionals and policy makers to overlook social factors that might contribute to African American hypertension," such as "the added stressor of living in a racist society" (Adelman 2003). According to a 2011 review of research, Elizabeth Brondolo and her colleagues argue that racism can cause "acute stress" and also act as a "chronic stressor," and they conclude that, "taken together, the evidence suggests that institutional and interpersonal racism are likely to contribute to the development of [hypertension]" (Brondolo et al. 2011, 523, 526), though the effect may be complex. Racism may lead to higher rates of hypertension (1) because of stress exposure and (2) because it fosters conditions that undermine good health behaviors. Regarding the latter, impoverished environments add additional stress and raise barriers to achieving healthy lifestyles (e.g., living in unsafe communities or communities without trails or sidewalks make it difficult to exercise outside and lack of money prevents joining gyms or having leisure time to exercise).

For further discussion of how stress from discrimination can directly affect the health of people of color in the United States, see Q16.

A final example illustrating the importance of external factors on health is alcoholism among Native Americans. Alcohol abuse has long plagued the Native American community, and a commonly held stereotype is that Native Americans are uniquely predisposed to alcoholism. A 2016 study, however, found that after adjusting for factors such as income and education, rates of alcoholism were about the *same* between whites and Native Americans, suggesting that external factors may be better predictors of alcohol abuse (Cunningham, Soloman, and Muramoto 2016). Further, there is no scientific evidence to support the belief that Native Americans are genetically predisposed to alcoholism. In fact, Joseph Gone, an associate professor of psychology at the University of Michigan, argues that there is *no* research that shows that Native Americans metabolize or react differently to alcohol as compared to other groups, and they have no known risk genes for alcoholism (Szalavitz 2015).

These findings, however, do not mean alcoholism is not a problem in Indigenous communities. According to social epidemiologist James K. Cunningham, "debunking a stereotype doesn't mean that alcohol problems don't exist." Teshia Solomon, an associate professor at the Native American Research and Training Center at the University of Arizona, adds that "Native Americans as a group have less access to medical care, safe housing and quality food, which can amplify health problems connected to alcohol" (University of Arizona 2016). Finally, studies show that alcohol abuse is prevalent in other Indigenous peoples outside of the United States—for example, among Aboriginal Australians. Native Americans and Aboriginal Australians do not share genes that make them vulnerable to alcoholism; rather, they share the "ongoing multi-generational experience of trauma" as members of oppressed, colonized groups (Szalavitz 2015). They are also more likely to be impoverished and marginalized in the societies in which they live.

Genetic Variability Exists, but It Does Not Follow Racial Lines

Many diseases and afflictions have external explanations, but what of ailments that are clearly genetic? Some diseases, such as cystic fibrosis, Tay-Sachs disease, and sickle cell anemia, are not caused by environmental factors; they are inherited and biological. Sickle cell anemia, for instance, is an inherited disease passed from parent(s) to child via the sickle cell allele and, according to the Centers for Disease Control and Prevention (CDC), the incident estimate for the trait is about 73 in 1,000 in Black American newborn babies, as compared to only 3 in 1,000 white American newborns (CDC 2014). Because the disease is genetic, this debilitating red blood cell disorder has long been referred to as an "African American disease"—even by many medical professionals (Roberts 2011). Sickle cell anemia, however, is found among peoples of Central and West Africa but not North, Southern, or East Africa. Hence, having African ancestry does not mean that one is more susceptible to the disease—knowing where in the world (specifically speaking) one's ancestors originated is a more powerful predictor of who is likely to inherit the disease. Moreover, the sickle cell trait is also carried by many non-African populations, including those in parts of the Middle East (e.g., Yemen and Saudi Arabia), Central and South America, India, and Europe (in particular, in Mediterranean countries such as Turkey, Italy, and Greece). People in Orchomenos, in central Greece, for instance, have double the rate of sickle cell disease than African Americans (Roberts 2011).

Importantly, in all of these regions, malaria is common. Scientists believe that sickle cell is prevalent in these populations because it arose several thousand years ago as a genetic mutation that conferred some measure of resistance to malaria. Inheriting a sickle cell allele provided a selective advantage in malarial regions, though inheriting two of the alleles caused the sickle cell disease (Adelman 2003). As such, Larry Adelman (2003) writes that "sickle cell . . . is a marker not of skin color or race but ancestry, or more precisely, having ancestors from where malaria was common." Reducing sickle cell to a "Black disease" is not merely overly simplistic and outright false but a potentially harmful assumption for health-care providers to make.

Though racial variations in inheritable diseases may suggest a biological basis of race, Alan Goodman warns against making this assumption. Even with genetic diseases, he argues, it is erroneous to equate "genetic with pan-racial" (2001, 39). We should instead talk of variation between populations—in other words, genetic variations found between localized groups of people. Some gene forms show up more often in some populations as compared to others (Adelman 2003), and as such, there may be genetic variability (albeit small) from one population to another; however, genetic variability does *not* exist from race to race. Racial differences in disease do not exist because (1) genetic variability does not follow racial lines, (2) there are no genes unique to any racial group (not even one), and (3) racial groups are socially constructed, ill-defined, and, according to Goodman, "too broad to be meaningful" (Goodman 2001, 40) (refer to Q1 and Q2 for in-depth discussions of these points).

If disparate rates of diseases and health afflictions are not biological, is knowing the race of patients essential to their care by physicians? Yes and no. In 1993, the Centers for Disease Control and Prevention (CDC) in a report on race in medical research concluded that "because most associations between disease and race have no biological basis, race—as a biological concept—is not useful in public health surveillance" (as cited in Goodman 2001, 40). However, although biological race is meaningless, social race is not. Racism is real; so too is inequality in education, income, nutrition, access to health care, and exposure to pollution. Perhaps knowing someone's race is important, not because it tells physicians anything about a patient's biology or genes, but rather because it has the potential to provide information about the social circumstances in which persons live and the external factors that may have adverse effects on their health.

FURTHER READING

Adelman, Larry. 2003. "Race and Gene Studies: What Difference Makes a Difference?" California Newsreel. Retrieved on November 22, 2020, at http://newsreel.org/guides/race/whatdiff.htm.

Brondolo, Elizabeth, Erica E. Love, Melissa Pencille, Antoinette Schoenthaler, and Gbenga Ogedegbe. 2011. "Racism and Hypertension: A Review of the Empirical Evidence and Implications for Clinical Practice." *American Journal of Hypertension* 24(5): 518–529.

Centers for Disease Control and Prevention (CDC). 2014. "Incidence of Sickle Cell Trait—United States." *Morbidity and Mortality Weekly Report* 63(49): 1155–1158. Retrieved on November 22, 2020, at https://www.cdc.gov/mmwr/preview/mmwrhtml/mm6349a3.htm?s_cid =mm6349a3_w.

Centers for Disease Control and Prevention (CDC). 2018. "Breast Cancer Rates among Black Women and White Women." Retrieved on July 9, 2020, at https://www.cdc.gov/cancer/dcpc/research/articles/breast _cancer_rates_women.htm.

Cunningham, James K., Teshia Solomon, and Myra L. Muramoto. 2016. "Alcohol Use among Native Americans Compared to Whites: Examining the Veracity of the 'Native American Elevated Alcohol Consumption' Belief." *Drug and Alcohol Dependence* 160: 65–75.

Goodman, Alan. 2001. "Biological Diversity and Cultural Diversity: From Race to Radical Bioculturalism." Pp. 29–45 in *Cultural Diversity in the United States: A Critical Reader*, edited by Ida Susser and Thomas C. Patterson. Malden, MA: Blackwell Publishers.

McClurg Lesley. 2016. "Scientists Seek Genetic Clues to Asthma's Toll on Black Children." NPR, June 7. Retrieved on May 1, 2019, at https://

www.npr.org/sections/health-shots/2016/06/07/481092103/scientsts
-seek-genetic-clues-to-why-asthma-is-deadlier-in-blacks.

Preidt, Robert. 2017. "Asthma Much More Lethal for Black Children,
Study Finds." WebMD. Retrieved on May 1, 2019, at https://www
.webmd.com/asthma/news/20170304/asthma-much-more-lethal-for
-black-children-study-finds.

Roberts, Dorothy. 2011. *Fatal Invention: How Science, Politics, and Big
Business Re-Create Race in the Twenty-First Century.* New York: The
New Press.

Rubin, Rita. 2017. "Lack of Insurance Plays a Key Role in Why Black
Women Are More Likely to Die of Breast Cancer." *Forbes*, October 17.
Retrieved on May 1, 2019, at https://www.forbes.com/sites/ritarubin
/2017/10/17/lack-of-insurance-plays-a-key-role-in-why-black-women
-are-more-likely-to-die-of-breast-cancer/#5cb8be27e17e.

Szalavitz, Maia. 2015. "No, Native Americans Aren't Genetically More
Susceptible to Alcoholism." The Verge, October 2. Retrieved on May
3, 2019, at https://www.theverge.com/2015/10/2/9428659/firewater
-racist-myth-alcoholism-native-americans.

Tessum, Christopher W., Joshua S. Apte, Andrew L. Goodkind, Nicholas
Z. Muller, Kimberley A. Mullins, David A. Paolella, Stephen Polasky,
Nathaniel P. Springer, Sumil K. Thakrar, Julian D. Marshall, and Jason
D. Hill. 2019. "Inequity in Consumption of Goods and Services Adds
to Racial-Ethnic Disparities in Air Pollution Exposure." *Proceedings of
the National Academy of Sciences of the United States of America* 116(13):
6001–6006.

University of Arizona. 2016. "Stereotypes about Native Americans and
Alcohol Debunked by UA Study." Office of Public Affairs, February
8. Retrieved on May 1, 2019, at https://opa.uahs.arizona.edu/news
room/news/2016/stereotypes-about-native-americans-and-alcohol
-debunked-ua-study.

2

❖

Power and Privilege

The women recline peacefully in their salon chairs, some with their feet soaking in the warm water before them. A few chat and laugh together, while others sit quietly peering at their phones and flipping through magazines. All are enjoying their relaxing pedicures and foot massages. At first glance, this seems like an everyday scene at an American nail salon, though this image, captured in a glossy color photograph, is strikingly different. This is because all of the pampered female customers are Asian American, while the apron-clad nail technicians perched on the small stools at their feet are white.

The photograph was included in a three-picture exposé that appeared in O, *The Oprah Magazine* in May 2017. The aim of the project was to invert racial stereotypes and, perhaps even more importantly, to draw attention to uneven power dynamics in the United States. For many readers, it was surprising, if not jarring, to see a familiar salon scene but one that portrayed white women waiting on women of color. In the two other pictures, the photographer, Chris Buck, depicted similar role reversals intended to challenge conventional expectations. In one, a young white girl looks up at an imposing wall of toy store shelves lined end to end with brown-skinned dolls. In the other, a glamorous stiletto-wearing Latina sits in her lavish apartment and, with her sparkly phone pressed to her ear and a Yorkshire terrier balanced on her lap, smiles as a white maid bends subserviently to pour her tea.

Buck's photographs were created to spark dialogue about race in American society, and they did just that. The images went viral, and many Americans shared their reactions across social media. Some found the images powerful and thought provoking; others argued that the photos merely perpetuated "reverse racism" toward white people. However, journalist Mia Mercado of *Bustle* magazine observed that the provocative pictures reveal that race is so deeply entrenched in our culture that we are often blind to the "racial power dynamics we encounter on a regular basis."

This chapter sheds further light on power and its consequences for different racial groups in American society by examining several frequently asked questions on a variety of race-related topics; none can be answered without considering the unequal power dynamics that exist between different races in the United States. The first three questions focus on the concept of privilege—the notion that some groups are advantaged over others in society. Question 5, "Does white privilege really exist?," looks at whether members of the dominant racial group, white Americans, hold special advantages in American society solely because of their race. Further, some people wonder whether other racial groups similarly experience privilege. Question 6 turns its attention to the question, "Does Asian American privilege exist?" Question 7 shifts focus from race privilege to examine skin color privilege—particularly among people of color—and asks, "Among people of color, are those with light skin advantaged over those with dark skin?" People come in all shades, and to answer this question, this essay looks at social dynamics within groups, such as those among African Americans, Latinx populations (in the United States and in Latin America), Native Americans, Asian Americans, and Asians. It addresses skin color biases that occur between racial groups, though also examines how whites privilege people of color with light skin over those with darker skin tones.

The second half of this chapter further addresses commonly asked questions that cannot be answered without bearing in mind the unequal power dynamics among different racial groups in American society. Question 8 asks, "Is it true that whites will soon become a racial minority in the United States?" Media headlines, particularly in the 2010s, have claimed that white America is nearing its end—but are the headlines true? To address this question, this entry examines what we, as a society, mean when we use the terms *white* and *minority*. The former term is more flexible that most people realize, complicating claims of an impending white demise. The latter is more than a mere population count; access to power is central to defining who is and who is not a minority.

Question 9 looks at the controversy over cultural appropriation (also known as cultural misappropriation), which refers to the borrowing or taking of elements of one culture by another. Much of the debate over cultural appropriation revolves around white Americans who adopt elements of minority cultures, and some Americans ask, "Is cultural appropriation of minority cultures by white Americans equivalent to American minorities adopting white culture?" To answer this question, scholars consider the uneven power between whites and minorities and the motives and pressures that may compel them to adopt aspects of another culture.

Finally, the closing question of this chapter looks at the controversy over blackface in the United States. Drawing on opinion polls, Question 10 asks, "Why do many Americans find blackface offensive?" Some Americans, particularly if they are non-Black, are baffled by the criticism and condemnation of blackface and ask, "Why all the fuss?" Understanding the history of blackface in the United States and uneven power dynamics between whites and Blacks is essential to answering this question.

Q5. DOES WHITE PRIVILEGE REALLY EXIST?

Answer: Yes. White privilege refers to the unearned advantages experienced by white people in the United States given their position as the dominant racial group. In her pioneering work of the late 1980s, scholar Peggy McIntosh introduced the concept of white privilege and compiled a list of the tangible advantages of whiteness in American society by reflecting on the daily effects of white privilege in her own life. Subsequent empirical research further illustrates that white Americans are privileged in many facets of U.S. society—though most remain unaware of their advantages. It is important to note, however, that while whites experience race privilege, not all white Americans experience privilege in the same way. White Americans hold many different social identities (in addition to race) that affect how they move through and experience the world.

The Facts: According to anti-racism activist and scholar Peggy McIntosh, people are often taught about racism in the United States in a way that focuses on how people of color are *disadvantaged*, though they often fail to see the flip side of racism—how some people, namely whites, are *advantaged* (or *privileged*). White privilege, according to McIntosh, refers to the "unearned advantages and benefits" accrued to whites by virtue of a system that establishes their racial group as "the norm" (1989). She writes of white privilege as unearned because whiteness is not something that people work for or earn by merit; rather, they are simply born white. Nonetheless, white Americans experience many advantages because, in American society, they are the dominant racial group.

To further understand this concept, consider what hand you write with—are you a "lefty" or a "righty"? In American society, right-handed people are the dominant group, and, as such, society is organized around right-handedness. Everyday products are geared toward "righties," such as cameras, power tools, firearms, school desks, spiral notebooks, scissors, measuring cups, can openers, cork screws, and more. Right-handed people benefit because most Americans are right-handed, though it is important to note that dominance is not simply based on population numbers. In the case of race, whites are dominant in the United States because they are the numerical majority (63.7 percent of the population in 2010) but also because they are the most powerful group. In some societies, whites are the dominant group not because they are the most numerous but because they hold the most power. Consider whites in South Africa during Apartheid or whites in India under British colonial rule. In both contexts, whites were the numerical minority, but they held the most power; hence, they were the most privileged racial group.

Returning to the handedness example, right-handed people probably do not spend their days thinking about how society is geared around them and how they benefit from this. In fact, most right-handed people are completely unaware of the benefits of being righties. Likewise, most whites are unaware of how they benefit from their whiteness. For example, a 2017 poll by the Pew Research Center found that although most African Americans (92 percent) believed that whites benefit a "great deal or fair amount" from being white, more than half of all white Americans, 54 percent, believed that they receive "little or no advantage" from their race (Oliphant 2017). McIntosh, however, reflecting on her white privilege, writes, "I have come to see white privilege as an invisible package of unearned assets that I can count on cashing in each day, but about which I was 'meant' to remain oblivious" (1989). She continues by describing white privilege as "like an invisible weightless knapsack" of special provisions that she carries with her each day (1989). To make the daily effects of white privilege more readily visible to herself and others, McIntosh assembled a list of examples of white privilege in her life. Some examples from her 50-item list include the following:

- I can, if I wish, arrange to be in the company of people of my race most of the time.
- I can turn on the television or open the front page of the paper and see people of my race widely represented.

- When I am told about our national heritage or about "civilization," I am shown that people of my color made it what it is.
- I can be sure that my children will be given curricular materials that testify to the existence of their race.
- I can arrange to protect my children most of the time from people who might not like them.
- I can do well in a challenging situation without being called a credit to my race.
- I am never asked to speak for all people of my racial group.
- If a traffic cop pulls me over, or if the IRS audits my tax return, I can be sure I haven't been singled out because of my race.
- I can easily buy posters, postcards, picture books, greeting cards, dolls, toys, and children's magazines featuring people of my race.
- I can choose blemish cover or bandages in "flesh" color that more or less match my skin.

Others have added to her list of examples:

- When people describe me, they usually don't refer to the color of my skin.
- When I speak in an eloquent manner, no one perceives me as an anomaly of my racial group, nor do they describe me as "articulate."
- When watching a film or reading a book, I can be reasonably sure that the lead characters will be of my racial group.
- I can easily buy dolls and action figures that are the same color as my children and purchase children's books whose central characters reflect their race.
- I can go to almost any meeting or gathering and see mostly faces of my color.
- If I'm an actor, almost every part is for my racial group, and even when they're not, I can sometimes get away from playing them anyway.
- The history of my racial group is part of the core curriculum, not relegated to a single month of the year, a college elective, or separate college department.
- "Beauty" is defined by the physical characteristics of my racial group (e.g., an image search on Google of "beautiful women" reveals mostly white-appearing women).
- When purchasing "nude" clothing, shoes, and makeup, I can be sure that the color will generally match my skin tone.

In addition to these examples, quantifiable evidence reveals that white privilege is omnipresent in just about every aspect of American society. For example, white privilege is palpably visible in the 2015 short film *Racism Is Real* (by Brave New Films). The film follows two men, one white (David) and one Black (Dante), through a day in their lives (Ramsey 2015). In every facet of life, David is advantaged over Dante: (1) when applying for a job (research shows that having a white-sounding name means 50 percent more callbacks for job interviews than having a Black-sounding name); (2) when buying a car (white people are charged, on average, $700 less than Black people); (3) when driving (white drivers are less likely to be pulled over by police than Black drivers); (4) when searching for a new home (white buyers are shown 17.7 percent more homes by real estate agents than their Black counterparts); (5) when seeking health care (white patients were more likely than Black patients to be informed of important medical procedures necessary to their treatment); and (6) when engaging in politics (white legislators respond more often to e-mails from constituents with white-sounding names versus those with Black-sounding names—regardless of political party).

Additional examples of white privilege in the United States, as supported by quantifiable data and empirical studies, include the following (these examples are documented throughout this book):

- White privilege in education: White students are more likely to be tracked into gifted programs than Black students—even when they have the same standardized test scores (see Q14).
- White privilege in the workplace: Whites are more likely to be hired and paid more than their nonwhite counterparts—even when they have identical credentials (see Q15).
- White privilege in health care: Whites are more likely to receive adequate pain management treatment in hospitals than their Black counterparts—even when their symptoms are the same (see Q16).
- White privilege in the environment: Whites are less likely than nonwhites to have polluters (such as factories, landfills, and toxic waste facilities) located in their communities. Data show that the racial makeup of community members is a more powerful predictor of where these polluters are placed than their social class (see Q16).
- White privilege in lending: Whites often pay lower interest rates on car loans than their Black counterparts—even when incomes and creditworthiness are controlled (see Q17).
- White privilege in criminal justice: Whites are less likely to be arrested and imprisoned for drug use than Blacks—even though both groups use drugs at similar rates (see Q18).

- Whites in the media: White mass shooters are far more likely than nonwhite mass shooters to be described as mentally ill; this narrative diverts direct blame from whites to external factors allegedly beyond their control (see Q23).

For further quantifiable examples of how white Americans experience privilege, see section 3 for examples of how whites are advantaged in housing, education, work, health, and banking and lending. Also see section 4 for examples of how whites are advantaged in the criminal justice system (Q19 and Q20) and in media coverage of crime (Q23).

Though white privilege in the United States is widely documented, some whites nonetheless struggle with the concept. Gina Crosley-Corcoran, a white woman raised in extreme poverty, writes of her own negative reaction when someone on the internet first told her she was racially privileged. Her initial response was "THE F**K!?!? . . . My white skin didn't do s— to prevent me from experiencing poverty" (Crosley-Corcoran 2017). However, after reading Peggy McIntosh's work on white privilege, Crosley-Corcoran admits that it became "impossible to deny that being born with white skin in America affords people certain unearned privileges in life."

Based on Crosley-Corcoran's experience, there are two important points to make about white privilege. First, possessing white privilege does not mean that one's life is easy. It simply means that for white people living in the United States, skin color is not a factor that makes their lives difficult. In other words, for whites, life may be challenging for a number of reasons (perhaps because they are poor, disabled, or gay) but not because they have white skin. Second, all whites do not experience privilege in the same way. There are many social statuses that people possess that intersect with their white privilege to determine how they move through and experience the world (such as those based on gender, sexuality, social class, age, nationality, religion, weight, and even physical attractiveness). Thus, a white, wealthy, heterosexual man may experience life very differently than a white, poor, lesbian woman. Crosley-Corcoran continues, "I, maybe more than most people, can completely understand why broke white folks get p—d when the word 'Privilege' is thrown around. As a child, I was constantly discriminated against because of my poverty. . . . But luckily my college education introduced me to a more nuanced concept of Privilege; the term Intersectionality. The concept of Intersectionality recognizes that people can be privileged in some ways and definitely not privileged in others."

Psychologist and racism expert Beverly Tatum similarly describes the concept of *intersectionality* and the importance of understanding the ways in which individuals can simultaneously experience privilege and lack thereof:

> It is important to acknowledge that while all Whites benefit from racism, they do not all benefit equally. Other factors, such as socioeconomic status, gender, age, religious affiliation, sexual orientation, and mental and physical ability, also play a role. . . . It is also true that not all people of color are equally targeted by racism. We all have multiple identities that shape our experiences. I can describe myself as a light-skinned, well-educated, heterosexual, able-bodied, Christian African American woman raised in a two-parent middle-class family. . . . I am systematically disadvantaged by race and by gender, but I systematically receive benefits in the other categories. (Tatum 2017, 92)

A final note—white privilege, as described here, exists in the United States because whites are the dominant racial group (i.e., the most numerous and most powerful). This is not to say, however, that other racial or ethnic groups are not privileged in other settings (e.g., Japanese in Japan). Clearly, privilege exists for those groups deemed the dominant group in any given society. Regardless, it is important to point out that white privilege often extends beyond white-dominant societies. When traveling or living in Asia, Africa, and South America, for example, whites may find that their skin color provides them certain advantages, such as undue respect, deferential treatment, and positive attention.

For example, one online blogger writes about the white privilege she experiences in Southeast Asia. She attracts positive attention because whiteness is frequently equated to beauty in Asia; she has also noticed that she travels effortlessly through airport security as compared to her darker-skinned companions (Anonymous 2017). Other travelers similarly document white privilege in other parts of the world. In Africa, one traveler described the first-class treatment often given to white people—from staff at restaurants and banks who serve white people first (even if African patrons had already been waiting) to security guards opting not to search the belongings of whites at security checkpoints for malls and other public spaces (Sawlani 2014). She attributes the privileged treatment given to whites to an internalized colonial mentality in which many Africans continue to revere white people and whiteness itself. This does not mean that whites are immune to discrimination (or at the extreme, terrorism) in parts of the world where they are the minority. However, it does mean that in many parts of the world, just as in the United States, whiteness comes with advantages.

FURTHER READING

Anonymous. 2017. "Acknowledging My White Privilege in Southeast Asia." Her Travel Therapy. Retrieved on August 2, 2019, at http://hertraveltherapy.com/acknowledging-white-privilege-southeast-asia/.

Crosley-Corcoran, Gina. 2017. "Explaining White Privilege to a Broke White Person." HuffPost, December 6. Retrieved on August 2, 2019, at https://www.huffpost.com/entry/explaining-white-privilege-to-a-broke -white-person_b_5269255.

McIntosh, Peggy. 1989. "White Privilege: Unpacking the Invisible Knapsack." *Peace and Freedom* (July/August): 10–12.

Oliphant, J. Baxter. 2017. "Views about Whether Whites Benefit from Societal Advantages Split Sharply along Racial and Partisan Lines." Pew Research Center, September 28. Retrieved on November 22, 2020, at https://www.pewresearch.org/fact-tank/2017/09/28/views -about-whether-whites-benefit-from-societal-advantages-split-shar ply-along-racial-and-partisan-lines/.

Ramsey, Franchesca. 2015. "Dante and David Apply for the Same Job but Only One Gets an Interview. Here's the Rest of Their Day." Upworthy, April 30. Retrieved on August 2, 2019, at https://www.upworthy .com/dante-and-david-apply-for-the-same-job-but-only-one-gets-an -interview-heres-the-rest-of-their-day.

Sawlani, Samira. 2014. "Tourism, White Privilege and Colonial Mentality in East Africa." Media Diversified. Retrieved on August 2, 2019, at https://mediadiversified.org/2014/10/14/tourism-white-privilege-and -colonial-mentality-in-east-africa/.

Tatum, Beverly Daniel. 2017. *Why Are All the Black Kids Sitting Together in the Cafeteria? And Other Conversations about Race.* 2nd ed. New York: Basic Books.

Q6. DOES ASIAN AMERICAN PRIVILEGE EXIST?

Answer: To challenge the concept of white privilege, some critics point to so-called Asian American privilege. Highlighting their educational and economic successes in American society, these skeptics of white privilege argue that Asian Americans are a "model minority" (a group so successful that they should be held up as a model for other minority groups), and, by extension, they assert that they must be a privileged racial group in American society. Is this depiction of Asian Americans as a privileged race accurate? Mostly, no. Though aggregate data suggest an overall higher socioeconomic status for Asian Americans than for other racial groups in the United States, a closer look reveals wide within-group social class disparities. Moreover, persistent racial barriers and anti-Asian discrimination show that Asian Americans do not experience race privilege in American society that is comparable to that experienced by white Americans.

The Facts: On the Fox News cable show *The O'Reilly Factor* in 2014, conservative host Bill O'Reilly highlighted some of the quantifiable successes of Asian Americans. He pointed to their enviable employment rate, median household income, high school graduate rate, and percentage of intact families. Based on these measures, he showed that Asian Americans outpace all other racial groups, including white Americans. He then asked viewers, "So do we have Asian privilege in America?" (O'Reilly 2014).

O'Reilly's question was largely in response to an earlier segment in which he challenged the concept of white privilege by pointing to the high status of Asian Americans in the United States. He argued that the "Asian American community is not a troubled situation" (Lee 2014), and his words suggested that if other minority groups simply followed the disciplined example of Asian Americans, they too could be as successful. O'Reilly was, in effect, invoking the *model minority* stereotype of Asian Americans (the notion that they are so successful that they should be held up as a model for other minority groups) as evidence that white privilege is not real. He argued that Asian Americans work hard and value education (just as whites presumably do), and as a result, they are successful—and perhaps even more so than their white counterparts.

However, though Asian Americans appear to be thriving in American society, their reality is much more complicated. In fact, evidence shows that the model minority stereotype is a myth and that Asian Americans continue to face racial barriers and persistent anti-Asian discrimination. Taken together, these realities challenge any notion that they experience race privilege comparable to that experienced by white Americans.

The model minority stereotype, for example, is misleading. On the surface, Asian Americans appear highly successful in American society. They are the highest income earning racial group in the United States today; in 2015, their median annual household income was $73,060 as compared to just $53,600 for all U.S. households (López, Ruiz, and Patten 2017). Asian Americans also have, on average, the highest educational levels of any racial group. More than half of all Asian Americans aged 25 and older have at least a bachelor's degree (51 percent), compared with 30 percent of all Americans in this age group (López, Ruiz, and Patten 2017).

These two socioeconomic indicators, among others, have been used to promote the view of Asian Americans as a model minority—a seemingly positive stereotype that privileges Asian Americans in the American racial hierarchy.

Proponents of the model minority stereotype maintain that because they have the "correct" cultural values (e.g., they are often praised for valuing education, family, and hard work), they are prosperous and thriving in American society. This perspective has led many Americans to believe in (1) the "bootstraps" argument, the idea that anyone can achieve success in the United States if they simply work hard (i.e., pull themselves up by their own bootstraps), and (2) a *post-racial* America, the notion that race no longer matters in contemporary U.S. society. Both views imply that no individual or racial group (including minorities) is hindered from success and advancement.

Such assertions are not borne out by the facts, however. In actuality, Asian Americans are an extremely heterogeneous racial group—not only in terms of country of origin (over 20 nationalities) and ethnicity but also in regard to their motive for migration, immigration status, and social class. A close examination of census data, for example, reveals wide variations in social class among Asian Americans; this is evident in measures for household income, educational attainment, poverty, and welfare usage (Park 2008). The median income of Asian American households outpaces the median income of all U.S. households, but wide variability in income exists among specific Asian American ethnic groups. Asian Indian households have the highest median income ($100,000), while Burmese ($36,000), Nepalese ($43,500), and Hmong ($48,000) have household incomes well below the median household income for all Americans (López, Ruiz, and Patten 2017). See figure 6.1 for a comparison of household incomes by Asian ethnicities, Asian Americans as a whole, and all U.S. households.

Asian Americans also have higher educational attainment than all other racial groups, but fortunes vary widely among Asian American subgroups in this area as well. Indians have the highest level of education among Asian Americans, with 72 percent holding at least a bachelor's degree. On the other hand, far fewer adults have a bachelor's degree among the Hmong (17 percent), Laotians (16 percent), and Bhutanese (9 percent).

Asian Americans are also less likely than the general U.S. population to live in poverty, but, again, there are large subgroup variations. Filipinos (7.5 percent) and Indians (7.5 percent) have the lowest poverty rates, and the highest rates are found among Hmong (28.3 percent), Bhutanese

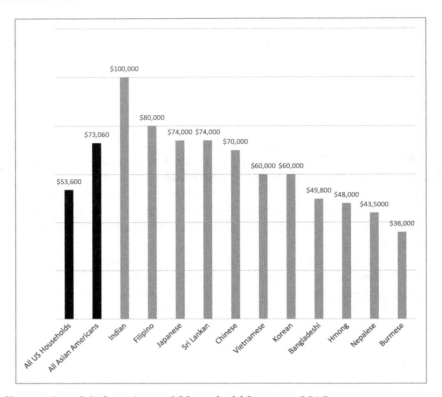

Figure 6.1. Median Annual Household Income, 2015.
(*Source*: Pew Research Center. Figure constructed from data in Lopez, Ruiz, and Patten [2017] and Budiman, Cilluffo, and Ruiz [2019]. *Not all Asian American groups are represented here)

(33.3 percent), and Burmese (35 percent) (López, Ruiz, and Patten 2017). Indeed, each of the three latter ethnic groups have poverty rates higher than that of African Americans (whose poverty rate was 21.2 percent in 2017) (Fontenot, Semega, and Kollar 2018). Further, some Asian American ethnic groups have relatively high rates of welfare utilization (Fong [1998] 2008). For example, in 2010, more than a third of Hmong Americans used public assistance (34.4 percent) as compared to 19.2 percent for the U.S. population as a whole (Bankston and Hidalgo 2016). Moreover, in 2015, less than 3 percent of Thai Americans and Japanese Americans participated in the Supplemental Nutrition Assistance Program (SNAP), which was formally known as "food stamps," as compared to nearly 70 percent of Bhutanese Americans and approximately half of all Burmese Americans (Tran 2018).

Furthermore, though the gap between rich and poor has risen in the United States since the 1970s, the disparity has grown faster among Asian Americans than for any other racial group between 1970 and 2016 (Kochhar and Cilluffo 2018). Today, they are the most economically divided racial group (Kochhar and Cilluffo 2018), and data show that those in the top tenth of the income distribution scale earn nearly eleven times that of the bottom tenth. Because of this gap, University of California professor Frank Wu describes Asian Americans as a "bipolar" population—disproportionately either rich or poor (2020). Nonetheless, the wealthiest tend to dominate the public imagination regarding Asian Americans, while the poorest generally remain invisible in the United States.

Economic disparities among Asian Americans stem from contemporary migration streams that widely differ in terms of class background. The Hart-Celler Act of 1965, the immigration act that for the first time allowed Asian immigrants into the United States in large numbers, favored two distinct types of immigrants: (1) highly skilled professionals (e.g., scientists, physicians, and engineers) and (2) immigrants joining family already in the United States (known as *family reunification*). The first group included highly educated professionals who arrived on American shores with education and job skills in hand. They represented the most educated, skilled, and privileged people from their home countries, which allowed for their rapid social ascent. The second group was more heterogenous regarding social class and included lower-class immigrants who were reuniting with family members. Additionally, in the 1970s, refugees began to arrive on American shores from war-torn regions of Southeast Asia (e.g., Cambodians, Hmong, Laotians, and Vietnamese). Because refugees tend to arrive with few resources, they experience higher than average rates of poverty and often have a more difficult time adjusting to life in the United States. In 2014, journalist Tina Nguyen summarized these stark differences in prospects and resources for Asian immigrants:

> For every Indian accountant who saved up money to immigrate to America—likely with a cushy job waiting for them at the other end by a company that sponsored their green card—there was a Cambodian refugee, fleeing from the promises of certain death with nothing but the clothes on their backs. For every Taiwanese expat with a college degree and fluency in English, there was a Hmong refugee from rural Laos. For every South Korean who came here with some investment money and business partners, to start a business and send

their kids to college, there were at least two terrified Vietnamese refugees who had lost everything they'd known, had no idea what was going to happen to them. (Nguyen 2014)

In addition, research shows that social class diversity, across and within Asian American groups, can have significant effects on the future successes of their children. One study of Korean American youth found that the primary factors predicting educational achievement were parental class background and social networks that reflect their social standing (Lew 2006). Lacking both economic resources and networks, lower-class Korean American students were more likely to drop out of high school than their higher-class Korean American counterparts. Such findings mirror the experiences of refugee groups from Southeast Asia, who often arrive in the United States with few resources—they, too, show high dropout rates. These findings challenge the model minority stereotype, which assumes that the positive cultural values of the minority group, such as the high value placed on education, solely explain their educational success. If this was indeed true, all Asian Americans (or at the very least, in this case, all Korean Americans) would graduate high school and perhaps college, regardless of social class. Instead, researchers find that social class background has far-reaching implications for educational achievement— just as it does for other racial minority groups in the United States.

How and when did the model minority stereotype emerge? And why does this trope continue to hold sway over the public mind despite ample evidence to the contrary? The idea of Asian Americans as the model minority became prevalent in the late 1960s. Scholars used the term to describe what appeared to be the exceptional educational achievement and upward mobility among Chinese and Japanese Americans despite the institutional discrimination and adversity that these groups had historically faced in the United States—including widespread anti-Asian hostility and Japanese American internment as recently as World War II. Some used the successes of Asian Americans to buttress the view that in the post–Jim Crow era, discrimination no longer existed that would prevent the assimilation and upward mobility of people of color. Asian Americans were held out as an example of the nation's capacity to incorporate all peoples and proof that all Americans, regardless of race, are afforded equal opportunity. This myth was mobilized as evidence that the nation was overcoming its history of racism and used to downplay or reject evidence of persistent racial oppression (Bascara 2006).

The model minority stereotype also became useful to explain existing racial inequality as a result of the individual and collective failings of other racial minorities (such as African Americans and Hispanic Americans) rather than due to systemic racism. Racial disadvantage was thus rationalized not as a problem of American society but as the failing of particular racial groups (and therefore not demanding of government intervention) since, as the argument goes, Asian Americans are raising themselves up by their own bootstraps despite their minority status (Kibria 1998; Zhou 2004). In short, some people said, "If Asian Americans can do it, why can't other groups?"

Some scholars further argue that the concept operates as an instrument of white supremacy by pitting Asian Americans and other minorities against each other (Chou and Feagin 2010; Kibria 1998; Zhou 2004). They assert that it was intended to create a "racial wedge" between minorities—particularly between Asian Americans and African Americans (Chow 2017). However, Janelle Wong, the director of Asian American Studies at the University of Maryland, argues that the stereotype makes a "a flawed comparison between Asian Americans and other groups, particularly Black Americans, to argue that racism, including more than two centuries of black enslavement, can be overcome by hard work and strong family values" (Chow 2017).

This apples-to-oranges comparison is echoed in the words of Bill O'Reilly in 2014 when he argued on-air that if African Americans only studied harder and maintained intact families, they could be as successful as Asian Americans (and by extension, white Americans) (O'Reilly 2014). This comparison, however, willfully ignores the advantaged position that accompanied many Asian immigrants when they arrived to American shores (particularly those most successful today, such as Indians, Filipinos, and Japanese Americans) and overlooks the fact that many were among the most privileged back home in their native countries (Wu 2020).

Moreover, one would assume that privileged racial groups would not face discrimination or racial barriers (at least not a significant amount), but this is not true of Asian Americans. Though they arguably face less discrimination than African Americans, they are not immune from systemic discrimination. They tend to receive a lower rate of return on educational achievement than similarly educated whites. Studies in the 2010s found that Asian American men earn 8 percent less than their white counterparts of comparable status and that, even in professional occupations, Asians cannot avoid unequal treatment (Dhingra 2016; Kim and Sakamoto 2010). They often face a "glass ceiling" that limits promotion and career advancement, as evidenced by their relative absence from top executive positions (Chou and Feagin 2010; Kibria 1998).

In the world of sports, meanwhile, Asian players frequently confront negative assumptions about their athletic ability. For example, scholar Maxwell Leung (2013) asserted that the reason basketball player Jeremy Lin was not drafted right out of college was that recruiters overlooked him because of his race. Even during his rapid ascent to NBA stardom in 2012, Lin's success continued to be framed according to the model minority narrative—the media, for example, attributed his on-court achievements to his "intelligence" and Ivy League education rather than his athletic ability (Leung 2013).

Further evidence that Asian Americans do not possess race privilege comparable to that of white Americans is reflected in their lack of full acceptance into American society. Even in the twenty-first century, Asian Americans are often seen by other Americans as "foreigners," no matter how many generations their families have lived in the United States. U.S.-born Asians, including those of the third and fourth generations, are still frequently asked where they are from, when and where they learned English (or praised for speaking "good English" or for having no accent), or are told in hostility to "go back to your country" by non-Asian Americans (Luo 2016; Tuan 1998). Ted Lieu, an Asian American politician, noted that even though he once served in the U.S. Air Force and currently serves as a U.S. congressman, he still experiences people telling him to "go back" to China or North Korea or Japan (Lieu 2019). In the post-9/11 era, South and Southeast Asian Americans (many of whom have dark skin) also often face added anti-Muslim sentiment and are treated as outsiders—though not all are Muslim (Fuchs 2017).

Moreover, in 2020, anti-Asian bias dramatically increased during the coronavirus/COVID-19 pandemic, adding further doubt about their so-called privilege in American society. The first months of 2020 saw a dramatic rise in anti-Asian discrimination, and according to one poll taken less than three months into the pandemic's presence in the United States, about a third of Americans reported that they had already witnessed someone blaming Asian people for the virus itself (Ellerbeck 2020). President Donald Trump repeatedly referred to COVID-19 as the "Chinese virus" or "Wuhan [China] virus" in 2020 and, at least once, as the "kung flu," though critics warned that his words might inflame anti-Asian xenophobia and potentially put Asian Americans in further danger of harassment and violence.

According to critics such as Cecillia Wang, of the American Civil Liberties Union, Trump's racialized labeling of the virus defied the advice of the World Health Organization (WHO) and Centers for Disease Control and Prevention (CDC) and escalated the risk that non-Asian Americans might engage in "dangerous scapegoating" of Asian Americans. She points out that, according to the civil rights organizations Chinese for Affirmative Action and the Asian Pacific Policy and Planning Council, there were more than 650 reports of anti-Asian attacks recorded in just a two-week period in March 2020—including denials of service at grocery stores, verbal harassments and slurs, and physical assaults. Regarding the latter, three members of an Asian American family were stabbed in March 2020 while shopping at a Sam's Club store in Midland, Texas. The attacker said he stabbed the family (including a two-year-old and a six-year-old child) because he believed that, because they were of Asian descent, they must have been spreading the virus (Wang 2020). A Pew Research Center poll conducted in June 2020 further found that many Asian Americans experienced discrimination amid the COVID-19 outbreak. Though only several months into the epidemic at the time of the survey, nearly a third of Asian American adults polled reported that they had been subject to slurs and racist jokes because of their race or ethnicity (Ruiz, Horowitz, and Tamir 2020).

The broad social class variability among Asian Americans and persistent systemic discrimination suggest that Asian American privilege does not yet exist in American society—at least that which might be comparable to privilege experienced by white Americans. However, it bears noting that this does not mean that Asian Americans possess no privilege at all. Privilege is relative. Although they do not experience race privilege as their white counterparts do, they arguably have more privilege than Black Americans. University of California–Irvine professor Claire Jean Kim asserts that the "racism that Asian-Americans have experienced is not what black people have experienced. . . . Asians have faced various forms of discrimination, but never the systematic dehumanization" that Black people have faced (Chow 2017). In other words, Asian Americans have experienced and continue to experience racism; however, they were never enslaved in the United States, nor have they endured the same degree of segregation, police brutality, and systemic discrimination that African Americans have experienced over the course of American history (Chow 2017).

FURTHER READING

Bankston, Carl L., III, and Danielle Antoinette Hidalgo. 2016. "The Waves of War: Refugees, Immigrants, and New Americans from Southeast Asia." Pp. 129–151 in *Contemporary Asian America: A Multidisciplinary Reader*, 3rd ed., edited by Min Zhou and Anthony C. Ocampo. New York: NYU Press.

Bascara, Victor. 2006. *Model Minority Imperialism.* Minneapolis and London: University of Minnesota Press.

Budiman, Abby, Anthony Cilluffo, and Neil G. Ruiz. 2019. "Key Facts about Asian Origin Groups in the U.S." Pew Research Center, May 22. Retrieved on June 2, 2020, at https://www.pewresearch.org/fact-tank /2019/05/22/key-facts-about-asian-origin-groups-in-the-u-s/.

Chou, Rosalind S., and Joe R. Feagin. 2010. *The Myth of the Model Minority: Asian Americans Facing Racism.* 3rd ed. Boulder, CO, and London: Paradigm.

Chow, Kat. 2017. "'Model Minority' Myth Again Used as a Racial Wedge between Asians and Blacks." NPR, *Codeswitch.* Retrieved on January 28, 2020, at https://www.npr.org/sections/codeswitch/2017/04 /19/524571669/model-minority-myth-again-used-as-a-racial-wedge -between-asians-and-blacks.

Dhingra, Pawan. 2016. "Just Getting a Job Is Not Enough: How Indian Americans Navigate the Workplace." Pp. 217–235 in *Contemporary Asian America: A Multidisciplinary Reader,* 3rd ed., edited by Min Zhou and Anthony C. Ocampo. New York: NYU Press.

Ellerbeck, Alex. 2020. "Over 30 Percent of Americans Have Witnessed COVID-19 Bias against Asians, Poll Says." NBC News, April 28.

Fong, Timothy P. (1998) 2008. *The Contemporary Asian American Experience: Beyond the Model Minority.* 3rd ed. Upper Saddle River, NJ: Pearson.

Fontenot, Kayla, Jessica Semega, and Melissa Kollar. 2018. *Income and Poverty in the United States: 2017.* U.S. Census Bureau, Current Population Reports, P60-263. Washington, DC: U.S. Government Printing Office. Retrieved on November 3, 2020, at https://www.census.gov /content/dam/Census/library/publications/2018/demo/p60-263.pdf.

Fuchs, Chris. 2017. "Behind the 'Model Minority' Myth: Why the 'Studious Asian' Stereotype Hurts." NBC News, August 22. Retrieved on August 22, 2020, at https://www.nbcnews.com/news/asian-america /behind-model-minority-myth-why-studious-asian-stereotype -hurts-n792926.

Kibria, Nazli. 1998. "The Contested Meanings of 'Asian American': Racial Dilemmas in the Contemporary U.S." *Ethnic and Racial Studies* 21(5): 939–958.

Kim, Chang Hwan, and Arthur Sakamoto. 2010. "Have Asian American Men Achieved Labor Market Parity with White Men?" *American Sociological Review* 75(6): 934–957.

Kochhar, Rakesh, and Anthony Cilluffo. 2018. "Income Inequality in the U.S. Is Rising Most Rapidly among Asians." Pew Research Center, July

12. Retrieved on November 3, 2020, at https://www.pewsocialtrends.org /2018/07/12/income-inequality-in-the-u-s-is-rising-most-rapidly-among -asians/.

Lee, Marie Myung-Ok. 2014. "Bill O'Reilly's 'Asian Privilege' Disgrace: The Fox News Host Needs Some Basic History Lessons." *Salon*, August 29. Retrieved on November 22, 2020, at https://www.salon.com/2014 /08/29/bill_oreillys_asian_privilege_disgrace_the_fox_news_host _needs_some_basic_history_lessons/.

Leung, Maxwell. 2013. "Jeremy Lin's Model Minority Problem." *Contexts* 12(3): 52–56. doi:10.1177/1536504213499879.

Lew, Jamie. 2006. *Asian Americans in Class: Charting the Achievement Gap among Korean American Youth*. New York: Teachers College Press.

Lieu, Ted. 2019. "I Have Served in the Air Force and in Congress. People Still Tell Me to 'Go Back' to China." *Washington Post*, July 16.

López, Gustavo, Neil G. Ruiz, and Eileen Patten. 2017. "Key Facts about Asian Americans, a Diverse and Growing Population." Pew Research Center, September 8. Retrieved on November 3, 2020, at https:// www.pewresearch.org/fact-tank/2017/09/08/key-facts-about-asian -americans/.

Luo, Michael. 2016. "An Open Letter to the Woman Who Told My Family to Go Back to China." *New York Times*, October 9. Retrieved on November 3, 2020, at https://www.nytimes.com/2016/10/10/nyregion /to-the-woman-who-told-my-family-to-go-back-to-china.html.

Nguyen, Tina. 2014. "A Lesson for Bill O'Reilly on 'Asian Privilege.'" Medialte, August 27. Retrieved on November 22, 2020, at https://www .mediaite.com/online/a-lesson-for-bill-oreilly-on-asian-privilege/.

O'Reilly, Bill. 2014. "Bill O'Reilly on White Privilege Debate Is There Asian Privilege Too." *The O'Reilly Factor*. YouTube, September 25. Retrieved on May 20, 2020, at https://www.youtube.com/watch?v= K84I3E92IMg

Park, Lisa Sun-Hee. 2008. "Continuing Significance of the Model Minority Myth: The Second Generation." *Social Justice* 35(2): 134–144.

Ruiz, Neil G., Juliana Menasce Horowitz, and Christine Tamir. 2020. "Many Black and Asian Americans Say That They Have Experienced Discrimination amid the COVID-19 Outbreak." Pew Research Center, July 1.

Tran, Victoria. 2018. "Asian Americans Are Falling through the Cracks in Data Representation and Social Services." Urban Institute, June 19.

Tuan, Mia. 1998. *Forever Foreigners or Honorary Whites? The Asian Experience Today*. New Brunswick, NJ: Rutgers University Press.

Wang, Cecillia. 2020. "Let's Stop the Scapegoating during a Global Pandemic." ACLU, April 14.

Wu, Frank. 2020. "Asian Americans Are Not the 'Model Minority.'" Diverse: Issues in Higher Education, April 27.

Zhou, Min. 2004. "Are Asian Americans Becoming White?" *Contexts* 3(1): 29–37.

Q7. AMONG PEOPLE OF COLOR, ARE THOSE WITH LIGHT SKIN ADVANTAGED OVER THOSE WITH DARK SKIN?

Answer: Yes. In many societies around the world, light skin is privileged over dark. Even in the United States, people with light skin are typically advantaged over those with darker skin tones—in particular, among communities of color, such as African Americans, Latinx Americans, Native Americans, and Asian Americans. Skin color discrimination occurs within and between these communities, and studies also show that whites, too, tend to favor people of color with lighter skin than those with darker hues.

The Facts: In much of the world, including in the United States, skin shade is a socially important human physical characteristic and light skin an enviable asset. According to sociologist Margaret Hunter, most Americans have a general understanding of discrimination between racial groups and its insidious effects on people of color, but she notes that "hidden within the process of racial discrimination, is the often overlooked issue of colorism" (Hunter 2005, 1). *Colorism* refers to the practice of discrimination whereby light skin is privileged over dark—both within and between racial and ethnic groups.

Colorism affects racial and ethnic groups worldwide, and its harmful effects have been well documented in the United States, particularly for African Americans. Research shows that light-skinned African Americans tend to have better health, greater job prospects, higher-status occupations, higher earnings, greater wealth, and more years of schooling than those with darker skin; light skin is also linked to perceived intelligence and trustworthiness (for a review of this research, see Hunter 2005; Khanna 2020; Russell-Cole, Wilson, and Hall 2013). Dark-skinned African Americans face bias from fellow African Americans as well as from other racial groups, including whites, who tend to favor those with light skin. This practice dates back to slavery, when white slave owners privileged slaves with light skin over those with dark skin tones. They gave them more desirable indoor jobs (while darker-skinned slaves labored in the fields), opportunities for education and skilled labor (privileges unavailable to most slaves), and, for some, even their freedom. Long after the end of slavery, the preference for light skin continued and even persists today. When Barack Obama ran for his first term as president, Senator Harry Reid, then the Democratic majority leader, predicted that Obama could become the nation's first Black president because he had "no Negro dialect" and was "light skinned" (Zeleny 2010).

A closer look at colorism among African Americans further reveals that for Black women in particular, light skin is associated with physical attractiveness and hence success in the marriage "market." Scholar Mark E. Hill argues that light skin is more valuable to Black women than Black men, drawing attention to what he calls "gendered colorism" (2002, 88). Beauty, often defined in the American context as possessing light skin, is a form of social capital for women, and Hunter notes that "study after study has shown that light-skinned African American women marry spouses with higher levels of education, higher incomes, or higher levels of occupational prestige than their darker-skinned counterparts" (Hunter 2007, 247). Gendered colorism is further evident in American media. Most Black actresses cast in lead film roles have historically been light-skinned (e.g., Halle Berry, Thandie Newton, and Paula Patton), and in the music industry, Black women with light skin, such as Mariah Carey and Beyoncé, have often taken center stage. The bias for light skin is also found in mainstream media outlets, with some having been accused of photoshopping Black and brown women to appeal to the white masses. For example, actress Gabby Sidibe was unnaturally lightened for the cover of *Elle* in 2010, recording artist Beyoncé was lightened for a print advertisement for L'Oréal in 2012, and actress Kerry Washington was noticeably lightened on the cover of *InStyle* magazine in 2015.

There is also growing research on Latinx populations—both in Latin America and in the United States. Light skin in these communities is similarly privileged, and skin tone affects one's life chances and opportunities. Latinx populations show a wide range in skin tone, and studies suggest that, as with African Americans, light skin is linked to better mental and physical health, more years of education, higher occupational status, and higher income. Light-skinned Latinxs in the United States also tend to live in more affluent neighborhoods, are more likely to marry "higher-status" spouses (those with higher levels of education, income, and occupational prestige), and are often considered more attractive than those with darker skin tones (Reichard 2016).

Moreover, although Latinxs may discriminate against fellow Latinxs based on skin tone, skin color bias also stems from other groups, including whites. For example, sociologist Lance Hannon found that whites are more likely to view light-skinned Latinxs as smarter than their darker-skinned counterparts (Hannon 2015). If whites equate lighter skin with intelligence, it may impact classroom expectations of Latinx students, hiring, promotions, pay, and even access to political power. Raquel Reichard, a Latina feminist and scholar, observes that most Latinx politicians are "light-skinned or straight-up white-passing" (Reichard 2016). This phenomenon may make light-skinned Latinxs such as Republican senators Ted Cruz (of Texas) and Marco Rubio (Florida) more palatable to voters.

Scholars have given less attention to colorism among Native Americans, though Professor Donna Brown and her colleagues (2018) argue that following European conquest and colonization, Native Americans similarly began to idealize light skin. European settlers equated light skin with intelligence and morality, and some Native tribes began to do the same. "Mixed-blood" Cherokees began to take pride in their light skin, and in Cherokee-run schools, darker "full bloods" were frequently "scorned" and perceived as "backward" (Brown, Branden, and Hall 2018, 2026). Brown and her colleagues argue that colorism persists today among Native Americans and can be observed in access to tribal membership. In short, "mixed-blood" Native Americans with white ancestry (light-skinned) are more favored for membership than those "mixed" with Black ancestry (dark-skinned). Cherokee tribal leaders, for example, attempted to exclude "mixed-blood" Black Cherokees from tribal membership, though a U.S. district court ruled against the Cherokee Nation in a highly publicized trial in 2017.

As a final example, scholarly attention has recently turned to skin color bias among Asians and Asian Americans (see Khanna 2020; Rondilla and Spickard 2007). Colorism exists in just about every part of Asia and affects Asian diasporas, including most Asian American communities—most notably affecting those descended from South and Southeast Asia (e.g., India, Pakistan, Cambodia, Philippines, and Indonesia) as well as those from Japan, China, South Korea, and other parts of East Asia. The preference for light skin is deeply rooted both in Asian ethnic cultures (and dates back hundreds if not thousands of years) and in European colonization, when whiteness and light skin became celebrated and revered in an exploitative system that placed Caucasians at the top of the racial hierarchy. As such, much of Asia and Asian America (even today) has a preoccupation with light skin, and light skin is often equated to sophistication, high social class, intelligence, and, for women in particular, physical attractiveness.

The present-day obsession with light skin is evident in the multibillion-dollar global skin whitening industry that promises consumers "white," "fair," and "translucent" skin through a wide variety of products, including moisturizers, makeup foundations, night creams, serums, lip balms, face washes, soap bars, and foot creams. Light-skinned (and sometimes Caucasian or part Caucasian) models advertise whitening products to people of color with product names such as Snowz, Fair & Lovely, Lightenex, Whitenicious, Fairever, White Beauty, Dior Snow, and Blanc Expert, which explicitly link whiteness with physical beauty. Whitening deodorants (presumably to whiten underarms) and feminine washes (to lighten the most intimate areas of the body) are also available. Though these products are sold worldwide and typically outside of American markets, they can easily be found in niche stores across the United States (e.g., those catering to particular ethnic or racial groups—such as Asian Americans). Additional options for skin whitening (though more expensive) include whitening pills that can easily be purchased online as well as in-office laser treatments and whitening injections. These products and treatments are typically aimed at women, though in recent years, the industry has increased its advertising to men.

In many societies, light skin is valued and privileged over dark—and scholarly research illustrates the concrete benefits of possessing light skin around the world and within communities of color in the United States. Light skin is linked to many positive stereotypes (such as intelligence, trustworthiness, sophistication, high social class, and beauty) as well as tangible positive outcomes in regard to mental and physical health, education, hiring, promotions, occupations, earnings, wealth, marriageability, marketability in media (e.g., films and music), and access to political power. For more on how colorism affects African Americans, see Q14 (for how skin shade affects Black children with regard to school suspensions) and Q19 (for how skin shade affects Black people in the criminal justice system).

FURTHER READING

Brown, Donna, Karen Branden, and Ronald E. Hall. 2018. "Native American Colorism: From Historical Manifestations to the Current Era." *American Behavioral Scientist* 62(14): 2023–2036.

Hannon, Lance. 2015. "White Colorism." *Social Currents* 2(1): 13–21.

Hill, Mark E. 2002. "Skin Color and the Perception of Attractiveness among African Americans: Does Gender Make a Difference?" *Social Psychology Quarterly* 65: 77–91.

Hunter, Margaret L. 2005. *Race, Gender, and the Politics of Skin Tone*. New York: Routledge.

Hunter, Margaret L. 2007. "The Persistent Problem of Colorism: Skin Tone, Status, and Inequality." *Sociology Compass* 1(1): 237–254.

Khanna, Nikki. 2020. *Whiter: Asian American Women on Skin Color and Colorism*. New York: New York University Press.

Reichard, Raquel. 2016. "11 Examples of Light-Skin Privilege in Latinx Communities." Everyday Feminism, March 25. Retrieved on May 10, 2018, at https://everydayfeminism.com/2016/03/light-skin-privilege-latinxs/.

Rondilla, Joanne L., and Paul Spickard. 2007. *Is Lighter Better? Skin Tone Discrimination among Asian Americans*. Lanham, MD: Rowman & Littlefield.

Russell-Cole, Kathy, Midge Wilson, and Ronald E. Hall. 2013. *The Color Complex: The Politics of Skin Color in a New Millennium*. New York: Anchor Books.

Zeleny, Jeff. 2010. "Reid Apologizes for Remarks on Obama's Color and 'Dialect.'" *New York Times*, January 10. Retrieved on April 28, 2018, at https://www.nytimes.com/2010/01/10/us/politics/10reidweb.html.

Q8. IS IT TRUE THAT WHITES WILL SOON BECOME A RACIAL MINORITY IN THE UNITED STATES?

Answer: No. Despite census projections and media headlines that claim that whites will be a racial minority in the United States by the mid-twentieth century, this is false. The framing by the media of census projections made in 2014 about a white demise by 2044 is greatly exaggerated and misrepresentative of the data. Additionally, the census projections themselves are problematic in how they define who is or is not "white" and how they describe the term "minority."

The Facts: Since the dawn of the new millennium, sensationalized media headlines such as "Whites to Become Minority in US by 2050" (Garcia 2008) and "The End of White America?" (Hsu 2009) have garnered a great deal of attention from the American public, politicians, and media pundits. Much of this stems from population predictions released by the U.S. Census Bureau in 2014 claiming that whites will become a "minority" by 2044 (Bedard 2014).

When Yale psychologist Jennifer Richeson first heard about the census report, she remembered thinking, "This is probably freaking somebody out." Namely, she predicted that some white Americans would become "uneasy" at the potential loss of their racial majority status in the United States (Resnick 2017). For some whites (though certainly not all), the headlines have indeed fueled fear, anxiety, and anger. A 2018 study found that nearly half of white Democrats (46 percent) and 74 percent of white Republicans "expressed anger or anxiety" after reading a news story that claimed that whites would soon become a racial minority in the United States (Myers and Levy 2018).

But these dramatic headlines are not true. There are several problems with the claim of an impending white minority. First, the description of the data is misleading. According to 2044 census projections, whites will make up 49.7 percent of the population, as compared to 25 percent of Hispanics, 12.7 percent of Blacks/African Americans, 7.9 percent of Asians, and 3.7 percent of multiracial Americans (Frey 2014; see figure 8.1). Though these projected numbers suggest that racial minorities, as a collective group, will slightly outsize whites in 2044 (by less than 1 percent to be exact), the white population will remain the single largest racial

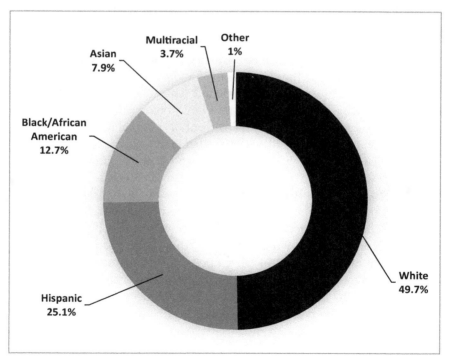

Figure 8.1. Projected U.S. Racial Population in 2044.
(*Source:* www.census.gov)

group in the United States—and nearly twice the size of Hispanics, the next largest projected group.

Second, who is defined as "white" in the U.S. Census is narrow. According to sociologist Richard Alba, the Census counts multiracial Americans (including those with partial white ancestry) as minorities. Alba argues, however, that "some of the mixed children now classified as minorities surely will think of themselves as white when they grow up." In fact, sociologists Jennifer Lee and Frank Bean reported in a 2010 study that parents of Asian-white and Hispanic-white children believed that their children would grow up to identify as "white or American often using these term[s] interchangeably" because, as they explain, their children were born in the United States, are strongly influenced by American culture, speak English, and are (as least in the case of respondents in the study) surrounded by white peers. For instance, an Asian Indian woman married to a white man explained that she believed her children would identify as white because "they were born here, and it's not like they're going to India." Her husband added, "I get the feeling that they'll probably identify themselves as white mostly because they probably won't speak Hindi. Plus, all of their friends are white" (Lee and Bean 2010, 105).

Moreover, many multiracial people identify with two or more races. If the census counted as white anyone who self-identifies as such (even if they also identify with another race or ethnicity), professors Dowell Myers and Morris Levy argue that the data then show that "the white population is not declining" but instead is "flourishing." This more inclusive definition of "whiteness," according to Myers and Levy, predicts a white population in the United States "in excess of 70 percent of the total for the foreseeable future" (Myers and Levy 2018). Alba further claims that multiracial Americans (particularly those with white ancestry) and even some minorities (e.g., light-skinned Latinxs and Asian Americans) are seen as "sociologically white"—meaning they are perceived essentially as white by other Americans (Alba 2015)—even if the census does not currently count them as such.

Additionally, definitions of "whiteness" have historically been subject to change (see Q2), and what is considered nonwhite today may indeed be redefined as white by 2044. In fact, American history illustrates the fluidity of whiteness. When some immigrant groups first arrived to American shores in the late 19th and early 20th centuries (such as the Irish, Italians, Greeks, and Eastern Europeans), they were not considered white. The Irish, for instance, were frequently referred to as "n*****s turned inside out" (Ignatiev 2009, 49), and they faced prejudice and discrimination for their perceived racial inferiority. They "became white" with time and assimilation, as did Southern and Eastern Europeans (Ignatiev 2009;

Yglesias 2018), illustrating that whiteness is an evolving social construct (see Q2 for additional coverage of the fluidity of whiteness over time). If the past is any indication of the future, the definition of whiteness will likely shift again, and perhaps by 2044, whiteness will expand once again to include groups that are today perceived as nonwhite (this may include some multiracial Americans and perhaps people of color with light skin).

Third, social scientists define *minority* as more than a mathematical description. The sociological meaning of the term *minority*, according to sociologist Martin N. Marger, is a group that "on the basis of their physical or cultural traits, are given differential and unequal treatment and receive fewer of the society's rewards" (Marger 2016, 578). Hence, the term *minority* is not simply about population numbers; it is about having comparatively less access to society's rewards. Power is a key example of a societal reward, and even if whites eventually become a numerical minority, it is unlikely that they will lose their hold on American power anytime soon. For example, in 2020, the *New York Times* reviewed 922 of the most powerful people in the United States (e.g., senators, mayors, governors, CEOs, university presidents) and found that only 180 of them were people of color—only about 20 percent, though 40 percent of Americans identify as Black, Indigenous, Asian, Native Americans, or another group of color (Lu et al. 2020). Perhaps there will be shifts in the coming decades in American leadership to better reflect the increasing diversity of the American people, though it is unlikely that these shifts in the power structure will significantly underrepresent or exclude whites. As described in Q5, Apartheid South Africa and colonial India are examples where power was concentrated in the hands of a numerically small racial group (i.e., whites). Though relatively small in number, their immense power over other races precluded classifying whites in these societies as racial minorities.

FURTHER READING

Alba, Richard. 2015. "The Myth of a White Minority." *New York Times*, June 11. Retrieved on May 28, 2019, at https://www.nytimes.com/2015/06/11/opinion/the-myth-of-a-white-minority.html.

Bedard, Paul. 2014. "Census: Whites Become 'Minority' in 2044, Hispanic Population Twice Blacks." *Washington Examiner*, December 15. Retrieved on May 28, 2019, at https://www.washingtonexaminer.com/census-whites-become-minority-in-2044-hispanic-population-twice-blacks.

Frey, William H. 2014. "New Projections Point to a Majority Minority Nation in 2044." Brookings, December 12. Retrieved on May 28,

2019, at https://www.brookings.edu/blog/the-avenue/2014/12/12/new
-projections-point-to-a-majority-minority-nation-in-2044/.

Garcia, Adriana. 2008. "Whites to Become Minority in U.S. by 2050." Reuters, February 11. Retrieved on May 28, 2019, at https://www.reuters.com
/article/us-usa-population-immigration-idUSN1110177520080212.

Hsu, Hua. 2009. "The End of White America?" *The Atlantic* (January/
February). Retrieved on May 28, 2019, at https://www.theatlantic.com
/magazine/archive/2009/01/the-end-of-white-america/307208/.

Ignatiev, Noel. 2009. *How the Irish Became White*. London: Routledge.

Lee, Jennifer, and Frank D. Bean. 2010. *The Diversity Paradox: Immigration and the Color Line in 21st Century America*. New York: Russell Sage.

Lu, Denise, Jon Huang, Ashwin Sheshagiri, Haeyoun Park, and Troy
Griggs. 2020. "Faces of Power: 80% are White, Even as U.S. Becomes
More Diverse." *New York Times*, September 9. Retrieved on November
22, 2020, at https://www.nytimes.com/interactive/2020/09/09/us/power
ful-people-race-us.html.

Marger, Martin N. 2016. *Race and Ethnic Relations: American and Global
Perspectives*. 7th ed. Belmont, CA: Thomson Wadsworth.

Myers, Dowell, and Morris Levy. 2018. "The Demise of the White
Majority Is a Myth." *Washington Post*, May 18. Retrieved on May 28,
2019, at https://www.washingtonpost.com/opinions/the-demise-of
-the-white-majority-is-a-myth/2018/05/18/60fc897c-5233-11e8-abd8
-265bd07a9859_story.html.

Resnick, Brian. 2017. "White Fear of Demographic Change Is a Powerful
Psychological Force." Vox, January 28. Retrieved on May 28, 2019, at
https://www.vox.com/science-and-health/2017/1/26/14340542/white
-fear-trump-psychology-minority-majority.

Yglesias, Matthew. 2018. "Study: Overhyped Media Narratives about
America's Fading White Majority Fuel Anxiety." Vox, May 2. Retrieved
on May 28, 2019, at https://www.vox.com/policy-and-politics/2018
/5/2/17305402/majority-minority-demographic-forecast.

Q9. IS CULTURAL APPROPRIATION OF MINORITY CULTURES BY WHITE AMERICANS EQUIVALENT TO AMERICAN MINORITIES ADOPTING WHITE CULTURE?

Answer: No (at least within the context of the United States). Cultural appropriation is not merely the taking of elements of one culture by another (such as food, music, or language); rather, it involves members of a dominant group who take from the culture of a subordinate minority group. Thus, the defining feature of cultural appropriation is power. A power imbalance between dominant and minority groups is problematic because racial minorities, who have relatively less power, often have little control over how their culture is represented and used by the dominant group. Dominant groups can also appropriate from minority cultures for gain (e.g., fame, attention, and money) with little appreciation of the culture nor acknowledgment of how the group has been marginalized in American society for practicing that culture. By contrast, when minorities adopt aspects of a dominant group's culture, they typically do so for the purposes of assimilation and survival in a white-dominated society.

The Facts: The topic of cultural appropriation is controversial and frequently misunderstood. *Cultural appropriation* (also called *cultural misappropriation*) typically refers to the adoption or use of elements of one culture by members of another. This may include (but is not limited to) the use of dialect/language, clothing, hairstyles, music, dance, cuisine, art, cultural artifacts, and religious symbols. Cultural appropriation should not be confused with *cultural exchange*. Cultural exchange involves a mutual exchange and respectful sharing between two or more cultures who are on a relatively level playing field—such as, for example, the fusion of Indian and Chinese cuisines in border regions of the two nations or when two Native American tribes (of relatively similar status) voluntarily exchange cultural traditions such as dance and art. Cultural appropriation, on the other hand, is less reciprocal. It typically involves a *power imbalance* whereby members of a privileged group take from a marginalized group.

This imbalance of power is problematic for several reasons. First, cultural appropriation generally refers to situations when one group borrows from the culture of another without any real understanding or knowledge of the culture. As such, the appropriation often oversimplifies, misrepresents, and distorts the culture, which is especially problematic for marginalized groups. For instance, Native American costumes are popular at Halloween and are commonly sold online and in stores throughout the United States. Every year, non-Native people play dress up in factory-produced costumes that exploit Native American cultures. They are exploitative because: (1) the costumes commodify Native American culture, (2) non-Native peoples profit from their sale, (3) the costumes reduce hundreds of tribes into a one-dimensional stereotype (usually a clichéd image of loin cloths, fringe, and feathers), and (4) in costumes marketed to adults, they frequently misrepresent the culture by hypersexualizing Native Americans—especially Native women. Because Native peoples are small in number and marginalized in American society, they have little power to counter these mass-produced images of themselves created by the dominant group.

Second, cultural appropriation occurs when one borrows or takes from another's culture without permission. According to journalist Katie J. M. Baker, cultural appropriation without consent is problematic for minority groups because they typically have little say in how their culture is used. Borrowing without permission is particularly harmful when the objects of appropriation are sensitive to the culture—such as sacred objects—that are then used for other purposes by those outside their group (Baker 2012). For instance, yoga practices in the West typically draw upon sacred Hindu symbols (e.g., the ohm and gods and goddesses) for decoration on yoga mats and T-shirts, often with little understanding or consideration of their religious meanings to Hindus. Even the practice of yoga itself in the West is often divorced from its original religious meaning, and in some cases, Western permutations debase the Hindu practice. For example, in "rage yoga," a 2019 trend in some parts of the United States, participants were encouraged to drink alcohol and "yell, scream, cuss and make obscene gestures" ("'Rage Yoga'" 2019).

Additionally, thousands of schools across the United States use Native peoples as mascots (often representing majority white schools), and in pep rallies and games, the mascots frequently don items sacred to Native American tribes without the permission of the cultures to whom the items belong. For instance, eagle feather bonnets are commonplace among school mascots, though they are symbols of honor to many tribes and typically worn only by Native chiefs and warriors. These items are used by the dominant group for entertainment and often with little to no understanding of their underlying sacred or cultural meanings. Jennifer Weston, of the Hunkpapa Lakota tribe at Standing Rock, asks that Native peoples fight back against these appropriations, arguing that when dressing up as Native peoples is "devoid of knowledge of our real cultures and religions, AND misrepresenting and misappropriating these sacred symbolic articles, we must demand respect for our religious practices" (as cited in Baker 2012).

Moreover, as previously described, obtaining permission is particularly important so that minority groups have a voice in how their cultures are represented. However, the issues of permission and who has authority to give consent are nuanced. A Nigerian bride who asks her white guests to wear traditional Nigerian attire to her wedding arguably has authority. A local Cherokee leader who invites non-Natives to a pow-wow has authority to give consent if they ask to participate in the tribe's traditional dances. However, authority is not absolute; for example, the tribal leader has some degree of authority, but does not necessarily have the right to give a multinational clothing company permission to usurp Native (or even Cherokee) clothing for its new fall fashion line. No one person represents or speaks for all Native Americans or even all Cherokees.

Finally, cultural appropriation is problematic because it frequently involves members of a dominant group who appropriate the culture of a historically oppressed group without an understanding of the ways in which these groups have been marginalized in American society for practicing this culture. Some examples include the following:

- Non-Arab/non-Muslim Americans wearing "Arab girl" costumes for Halloween (complete with hijab): They may wear it for fun, but they remain blissfully unaware of the religious and cultural meaning of such dress and the challenges faced by those who wear it as part of their daily lives in American society. For instance, according to a 2018 New York survey, one in four Muslim women reported that they had been pushed on subway platforms while wearing their hijabs (Croft 2018). Additionally, these costumes are often overtly sexual; thus, they sexualize a culture centered on modesty.
- Non-Indian women who wear bindis—colored dots worn in the middle of the forehead—as fashion accessories: They may perceive bindis as "trendy," "cute," or "exotic," but they typically have little understanding of their cultural/religious significance and no recognition of how Indian women in the United States have been marginalized, othered, and targeted for wearing them. For instance, in the 1980s, Indians were harassed and terrorized in a New Jersey community by a group calling themselves "the Dotbusters" (an apparent reference to the bindi); some Indian women abandoned their bindis to avoid harassment and violence (Marriott 1987).
- Non-Black celebrities who arrange their hair into box braids, cornrows, twists, or knots: Though the origins of each of these styles are debated, these styles are commonplace in Black culture. In 2017, reality show star Khloe Kardashian faced criticism for styling her hair into "Bantu knots" (named for an ethnic group in Africa). According to activist Francesca Ramsey, the problem is that non-Black celebrities, like Kardashian, are often praised for being "edgy" or "stylish," with little recognition that Black women are often disparaged and penalized for wearing the same hairstyles. Many schools prohibit Black girls from wearing these hairstyles, and Black women have even been fired for sporting these styles in the workplace.

- Iggy Azalea, white Australian-born rapper, who uses Southern Black dialect in her music: Though musicians have long shared and exchanged musical styles, Azalea's striking shift in accent and dialect (from middle-class Australian English to African American Vernacular English [AAVE]) for professional and financial gain is seen by critics as problematic. This does not mean that white musicians cannot perform musical styles that originated in Black culture. In fact, the United States has a long history of white artists borrowing aspects of Black music, ranging from Elvis to Eminem to Robin Thicke. One commentator, however, contends that the situation with Iggy Azalea (otherwise known as Amethyst Amelia Kelly) is different: "While Iggy Azalea might seem to be continuing this tradition of white artists emulating black culture, there is a major difference between these other artists and her: other white Hip Hop artists who have achieved mainstream success rap in their own dialect and use lyrics which authentically reflect their backgrounds, they do not speak in a way which is completely outside of their cultural frameworks in order to appeal to a particular audience" (Andrews 2014).

  By contrast, detractors contend that Azalea puts on and takes off Black culture like clothing (she speaks with her natural Australian accent in interviews but shifts to Southern Black dialect in her music), all the while remaining silent on social issues important to many African American, such as how they are stigmatized for speaking AAVE. She has also been accused by detractors of being indifferent to the Black Lives Matter movement.

Critics of the concept of cultural appropriation argue that while white Americans occasionally adopt aspects of minority cultures, people of color adopt elements of white Western culture, too. Black women straighten their hair, Indian immigrants trade saris for jeans, and Mexican immigrants adopt English. Aren't these examples of cultural appropriation, they ask?

The answer is no because of the unequal social positions of different racial groups. While the dominant group may borrow aspects of a marginalized group's culture because it is "cute," "cool," or because they can profit off the culture, marginalized groups adopt the dominant group's culture for conformity and assimilation into American society. For instance, some Black women straighten their hair not simply because they think it stylish but because larger American society deems straight hair more professional and attractive than the tightly curled hair typical of African Americans.

Style and beauty writer Shayna Watson argues that there is "a difference between voluntary adoption and forced conformity" and writes:

> Emphasis placed on European standards of beauty for black people . . . stems from actual monetary value. The notion that kinky, textured hair was worthless came from the fact that slaves with more distinct African features were actually valued less. Slaves with lighter skin and straight hair commanded higher prices at auctions. . . . Even after slavery ended, black women who straightened their hair were seen as being more "well-adjusted" and had an easier time gaining employment from white employers. . . . Straight hair was mandatory for blacks to gain entry into schools, businesses and social organizations after emancipation. So black people's decision to straighten their natural hair texture . . . has a foundation in a century-long rule set that conformity is necessary for survival. (Watson 2016)

The pressure to conform to white norms is exemplified in a study conducted by the beauty brand Dove, which found that 80 percent of Black women reported changing their hair from its natural state to fit in at work; they were also 50 percent more likely than white women to report having been sent home or knowing of other Black women sent home from work because of hair (*Glamour* 2020). Anti-Black hair discrimination also takes the form of policies in the workplace and K-12 schools that ban styles common among Black women and girls, including natural Black hair, such as afros. For example, in 2013, one Ohio school banned "afro-puffs and small twisted braids," which are styles popular among Black girls (Klein 2018). In 2016, a Kentucky high school banned cornrows, twists, and dreadlocks. One parent noted that the school policy stated that students' hair must be "neat and clean," implying, she argued, that Black hair is not (Quinn 2016). Additionally, it was not until 2014 that the U.S. military lifted a ban on Black hairstyles such as twists and multiple braids (Rhodan 2014).

In 2019, California became the first state to prohibit workplace and school policies banning natural hair (i.e., afros) as well as other hairstyles, such as twists, cornrows, and dreadlocks. By 2020, six other states—New York, New Jersey, Maryland, Virginia, Colorado, and Washington—followed suit (*Glamour* 2020), but Black women and girls continue to face hair discrimination across most of the nation. Furthermore, a study conducted by researchers at Duke University in 2020 found that hair matters in hiring. The study's participants (who were of different races) were asked to pretend they were job recruiters and then instructed to screen fictitious female job candidates via mocked-up social media accounts; as is typical with social media, photographs of the women were included. Participants rated Black women with natural hairstyles as less professional as compared to Black women with straightened hair. They were also less likely to recommend them for job interviews, suggesting that bias for white cultural norms is systemic and economically injurious for Black women who choose not to conform (Guy 2020).

Moreover, in contexts where their hairstyles are not prohibited, Black women still face intense cultural pressure to conform to white hair norms. Comedian Paul Rooney once joked, "If your hair is relaxed, white people are relaxed. If your hair is nappy, they're not happy" (Louis 2009). Consider former first lady Michelle Obama and the potential public reaction by whites (also the largest voting bloc) if, during her husband's presidency, she had let her hair grow naturally into an afro (or styled it into cornrows, Bantu knots, or another African/Black cultural style). Perhaps some would have applauded her hair, but others would have certainly criticized it as unbecoming of her position as First Lady of the United States if they perceived the style to be unprofessional (see the 2020 Duke study previously discussed). When Black women straighten their hair or when non-Western immigrants to the United States dress in Western clothing or adopt English, they often do so because the dominant group expects and demands it: they do so for the purposes of cultural integration. To survive and thrive in American society, there is immense pressure to conform to dominant white culture.

Finally, cultural appropriation is not something that only white people do. People of color can also be guilty of cultural appropriation, especially when it involves a more privileged minority group appropriating the culture of a more marginalized group. Scholar and educator Rachel Kuo argues, "As a person of color, I can absolutely be complicit in cultural appropriation," and she admits that she does not automatically receive a "pass" simply because she is Asian American (2016). Even among minority groups in the United States, there are groups that are more or less privileged than others. The following are two examples of cultural appropriation among people of color:

- Asian American celebrities who appropriate aspects of Black culture (e.g., speaking in AAVE) because they perceive it as profitable to their careers and bank accounts—without recognizing or acknowledging anti-Black bias within their own communities. For instance, Asian American actress Awkwafina has been accused of exploiting Black culture for personal fame and fortune. According to one critic, she "has made a career out of performing a caricatured interpretation of Blackness" by speaking in "blaccent" (AAVE) and by wearing "Blackness like a costume, putting it on when it commercially rewards her . . . and taking it off when it does not" (Miao 2020).

- African Americans who appropriate aspects of Native cultures in ways that misrepresent or misuse the culture. In 2014, African American entertainer Pharrell Williams donned a traditional Native headdress on the cover of *Elle* magazine, causing backlash on social media with comments such as "My culture is not a costume or a hat" and "You have no right to wear a headdress that is so sacred to native people. Those headdresses are earned and not worn to make a buck" (MTV UK 2014; Wilson 2017). Williams subsequently apologized, saying that he was "genuinely sorry" for posing with the headdress (Blistein 2014).

FURTHER READING

Andrews, Grant. 2014. "Iggy Azalea and Black Culture: Homage or Appropriation?" Cutlurecrit, July 1. Retrieved on May 30, 2019, at http://www.culturecrit.com/2014/07/iggy-azalea-and-black-culture-homage-or.html.

Baker, Katie J. M. 2012. "A Much-Needed Primer on Cultural Appropriation." Jezebel, November 13. Retrieved on May 30, 2019, at https://jezebel.com/a-much-needed-primer-on-cultural-appropriation-30768539.

Blistein, Jon. 2014. "Pharrell Apologizes for Wearing Headdress on Magazine Cover." *Rolling Stone*, June 5.

Croft, Jay. 2018. "1 in 4 Muslim Women in New York Say They've Been Pushed on a Subway Platform while Wearing a Hijab." CNN, June 19.

Glamour. 2020. "The Crown Act: Every State That's Passed Legislation Banning Hair Discrimination." July 3. Retrieved on November 23, 2020, at https://glamor.news/the-crown-act-every-state-thats-passed-legislature-banning-hair-discrimination/.

Guy, Jack. 2020. "Black Women with Natural Hairstyles Are Less Likely to Get Job Interviews." CNN, August 12.

Klein, Rebecca. 2018. "Schools See Major Uptick in Racial Harassment, New Data Suggests." HuffPost, February 23.

Kuo, Rachel. 2016. "Yes, People of Color Can Practice Cultural Appropriation—Here Are 3 Ways How." Everyday Feminism, June 14. Retrieved on May 30, 2019, at https://everydayfeminism.com/2016/06/poc-cultural-appropriation/.

Louis, Catherine Saint. 2009. "Black Hair, Still Tangled in Politics." *New York Times*, August 26.

Marriott, Michel. 1987. "In Jersey City, Indians Protest Violence." *New York Times*, October 12.

Miao, Hannah. 2020. "On Awkwafina, Appropriation and Asian American Identity." *The Chronicle*, January 23.

MTV News. 2015. "7 Myths about Cultural Appropriation Debunked." Video. YouTube, November 11. Retrieved on May 30, 2019, at https://www.youtube.com/watch?v=KXejDhRGOuI.

MTV UK. 2014. "Pharrell's Elle Headdress Cover Causes Controversy." June 4. Retrieved on May 30, 2019, at http://www.mtv.co.uk/pharrell-williams/news/pharrells-elle-headdress-cover-causes-controversy.

Quinn, Dave. 2016. "Kentucky High School Lifts Hairstyle Ban after Furious Parents and Students Call Policy Racist." *People*, August 4.

"'Rage Yoga' Releases 'Negative Energy' with Alcohol, Profanity and Obscene Gestures." 2019. CBS Philly, October 16. Retrieved on October 17, 2019, from https://philadelphia.cbslocal.com/2019/10/16/rage-yoga-releases-negative-energy-with-alcohol-profanity-and-obscene-gestures/.

Rhodan, Maya. 2014. "US Military Rolls Back Restrictions on Black Hairstyles." *TIME*, August 13.

Watson, Shayna. 2016. "Black People, Please Stop Saying Straightening Our Hair Is Appropriation." The Root, October 22. Retrieved on May 30, 2019, at https://www.theroot.com/black-people-please-stop-saying-straightening-our-hair-1790857373.

Wilson, Julee. 2017. "Not Everyone Is Happy about Pharrell Williams' Elle UK Cover." HuffPost, December 6. Retrieved on May 30, 2019, at https://www.huffpost.com/entry/pharrell-williams-elle-uk-cover_n_5444351.

Q10. WHY DO MANY AMERICANS FIND BLACKFACE OFFENSIVE?

Answer: According to a 2019 poll, nearly 60 percent of all Americans and roughly 75 percent of African Americans found it unacceptable for a white person to wear blackface makeup—though, notably, views toward blackface are not universal. Americans have varying opinions on the practice, and in some cases, people are puzzled by the controversy and ask, "Why is blackface seen as offensive?" In response, historians point out that blackface has a long and racist history in the United States and is the product of a power imbalance between white and Black Americans. Whites historically donned blackface in widely popular minstrel shows to parody and ridicule African Americans (who had little power to fight back against these portrayals), and even today, blackface is used to mock, demean, and dehumanize African Americans.

The Facts: In 2019, the media was abuzz when an old yearbook photo surfaced of Virginia's governor, Ralph Northam. His offense? In the grainy 1984 photo, a young Northam, then a medical student at Eastern Virginia Medical School, allegedly appears in blackface—complete with blackened face and hands and a black curly wig (notably, he is also posing with a fellow student decked out in a white Ku Klux Klan robe and pointed white hat). Northam, a Democrat, confirmed that he was in the photo and admitted in a statement that the costumes were "clearly racist and offensive." He went on to apologize, saying that he was "deeply sorry" for the hurt that he caused to others (however, within 24 hours he had retracted the apology, claiming that he was not sure he was one of the men pictured in the photograph after all). Regardless, the head of the NAACP, the editorial board for the newspaper serving Virginia's capital, and politicians on both sides of the aisle called for his resignation (Kelly 2019).

Another highly publicized incident occurred in 2013, when white celebrity Julianne Hough donned blackface for a Halloween party by dressing up as her favorite character from the hit Netflix series *Orange Is the New Black* (she covered her face in black paint and styled her hair into small knots). She apologized to critics, though she added, "I am a huge fan of the show *Orange Is the New Black*, actress Uzo Aduba, and the character she has created. It certainly was never my intention to be disrespectful or demeaning to anyone in any way" (Sieczkowski 2017). Similarly, white reality star Luann de Lesseps (of *The Real Housewives of New York* fame) was perplexed when people criticized her 2018 blackface Halloween costume as "disrespectful" and "tone deaf" (Mar 2018). She admitted feeling horrified by the public backlash and explained that her costume (bronzed skin and oversized curly wig to impersonate Diana Ross) was intended merely as a "tribute" to the singer (Mar 2018). In 2015, country singer Jason Aldean was criticized for his blackface Halloween costume (he dressed up as Black rapper Lil Wayne, complete with darkened skin and dreadlock wig). He apologized, though he also added that "people are so sensitive" (Furdyk 2016).

Though some have offered apologies or expressed embarrassment for wearing blackface, others remain outright baffled by its condemnation.

For instance, in 2018, white talk show host Megyn Kelly was fired from NBC after she defended blackface on her morning show and claimed that it was seen as "okay" when she was a kid. After she received widespread backlash for her comments, she allegedly circulated an e-mail to coworkers asking, "What is racist" about dressing up in blackface? (Moniuszko 2018).

Put simply, many perceive blackface as problematic because of its long, racist history in the United States. Some people may see it as nothing more than darkening one's skin for fun (and think, "Well, what's the harm in that?"), but for others, blackface invokes a racist time in American history that was particularly degrading and demoralizing for African Americans. The practice of blackface is rooted in the widely popular minstrel shows of the nineteenth and twentieth centuries in which white men painted their faces with burnt cork, grease, or black shoe polish; donned curly black wigs; and painted their lips wide and bright white. They typically caricatured how they believed African Americans looked and acted, and in these vaudeville-type shows, they ridiculed them and made them the butt of their jokes for the entertainment of white audiences. In addition to altering their physical appearance to impersonate African Americans, they adopted heavy dialects (intentionally misusing the English language to garner laughs) and performed what they claimed were Black songs and dances. White actors in blackface also poked fun at Black enslavement and presented African Americans as foolish, naïve, ignorant, dim-witted, cowardly, lazy, and hypersexual—all white-created stereotypes of African Americans.

Blackface minstrelsy became a national sensation. In the second half of the nineteenth century, in fact, it was "the most popular form of entertainment in America," and for decades, minstrel shows "had few show-business competitors" (Grosvenor and Toll 2019). From the South to the West to the North, white audiences flocked to blackface minstrel shows. The spread of blackface comedy and the wild success of minstrel shows were rooted in a stark power imbalance. The white dominant group had immense power and control over how African Americans were depicted; by contrast, African Americans had little say in how whites portrayed them. Blackface minstrel shows flourished because African Americans had little power to fight back against these derogatory portrayals intended for comedy and entertainment. Furthermore, if African Americans had caricatured whites in a similar manner, the power imbalance meant that they risked certain violence and death.

The practice of white men dressed in blackface eventually moved from stage shows to other white-controlled entertainment platforms, such as radio, film, and television. As with stage shows, these new venues (1) discriminated against African Americans with negative portrayals, and (2) continued the tradition of excluding African Americans from show business altogether. Some notorious examples of blackface in American film include *The Birth of a Nation*, 1915 (white actors played racist caricatures of Black men; the film was so popular that it was screened by President Woodrow Wilson in the White House and is credited for the reemergence of the KKK in the post–Civil War era); *The Jazz Singer*, 1927 (starring a white Al Jolson who donned blackface for the duration of the film); and *Everybody Sing*, 1938 (white actress Judy Garland wore what some critics have described as "horrific" blackface makeup, which featured exaggerated clown-like bright white lips and blackened face and body) (Lee 2017). Other white celebrities who have donned blackface in film or television include Fred Astaire, Jack Benny, Oliver Hardy, Benny Hill, Bob Hope, Gene Kelly, Mickey Rooney, Frank Sinatra, Elizabeth Taylor, and Shirley Temple; more recent examples include Dan Aykroyd, Billy Crystal, Danny DeVito, Jimmy Kimmel, and Jimmy Fallon. In 2020, amid public pressure, both Kimmel and Fallon apologized for appearing in blackface early in their careers (in the mid-1990s and 2000, respectively), underscoring how American attitudes about the practice have evolved over time.

Though blackface was once widely popular in American entertainment, the majority of Americans view the practice as unacceptable today. In a 2019 poll, nearly 60 percent said it was "unacceptable" for white people to wear blackface makeup (*The Economist* and YouGov 2019). However, opinions about blackface vary widely depending on one's race, political party affiliation, political ideology, and gender; those who are Black, Democrat, liberal, and female are most likely to find the practice unacceptable (see table 10.1 for a breakdown by race, political party, ideology, and gender).

These differences in public opinion may be explained by (1) one's racial identity and whether one's racial group is the target of blackface, (2) varying opinions of "political correctness" and what should be defined as acceptable or unacceptable behavior, and perhaps most importantly, (3) varying levels of awareness of the history of minstrel shows and blackface in the United States.

Not surprisingly, African Americans are more likely than white Americans to view blackface as offensive or racially insensitive. More than half of all whites in the abovementioned national poll (57 percent) agreed

Table 10.1 "Is It Acceptable or Unacceptable for a White Person to Wear Blackface Makeup?"

	"Unacceptable" (percentage)
All Respondents	58
Race	
White	57
Black	73
Hispanic	55
Party ID	
Democrat	81
Republican	44
Independent	50
Ideology	
Liberal	85
Moderate	57
Conservative	48
Gender	
Male	54
Female	62

Source: The Economist/YouGov (2019).

that blackface was "unacceptable," though nearly three-quarters of African Americans agreed—in part because, even in the twenty-first century, blackface continues to be used to caricature, mock, and dehumanize African Americans:

- In 2001, white students at Auburn University posed for photos at a fraternity party in front of a Confederate flag, which for many is perceived as a symbol of white supremacy, Black enslavement, and anti-Black terror. One student also wore blackface with a noose around his neck (evoking lynching), and another donned a Ku Klux Klan robe.
- Also in 2001, white students at the University of Mississippi posed for a picture at a Halloween party. One student, dressed as a police officer, pointed a gun at the head of another white student who was dressed in blackface, and kneeling down and picking cotton.

- In 2010, white students at the University of California, San Diego, held an off-campus "Compton Cookout" party to mock Black History Month. The Facebook invitation promised partygoers a taste of "life in the ghetto" and urged attendees to dress in blackface. For example, women were instructed to dress as "ghetto chicks," who "usually have gold teeth, start fights and drama, and wear cheap clothes" (Gordon 2010).
- In 2019, two white students at the University of Oklahoma were filmed laughing as one student donned blackface (down to the palms of her hands) while allegedly spouting the N-word.
- In the same year, white Alabama high school student wore blackface paint in a Snapchat photo captioned, "Is this what being a n****r feels like?"
- Also in 2019, a photo of Florida secretary of state Mike Ertel surfaced showing him dressed in blackface. He wore black paint on his face, red lipstick, hoop earrings, a New Orleans Saints bandana, and fake breasts under a purple T-shirt that read "Katrina Victim." Given that most people who died from Hurricane Katrina in 2005 were Black, he appeared to be mocking Black victims.

Blackface can be found in yearbook photos, college parties, Halloween costumes, film, television, and even in other unexpected places. Luxury brands Prada and Gucci, for instance, came under fire in 2018 and 2019, respectively, for advertising and selling products with blackface imagery. Regarding the former, the company marketed what they called "Pradamalia imagery" on a range of products (from keychains to cell phone cases to clothing and more) online and in stores that appeared monkey-like, with jet-black skin and large, bright red lips—reminiscent of blackface imagery in the nineteenth and twentieth centuries. Though company representatives denied they were blackface, critics disagreed.

Blackface has garnered increased scrutiny in the twenty-first century, suggesting that attitudes about the practice are shifting. Nonetheless, some Americans (especially if non-Black) continue to see little problem with blackface or remain perplexed by the controversy. Increased education about America's history of minstrelsy and blackface is thus regarded as key to ending the practice.

FURTHER READING

The Economist and YouGov Poll. 2019. "*The Economist*/YouGov Poll: February 2–5, 2019—1500 US Adults: Table 43: Blackface Acceptable."

Retrieved on October 28, 2019, at https://d25d2506sfb94s.cloudfront
.net/cumulus_uploads/document/er2vitqfsn/econTabReport.pdf.

Furdyk, Brent. 2016. "Jason Aldean Apologizes for Controversial Blackface Halloween Costume: 'People Are So Sensitive.'" ET Canada, September 8.

Gordon, Larry. 2010. "UC San Diego Condemns Student Party Mocking
Black History Month." *Los Angeles Times*, February 18.

Grosvenor, Edwin S., and Robert C. Toll. 2019. "Blackface: The Sad
History of Minstrel Shows." *American Heritage* 64(1). Retrieved
on November 23, 2020, at https://www.americanheritage.com
/blackface-sad-history-minstrel-shows.

Kelly, Caroline. 2019. "Virginia Governor Apologizes for 'Racist and
Offensive' Costume in Photo Showing People in Blackface and KKK
Garb." CNN, February 7.

Lee, Youyoung. 2017. "A History of Blackface in Movies: From 'Birth of a
Nation' to 'White Chicks.'" HuffPost, December 6.

Mar, Kylie. 2018. "'Real Housewives' Star Denies Blackface Accusations."
Yahoo! Entertainment, April 5.

Moniuszko, Sara M. 2018. "Megyn Kelly Apologizes for Blackface
Comments on 'Today,' Gets Ripped by Don Lemon." *USA Today*,
October 24.

Sieczkowski, Cavan. 2017. "Julianne Hough Apologizes for Blackface
Costume, Is Sorry She Offended People." HuffPost, December 6.

3

❖❖❖

Systemic Racism in American Life

In 2020, retired NBA legend Kareem Abdul-Jabbar penned an opinion piece in the *Los Angeles Times* in the days immediately following the death of George Floyd, an unarmed Black man who died at the hands of Minneapolis police. Floyd, who allegedly passed a counterfeit $20 bill at a nearby food store, was forcibly pulled from his car, handcuffed, and pinned to the ground by a white officer for nearly 9 minutes with a controversial knee-to-neck restraining maneuver. With his face pressed to the pavement by the officer's weight, he sobbed, told officers more than 20 times that he could not breathe, cried out for his late mother, and then fell silent. For the final 2 minutes and 53 seconds, Floyd was completely unresponsive and his body lifeless, but the officer continued to press his knee into the back of Floyd's neck. Eventually, an ambulance was called, and Floyd was pronounced dead a short time later at an area hospital.

Reacting to his murder, angry protestors filled the nation's city streets by the thousands. Abdul-Jabbar observed that most of those protesting were people who had finally been "pushed to the edge." They were infuriated over recurrent police violence toward Black men and what they perceived as a general disregard for Black lives in American society. Many Americans of all races who watched the protests from home sided with protestors (some even joined in or added their voices to calls for nationwide reform); others, however, were perplexed, even incensed, by the protestors' fury. In his essay, Abdul-Jabbar addressed the public divide and offered an explanation for why some Americans may have been confused by or even resistant to protests. According to Abdul-Jabbar, racism in the United States is like "dust in the air." It hangs in the air all around us, and we breathe it in all day, every day. He added, however, that racism, like dust, is often "invisible—even if you're choking on it."

This chapter sheds light on systemic racism by examining frequently asked questions about racial disparities in American life—particularly in regard to housing, education, work, health, and banking and lending. Though seemingly invisible to some, research reveals clear and wide disparities between white Americans and Americans of color in these areas, and these inequalities affect how Americans of different races experience life in the United States.

The first two questions focus on housing in the United States. Question 11, "Is housing segregation a relic of the past?," considers whether Americans of different races are increasingly integrating or persist in living apart and looks at the impact of segregation on people of color. Question 12 examines whether segregation is simply due to personal preference: "Can residential segregation simply be attributed to people wanting to live with those like themselves?"

Questions 13 and 14 examine education in the United States and whether and how racial bias and systemic racism shape the experiences of American students (and hence their future trajectories). Question 13, "Did *Brown v. Board of Education* (1954) end racial segregation in education?," looks at whether the landmark U.S. Supreme Court case was successful in ending racially segregated education—as was intended. This entry also outlines some of the problems with educating students of different racial groups separately. Question 14 then poses an age-old question: "Is education the key to racial equality in America?" Undoubtedly, education has potential to benefit all Americans and is often believed to be the key to social mobility, though education may not be the "great equalizer" that many assume it to be.

The final questions of this chapter explore racial disparities in employment, health, and banking and lending. Question 15 asks, "Do all races have equal opportunity in the American workplace today?" Drawing on empirical research, this entry looks at whether the playing field is level for all racial groups regarding employment and work. Question 16 looks at health: "Does racial bias negatively affect the health of Americans of color?" People of color generally have worse health outcomes than white Americans, and researchers identify several explanatory social factors to explain these health disparities. This entry, however, focuses on whether systemic racial bias may also contribute to racial disparities in health. Finally, Question 17 asks, "Does racial inequality exist in banking and lending?" Given that differential treatment in this area can have tangible effects on the wealth of individuals, families, and entire racial groups, understanding racial bias in banking and lending is essential.

Q11. IS HOUSING SEGREGATION
A RELIC OF THE PAST?

Answer: No. Although there have been improvements in racial integration since the Jim Crow era, segregation in housing remains high across the United States. Census data show that racial minorities typically live separately from whites, and African Americans are the most segregated minority group in the United States. Residential segregation matters because race and social class are inextricably intertwined in the United States, leading to very different lived experiences for whites and people of color. As compared to those living in white areas, those living in high-minority areas, especially if Black, typically have worse schools, less frequent and inferior amenities and services, less access to affordable and healthy food, increased exposure to environmental toxins, less access to health care, fewer job opportunities, and suppressed real estate values. They are also more likely to live in social isolation, which further limits their economic opportunities.

The Facts: When many Americans think of racial segregation, they often imagine the first half of the twentieth century, when segregation was codified into law and regularly enforced through intimidation and violence. They perceive racial segregation as a relic of the nation's past, something to be filed away in history books, museums, and collective memory. However, present-day data show that the vast majority of Americans continue to live in communities and neighborhoods with people of their own racial group. In fact, according to multiple studies, housing in the United States is nearly as segregated as it was more than 50 years ago, when President Lyndon B. Johnson signed the Fair Housing Act of 1968, a groundbreaking law designed to foster residential integration in the United States (Williams 2018). Census data show modest improvements over time in advancing this goal. But these data also paint a picture of an America that remains deeply segregated in terms of housing—even as the nation becomes increasingly diverse (Frey 2015; Williams and Emamdjomeh 2018).

In 2015, the *New York Times* published a series of interactive maps of major American cities showing the geographic distribution of inhabitants based on race (to view the maps, see Bloch, Cox, and Giratikanon 2015). Featured cities included New York, Boston, Atlanta, Chicago, Los Angeles, Houston, Philadelphia, and Washington, DC, among others. The maps included color-coded dots, each color representing different races, that allowed readers to see the rigid racial segregation in American cities firsthand. For example, the distribution of colored dots across the map of Atlanta show that the north and east sides of the city are predominantly white, while the west and south are majority Black. The map of Houston shows whites living together on the west side and Hispanics in the east. The map of Washington, DC, reveals that whites mostly live on the west side of the city, and Blacks live in the east; Hispanic people are largely grouped together in a relatively small region in northeast DC. The remaining maps tell similar stories of highly segregated American cities, with large swaths of urban areas dominated by single racial groups.

The *New York Times'* maps are based on information gathered from the 2010 census, and a closer look at these data further points to significant segregation across the United States—not only in urban areas but also in suburbs, small towns, and rural communities. Census data further reveal that African Americans are the most segregated minority group in the country. All minorities live segregated from whites (to various degrees), but segregation is particularly high between Blacks and whites and between Blacks and *all* other races (Parisi, Lichter, and Taquino 2011). Sociologists Douglas S. Massey and Jonathan Tannen (2015), for example, find that approximately half of all Black metropolitan residents live in highly or "hypersegregated" cities (as based on five measures of segregation), and, as such, they tend to live in extreme isolation from other racial groups. See table 11.1 for a list of hypersegregated American cities in 2010.

Other minorities also live segregated from whites. Demographers typically use the dissimilarity index to measure racial segregation. Each minority group has its own dissimilarity index, and a higher index means a higher the level of segregation from the white majority. See table 11.2 for dissimilarity indices by race based on 2010 data.

These data show that Black Americans are the most segregated minority with a dissimilarity index of 61; this means that 61 percent of whites would have to move to another neighborhood to make whites and Blacks more evenly distributed. Based on the other dissimilarity indices shown here, nearly half of all whites would have to move to make American Indians and whites more evenly distributed, nearly 40 percent of whites would need to move to make Asians and whites more evenly distributed, and a little over a third of whites would need to move to evenly disperse Hispanics and whites.

Table 11.1 "Hypersegregated" Metropolitan Areas in 2010

Hypersegregated Metropolitan Areas Based on a High Score on 5 of 5 Measures of Segregation	Hypersegregated Metropolitan Areas Based on a High Score on 4 of 5 Measures of Segregation
Baltimore	Boston
Birmingham	Chattanooga
Chicago	Dayton
Cleveland	Gadsden
Detroit	Hartford
Flint	Kansas City
Milwaukee	Mobile
St. Louis	Monroe
	New York
	Philadelphia
	Rochester
	Syracuse
	Winston-Salem

Note: "Hypersegregation" is measured by five measures of segregation: (1) unevenness: the degree to which Blacks and whites are unevenly distributed across neighborhoods in a metropolitan area; (2) isolation: the extent to which African Americans live in predominantly Black neighborhoods; (3) clustering: the degree to which Black neighborhoods are clustered together in space; (4) concentration: the relative amount of physical space occupied by African Americans in a metropolitan area; and (5) centralization: the degree to which Blacks reside near the center of a metropolitan area. Massey and Tannen (2015) label metropolitan areas as "hypersegregated" if they score high on 4 or 5 of these 5 measures.

Source: Massey and Tannen (2015).

Table 11.2 Dissimilarity Indices by Race

Racial Group	Dissimilarity Index (with Whites)
White	—
Black	61.0
American Indian	44.6
Asian	38.1
Hispanic	34.5

Source: 2010 U.S. Census at http://www.censusscope.org/us/s39/p18000/chart _dissimilarity.html

Though Asian Americans show relatively less segregation from whites as compared to most other racial groups, 2010 census data show they are just as segregated as they were in 1980 (Logan and Stults 2011). Moreover, some Asian ethnic groups experience higher rates of segregation as compared to others; for example, Vietnamese Americans are highly segregated and live as separate from whites as do African Americans (Mientka 2013). Furthermore, Hispanic Americans appear to be the least segregated group on a national scale. In some parts of the country, however, they have become increasingly segregated from whites since 1980. There are also parts of the nation where they show particularly high rates of segregation, such as in New York City and Los Angeles (Iceland, Weinberg, and Steinmetz 2002).

These high levels of housing segregation are important because, as scholars have noted, "segregation is critical to understanding racial stratification in the United States today" (Massey and Tannen 2015, 1026). Because race remains highly correlated with social class, one's zip code affects one's opportunities and life chances. Segregation is particularly harmful for racial minorities segregated in poor communities, as numerous studies have documented (Brooks 2014; Campbell 2016; da Costa 2018; Kozol 1991; Massey and Denton 1998; Morello-Frosch and Jesdale 2006; Newkirk 2016; Williams and Collins 2001). Some examples of the negative effects of housing segregation for people of color include the following:

- *Fewer Educational Opportunities.* Because public schools are often funded by local property taxes, children living in poor high-minority areas are often educated in substandard public schools with comparatively fewer resources than children living in wealthier white areas. Because of lack of money, students in these schools have more limited curricula, fewer qualified teachers, and are more likely to be educated in overcrowded classrooms in older and deteriorating buildings. These underfunded schools also tend to have fewer advanced courses, personnel (e.g., counselors, librarians, and nurses), computers, textbooks, library books, art/music/physical education courses, gifted programs, and extracurricular activities. Poor Black children in segregated communities are also more likely than wealthier white children to attend elementary schools with no playgrounds, though research shows that recess is developmentally important and tied to cognitive, behavioral, and social benefits (Day 2012). Studies show that reduced educational resources and opportunities lead to higher high school dropout rates, lower college attendance, and diminished job prospects—hence perpetuating a cycle of poverty (for more on segregation in American public schools, see Q13).

- *Fewer Community Amenities and Less Frequent Public Services.* Those living in impoverished high-minority communities tend to see comparatively fewer amenities and less frequent public services as compared to those living in wealthier white communities. Those living in segregated Black communities, for example, are likely to see fewer trash pickups and less fire protection and emergency services. These communities are also less likely to have sidewalks and community spaces (e.g., green spaces, baseball fields, and bike trails), though studies show that these amenities affect quality of life, mental health, sense of community, and property values. Moreover, when cities need to cut costs, it is often high-minority areas that bear the brunt. For example, in the 1970s, when New York bureaucrats were looking for ways to trim the city's budget, they decided to shutter fire houses in predominantly Black areas, such as the Bronx (in part because they saw Black constituents as politically weak). Not surprisingly, a rash of fires spread through the community, and between 1970 and 1980, seven census tracts in the Bronx lost more than 97 percent of its buildings to fire and abandonment. Joe Flood, the author of a 2010 book about the Bronx fires, argues that though many people believe the fires were mostly caused by arson, the reality is that they were caused by politicians. They closed fire departments, reduced fire inspections by 70 percent, gutted fire marshal programs, and put ancient fire trucks into service with outmoded safety features; broken fire alarm boxes and water hydrants were rarely fixed (Flood 2010).
- *Less Access to Affordable and Healthy Food.* "Food deserts" (places with few food options because of the scarcity of supermarkets) are more abundant in minority communities, especially in poor Black communities. For example, in Atlanta, researchers found that there are four times as many supermarkets in predominantly white neighborhoods as in Black neighborhoods (NewsOne staff 2011). Residents in poor communities, especially those without easy access to transportation, are often limited to corner markets, convenience stores, and fast-food restaurants. Consequently, they tend to have less access to fresh and healthy foods (especially fruits, vegetables, meat, and dairy) and pay more for food than their white counterparts in wealthier areas. A study of food prices led by Caitlin E. Caspi, of the University of Minnesota's Department of Family Medicine and Community Health, found that smaller food stores typically charge higher prices for most staple foods as compared to supermarkets. Analyzing food

prices in Minneapolis/St. Paul, Minnesota, researchers discovered that, on average, prices at smaller food stores were 6–54 percent higher for fruit, milk, protein, and grain staples than those at the nearest supermarkets. For example, the price of eggs was 7 percent higher, milk was 11–14 percent higher, and bananas were 54 percent higher (Caspi et al. 2017). Faced with paying more for food, people living in food deserts often choose less costly options, and as a result, they exhibit high rates of obesity, diabetes, and cardiovascular disease, in part due to their consumption of cheaper foods, which are often highly processed and unhealthy (NewsOne staff 2011). To find out if you live in a "food desert," see the U.S. Department of Agriculture's interactive map at https://www.ers.usda.gov/data-products /food-access-research-atlas/go-to-the-atlas/.

- *Higher Exposure to Harmful Toxins.* Minority communities are more likely than white communities to be exposed to environmental toxins such as lead, air pollutants, and other environmental hazards. Research reveals that race is a more powerful predictor than social class of toxic exposure. This disproportionate exposure is highest in segregated minority communities and puts those residents at greater risk for various cancers, lung diseases, and other health problems (for more on toxic exposure in minority communities, see Q16).

- *Increased Vulnerability to Health-Care Facility Closures.* The data is mixed on whether high-minority areas typically have fewer health-care options (Caldwell et al. 2017). However, studies confirm that hospitals, clinics, psychological services, and pharmacies are more likely to close in poor and minority communities than in other areas. This means that even for people of color with health insurance, these closures limit their access to health care. For example, inner-city hospitals are at higher risk of closure than those located in wealthier suburban communities, which disproportionately disadvantages poor and minority patients. They are left with fewer options for care and increased wait times (such as in ER waiting rooms), and as a result, they are at greater risk of death (Williams 2019). Further, even if they find facilities in their segregated communities, the quality of the resources found in these facilities tend to lag those located in predominantly white areas. This is also especially problematic for Native Americans living on reservations (for more, see Q27).

- *Fewer Job Opportunities.* Since the 1970s, there has been a mass outmigration of low-skilled, high-paying manufacturing jobs from urban to suburban areas and overseas. This and a lack of public transportation from many urban areas to the suburbs have contributed to job losses mostly affecting Black Americans living in inner cities. Moreover, those without cars, usually the most impoverished, have fewer job options because they have few ways to reach these jobs now largely located outside of urban areas. It bears noting that the lack of public transportation from urban to suburban communities was and is often intentional, strategic, and rooted in anti-Black racism. White suburbanites in Atlanta, for example, have long resisted the expansion of its public transportation system (MARTA) from the city into their suburbs for fear its trains and buses would carry Black people into their communities. MARTA, an acronym that stands for Metropolitan Atlanta Rapid Transportation Authority, has been widely referred to as "Moving Africans Rapidly through Atlanta" (Monroe 2012) by white suburbanites, exposing the underlying racism that has stunted its expansion. In addition to closing off opportunities to poor people of color to jobs in the suburbs, the remaining jobs in urbans areas available to unskilled workers (like those in Atlanta and other American cities) are often low paying—thus continuing the cycle of poverty.

- *Stagnant or Declining Real Estate Values.* Because studies indicate that a majority of whites generally avoid living near Black people and other racial minorities (for more on this phenomenon, see Q12), the number of Americans looking to buy in segregated minority neighborhoods is relatively small. For instance, if Black neighborhoods typically attract only Black buyers, they have a smaller number of potential buyers (because Black Americans make up only about 13 percent of the population) than those living in predominantly white communities. Fewer potential buyers means stagnant or deflated property values. Conversely, those living in predominantly white communities are comparatively more likely to experience rising real estate values over time because they appeal to a wider market and have more people looking to buy in their neighborhoods.

- *Limited Social Networks.* Because racial groups live segregated from each other, their social networks are also segregated. Impoverished African Americans in hypersegregated urban areas live in social bubbles with little to no contact with other racial groups, and this isolation affects many things, including their economic opportunities. For one, Black hypersegregation has led to the development of cultural norms distinct from mainstream white society, such as the development of a separate Black speech pattern—what linguists term African American Vernacular English (AAVE). Undoubtedly, speaking AAVE, rather than standard American English, hurts job prospects and poses a significant barrier to socioeconomic advancement. Further, poor African Americans who live in hypersegregation, only surrounded by poor people like themselves, have limited social connections to find jobs. Sociologists Douglas S. Massey and Nancy A. Denton note that "this lack of connection from the rest of society carries profound costs, because personal contacts and friendship networks are among the most important means by which people get jobs" (Massey and Denton 1998, 161). Thus, extreme residential isolation puts Black Americans at a distinct disadvantage in the labor market.

Segregation in the United States persists in the twenty-first century and has important ramifications for people of color. This is especially true for African Americans, who are the most segregated racial minority group in the nation. Physical separation and, at times, social isolation from the rest of the American population underpins and perpetuates present-day racial inequality.

FURTHER READING

Bloch, Matthew, Amanda Cox, and Tom Giratikanon. 2015. "Mapping Segregation." *New York Times*, July 8.

Brooks, Kelly. 2014. "Research Shows Food Deserts More Abundant in Minority Neighborhoods." *Johns Hopkins Magazine* (Spring). Retrieved on November 23, 2020, at https://hub.jhu.edu/magazine/2014/spring/racial-food-deserts/.

Caldwell, Julia T., Chandra L. Ford, Steven P. Wallace, May C. Wang, and Lois M. Takahashi. 2017. "Racial and Ethnic Segregation and Access to Health Care in Rural Areas." *Health Place* 43: 104–112.

Campbell, Alexia Fernandez. 2016. "Inequality in American Public Parks." *The Atlantic*, September 29.

Caspi, Caitlin E., Jennifer E. Pelletier, Lisa J. Harnack, Darin J. Erickson, Kathleen Lenk, and Melissa N. Laska. 2017. "Pricing of Staple Foods at Supermarkets versus Small Food Stores." *International Journal of Environmental Research and Public Health* 14(8): 915.

Da Costa, Pedro Nicolaci. 2018. "There's a Major Hurdle to Employment That Many Americans Don't Even Think about—And It's Holding the Economy Back." Business Insider, January 27.

Day, Nicholas. 2012. "The Rebirth of Recess." Slate, August 29.

Flood, Joe. 2010. "Why the Bronx Burned." *New York Post*, May 16.

Frey, William H. 2015. "Census Shows Modest Declines in Black-White Segregation." Brookings, December 8.

Iceland, John, Daniel H. Weinberg, and Erika Steinmetz. 2002. *Racial and Ethnic Residential Segregation in the United States: 1980–2000.* U.S. Census Bureau, Series CENSR-3. Washington, DC: U.S. Government Printing Office. Retrieved on July 2, 2020, at https://www.census.gov /prod/2002pubs/censr-3.pdf.

Kozol, Jonathan. 1991. *Savage Inequalities: Children in America's Schools.* New York: Crown Publishing Group.

Logan, John R., and Brian J. Stults. 2011. "The Persistence of Segregation in the Metropolis: New Findings from the 2010 Census." Census Brief prepared for Project US2010.

Massey, Douglas S., and Nancy A. Denton. 1998. *American Apartheid.* Cambridge, MA: Harvard University Press.

Massey, Douglas S., and Jonathan Tannen. 2015. "A Research Note on Trends in Black Hypersegregation." *Demography* 52: 1025–1034.

Mientka, Matthew. 2013. "Asian Americans Nearly as Segregated as African Americans—But Richer." Medical Daily, June 26.

Monroe, Doug. 2012. "Where It All Went Wrong." *Atlanta Magazine,* August 1.

Morello-Frosch, Rachel, and Bill M. Jesdale. 2006. "Separate and Unequal: Residential Segregation and Estimated Cancer Risks Associated with Ambient Air Toxins in U.S. Metropolitan Areas." *Environmental Health Perspectives* 114(3): 386–393.

Newkirk, Vann R., II. 2016. "America's Health Segregation Problem." *The Atlantic,* May 18.

NewsOne staff. 2011. "America's Worst 9 Urban Food Deserts." NewsOne, September 22.

Parisi, Domenico, and Daniel T. Lichter, and Michael C. Taquino. 2011. "Multi-Scale Residential Segregation: Black Exceptionalism and America's Changing Color Line." *Social Forces* 89(3): 829–852.

Williams, Aaron, and Armand Emamdjomeh. 2018. "America Is More Diverse Than Ever—But Still Segregated." *Washington Post,* May 10.

Williams, David R., and Chiquita Collins. 2001. "Racial Residential Segregation: A Fundamental Cause of Racial Disparities in Health." *Public Health Reports* 116: 404–416.

Williams, Joseph P. 2018. "Segregation's Legacy." *U.S. News & World Report,* April 20.

Williams, Joseph P. 2019. "Code Red: The Grim State of Urban Hospitals." *U.S. News & World Report,* July 10.

Q12. CAN RESIDENTIAL SEGREGATION SIMPLY BE ATTRIBUTED TO PEOPLE WANTING TO LIVE WITH THOSE LIKE THEMSELVES?

Answer: Mostly, no. As described in Q11, racial segregation in housing remains high in the United States and can be observed nationwide. To explain the persistence of this phenomenon in American life, some people attribute it to the personal preference of Americans of different races "to live near people like themselves." Though there is some kernel of truth to this statement, historians and social scientists argue that today's segregation is better understood as a culmination of widespread historical and present-day discrimination toward people of color—and especially against African Americans, who remain the most segregated racial minority group in the United States.

The Facts: The personal preference to live with the same race partially explains housing segregation in the United States today. Studies show that some Americans prefer to live with same-race others—though this explanation largely pertains to the housing preferences of white Americans. Whites tend to favor predominantly white neighborhoods, and research studies have found that Blacks and Latinxs more often prefer neighborhoods that are racially integrated (see Havekes, Bader, and Krysan 2016). So what explains the patterns of racial segregation observed in the United States today? Scholars argue that while personal preferences to live with people like themselves (especially by whites) matters to some degree, historical and present-day discrimination against people of color better explain racial segregation across the nation.

Historical Discrimination

The segregation observed in the United States today did not happen by accident; rather, it is the direct result of decades of explicitly racist local, state, and federal policies combined with widespread violence against people of color. During the Jim Crow era, whites passed hundreds of laws to keep whites and Blacks segregated, especially in southern states. These laws, called Jim Crow laws, segregated just about every part of society, including schools and universities, public facilities (e.g., parks, water fountains, theaters, restrooms, and pools), public transportation, jails, hospitals, cemeteries, and even housing. To segregate housing, municipalities enacted overtly racist *zoning laws* that typically prohibited Black families from moving into white-dominated blocks.

Zoning laws could be found in many southern cities, including Atlanta, which enacted a racial zoning ordinance in the 1920s that assigned a racial designation to most city blocks (Rothstein 2017). Blacks and whites could only legally live in their racially assigned areas, and the ordinance forcibly shifted African Americans from the east side of Atlanta to the west (Silver 1997)—where they remain concentrated today. Zoning laws in other southern cities (e.g., Dallas, New Orleans, Charleston, Birmingham, and Richmond) similarly segregated residential areas, and in many cities, these patterns of segregation persist.

Racial zoning laws eventually expanded to northern, midwestern, and western cities, such as Los Angeles, Chicago, San Francisco, and many others. In 1917, the U.S. Supreme Court ruled such zoning laws unconstitutional in *Buchanan v. Warley*, but many cities simply ignored the ruling and continued the practice (Rothstein 2017). For example, Birmingham continued racial zoning until the 1950s, West Palm Beach until 1960, and Apopka (an Orlando suburb) until 1968 (Rothstein 2017).

In other places, these laws simply took on new forms. Richmond, Virginia, for example, continued racial zoning by barring people from moving into blocks where they were legally prohibited from marrying the majority of people residing there. Because Virginia, like many other states at the time, outlawed marriages between whites and Blacks, Black people were effectively blocked from white communities (Nodjimbadem 2017).

Cities across the United States (especially outside the South) also began implementing *restrictive covenants*. These were legally enforceable contracts written into housing deeds that prohibited their sale, lease, or transfer to minorities—including to Jews, Asians, Hispanics, Native Americans, and, most often, African Americans. The language of restrictive covenants was overtly and unapologetically racist. For example, one restrictive covenant that affected nearly a thousand homes in Seattle read: "said lots or buildings thereon shall never be rented, leased or sold, transferred or conveyed to, nor shall the same be occupied by any negro or colored person or person of negro blood" (Seattle Civil Rights Labor History n.d.).

Many other cities, including New York, Los Angeles, Detroit, Minneapolis, Chicago, Washington, DC, had similar covenants to "protect" white communities. By the late 1920s, for example, nearly 85 percent of housing in Chicago was covered by such covenants, restricting Black people to small areas in the city (Kamp 1987). Though ruled unenforceable in 1948, restrictive covenants nonetheless continued until the late 1960s in many parts of the United States. In 1968, restrictive covenants were finally declared unconstitutional, though the archaic racial restrictions, which are today toothless, can still be found in the language of many old housing deeds (Rose 2010). Furthermore, racial segregation created by these covenants endures in many cities across the nation.

The federal government furthered institutionalized segregation though a practice called *redlining*. Beginning in the 1930s and continuing through the 1970s, the Federal Housing Administration (FHA) refused mortgage loans to people living in and near minority neighborhoods; it was called *redlining* because the administration literally drew red lines on city maps around minority neighborhoods to signify where they would deny mortgages (more than 200 American cities were affected). They deemed redlined areas too risky to invest in, though the percentage of minorities living there primarily determined which communities were redlined—not the wages or wealth of residents or other traditional risk factors. Hence, people of color living in these communities were automatically denied home loans, while whites were granted loans by the FHA to buy homes in newly constructed suburbs outside of major urban areas. Between 1930 and 1950, three out of five homes purchased in the United States were financed by the federal government via the FHA, but only 2 percent of those loans went to people of color (California Newsreel 2003). African Americans and other minorities who wanted to leave redlined areas and purchase newly built homes in the suburbs (areas not redlined) were blocked by restrictive covenants. In fact, the FHA encouraged these new suburban communities to exclude minorities and promoted the use of restrictive covenants—even going so far as to provide model language for restrictive covenants to housing developers in their administration's *Underwriting Manual.*

One notable example of racially restrictive practices occurred in Levittown, New York—one of the nation's first suburbs. Constructed shortly after World War II, homes in Levittown, like those in other suburbs sprouting around the country at the time, were new, modern, and affordable to working-class American families. They were built especially for American GIs returning home from World War II—but there was a catch. Beginning in 1947, anyone who purchased a home in Levittown had to be white, and homebuyers were required to sign a restrictive covenant stating that the property they acquired could not be sold or rented to any individuals "other than members of the Caucasian race" (Galyean 2015); thus, the new suburb was closed to racial minorities. Even after restrictive covenants were outlawed in 1948, Levittown developers continued to exclude minorities, and they did so partly because of pressure from the FHA to keep the community all white or risk losing future FHA housing development loans (Rothstein 2017).

By 1953, Levittown was home to 70,000 people, and the sprawling sub-urb constituted the largest community in the United States with zero Black residents (Galyean 2015). One former resident who grew up in Levittown in the 1950s recalled that the question of whether Black people would live in Levittown was akin to asking whether there were going to be "Martians" in Levittown (California Newsreel 2003). Even today, Levittown is major-ity white. According to 2018 data from the U.S. Census Bureau, nearly three-quarters of residents were white, and only about one percent were Black. Like Levittown, the overwhelming whiteness of thousands of other American suburbs was no historical accident; rather, it can be attributed to the racist decisions of the federal government and housing developers during the mid-twentieth century to shut out minorities. According to sociologist James W. Loewen (2018), nearly *all* suburbs built between 1946 and 1968 were originally established as white-only communities.

These practices effectively segregated communities, but they also created a racial wealth gap. Family wealth is measured by adding together a family's assets (e.g., money, properties, and valuable possessions) and subtracting their debts. Using this measure, today's white families have nearly 10 times the wealth of Black families according to the Brookings Institute (McIntosh et al. 2020), and this is due in large part to the federal government leaving Black Americans out of the booming housing market post–World War II. Blacks were disenfranchised by the FHA, while whites were able to buy suburban houses subsidized by low-interest FHA loans. Consequently, they built equity and saw wealth gains as their homes appreciated in value over time (California Newsreel 2003). Homes in Levittown, for instance, ori-ginally sold to white families for about $7,000, which was very affordable at the time to blue-collar families; today, those same homes sell for about $300,000 to 400,000 (and, as such, are out of the reach of today's work-ing-class families) (Gross 2017). Given that most American family wealth is held in home equity, housing discrimination (in Levittown and other post–World War II suburbs) had an enormous financial impact, enriching whites at the expense of Black Americans and other racial minorities.

When government and developer policies failed to keep people of color out of white communities, whites often turned to intimidation and violence. In 1957, the first Black family (Daisy and Bill Myers and their three young children) moved to Levittown, Pennsylvania, a sister sub-urb of the original Levittown in New York. Though the owners of both Levittowns refused to sell to Black families, the Myers were able to pur-chase a Levittown home from a former homeowner who willfully ignored the restrictive covenant. As soon as the family moved in, pandemonium ensued: white mobs gathered nightly on their lawn, hurling racial slurs and threats, throwing Molotov cocktails, burning crosses, throwing rocks through windows, and blaring music day and night. State troopers eventually had to be called in to restore order after local police failed to stop the harassment (McCrary 1997; Rothstein 2017).

Many other Black families moving into historically white suburbs suffered similar harassment—or even worse. Scholar Richard Rothstein notes that Black families could not always count on local law enforcement, who sometimes turned a blind eye or were even complicit in the violence. Further, Rothstein writes that what the Myers endured "was not an aberration" but reflective of the "systematic and nationwide" violence and intimidation by whites to keep their communities white (Rothstein 2017, 143). For example, in 1945, a Black family of four was murdered when their new home in a white Los Angeles neighborhood was blown up. That city experienced even more housing-related violence between 1950 and 1965, as more than 100 bombings and vandalism greeted Black families attempting to move into white communities. In Philadelphia, in the first half of 1955 alone, 213 violent incidents ensured that Black residents remained out of white communities (Rothstein 2017). These are just a few of thousands of examples of violence and intimidation across the nation that prevailed for decades.

Additionally, sociologist James Loewen documented recurrent mass expulsions of minorities from cities and towns across the nation during the Jim Crow era by use of mob violence. "In town after town in the United States," he wrote, "especially between 1890 and the 1930s, whites forced out their African American neighbors violently, as they had the Chinese in the West" (Loewen 2018, 92). They attacked minority communities, set fire to their homes and business, and, in some cases, massacred people of color en masse. Some examples, according to Loewen, in which whites tried to "cleanse" their nonwhite populations included Denver (of Chinese), 1880; Seattle (of Chinese), 1886; Akron (of Blacks), 1900; Evansville, Indiana (of Blacks), 1903; Joplin, Missouri (of Blacks), 1903; Springfield, Ohio (of Blacks), 1904, 1906, and 1908; Springfield, Missouri (of Blacks), 1906; Springfield, Illinois (of Blacks), 1908; Youngstown, Ohio (of Blacks), 1917; East St. Louis, Illinois (of Blacks), 1917; Omaha (of Blacks), 1919; Knoxville (of Blacks), 1919; Tulsa (of Blacks), 1921; Johnstown, Pennsylvania (of Blacks), 1923; and Lincoln, Nebraska (of Blacks), 1929. This list is far from exhaustive.

Some cities and towns across the nation were more successful than others in driving out people of color. For example, when cities such as Seattle, San Francisco, and Los Angeles proved unable to completely drive out Chinese residents, they turned to racial zoning laws and restrictive covenants to restrict where they could live. It was during this time that Chinatowns—segregated ethnic communities of people of Chinese descent within larger urban areas—became the norm for Chinese Americans. These communities did not arise out of Chinese Americans' desire to self-segregate, but rather because they had few other residential options.

Nonetheless, Chinese Americans were not necessarily safe in Chinatowns either. In 1885, white mobs (composed largely of miners who felt their livelihoods threatened by the willingness of Chinese immigrants to work in mines for low wages) gave Chinatown residents in Rock Springs, Wyoming, one hour to pack up their belongings and leave before they attacked. Most fled immediately, leaving their homes, possessions, and money behind. Others hid in their homes and were burned alive as their homes were set ablaze by the white mob (Loewen 2018). Nearly 30 Chinese Americans were murdered, and of the 700 to 900 Chinatown residents in Rock Springs, not one remained the following day.

Soon after, copycat expulsions of Chinese Americans "swept the West" (Loewen 2018, 51), and similar violence targeting African Americans continued for decades. In Tulsa, in 1921, for example, after an alleged assault of white woman by a Black man (she never pressed charges), white mobs attacked the Black section of town, then known as the Greenwood District. The area had been informally branded the "Black Wall Street" because of its thriving business district and nice homes and because it was one of the wealthiest Black communities in the nation at the time. White mobs burned down all 35 city blocks of Greenwood, including all Black-owned homes and businesses; they then ransacked and looted anything that remained. Nearly 40 (and perhaps as many as 300) Black Tulsa residents were massacred over a two-day period, and thousands of others fled the city. Unlike the white mobs in Rock Springs who successfully expelled Chinese American residents, white residents of Tulsa were never able to fully drive out African Americans. Nonetheless, many other white communities pursued similarly brutal methods of expulsion. Census data, for example, show that minority populations in many jurisdictions nationwide declined dramatically—at times, in short spans of time—likely indicating their forced exodus (Loewen 2018).

Other communities established themselves as *sundown towns*—exclusively white towns (or suburbs or counties) that remained segregated by use of fear and violence (Loewen 2018). The term originated from signs posted at city limits that warned people of color to leave town by sunset or face unimaginable terror. Some examples include "Whites Only Within City Limits After Dark" or "N****r, Don't Let the Sun Set on You in [insert city name]." Many of these towns relied on bells or whistles at dusk to signal to minorities that it was time to leave, and if caught there after sunset, they faced arrest, assault, or even murder. These arrangements benefited white businesses because they allowed people of color, usually Black Americans, into town during the day to provide labor or spend money at white-owned businesses but ensured that they lived elsewhere.

One might assume that sundown towns were a rarity, but one scholar estimated that there were thousands of sundown towns that existed at one time or another in the United States (184 of which were known to have warning signs at their borders). Many were found in southern states, but they were most often located outside the South, in places such as New York, Maine, Wisconsin, California, Minnesota, Michigan, Connecticut, Indiana, and Ohio. Illinois, for example, is estimated to have had nearly 500 sundown towns. These racially restrictive towns proliferated throughout the early to mid-twentieth century, though some existed as late as the 1990s (and perhaps even later) (Loewen 2018).

Given their racist and violent histories, it should come as no surprise that many of these former sundown towns remain overwhelmingly white today. For example, white residents of Forsyth County, Georgia, forcibly expelled all Black residents in 1912 and for decades allegedly "attacked any nonwhite who dared step over the county line" (Phillips 2017). Though no longer a sundown town (or sundown county in this case), it was still only about 4 percent Black in 2019 (Census Reporter 2019).

Most Americans have no knowledge of the violent expulsions of people of color or of sundown towns because they are entirely absent from history textbooks and history curricula in American schools. Moreover, sundown towns are not ancient history—some endured to the end of the twentieth century. Some sundown towns "still flaunted their condition" as late as the 1990s "with signs saying 'Don't Let the Sun Go Down On You in ___,' according to credible reports from Arab, Alabama; Marlowe, Oklahoma; and Sullivan, Missouri" (Loewen 2018, 389).

Additionally, twentieth-century city, state, and federal planning further strengthened already existing segregation in some areas and fashioned new segregation in others. For example, urban planners physically isolated Black communities from white ones—first with railroad tracks and later with boulevards and highways—by running them right between neighboring racial communities. Newly built multilane highways in the 1950s and 1960s, for instance, were uncrossable, further ensuring little to no contact between once adjacent Black and white neighborhoods (Badger and Cameron 2015).

These midcentury bureaucratic decisions were important because strategic man-made barriers long segregated many city landscapes. Eight

Mile Road in Detroit, for instance, first began as a dirt road in the late 1920s and later morphed into a multilane road. The wide asphalt barrier sliced right between neighboring Black and white communities and, for decades, physically divided them (*Encyclopedia of Detroit*). A six-foot-tall, half-mile-long concrete wall was also constructed in the 1940s to further divide Black and white neighborhoods in Detroit; some local residents have termed it the "segregation wall" or the "Berlin Wall" (the latter term reminiscent of the wall separating East Germany from West Germany in the twentieth century). White developers constructed the wall to keep Black people out of white neighborhoods. One Detroit resident who grew up near the wall recalled that it was effective: "I didn't see white people, you know?" Beginning in the 1960s, however, whites fled Detroit for the suburbs (i.e., white flight), and the wall became less necessary for segregating Black and white neighborhoods. Today, Black residents live on both sides of the concrete barrier (Baker and Schwartz 2017).

Furthermore, officials repeatedly planned highways right through the middle of Black communities across the nation, devastating Black neighborhoods and tearing down Black homes and businesses in the process. This happened over and over throughout the twentieth century, destroying Black communities in cities such as Miami, New York, Los Angeles, Atlanta, Charlotte, Seattle, Philadelphia, Baltimore, and many others (Halsey 2016). Black families were disproportionately dislocated and typically given a pittance for their demolished homes because they were in redlined areas; hence, many had little option but to relocate to inner-city public housing. Consequently, the nationwide pattern of Blacks concentrated in cities and whites in suburbs was solidified.

Finally, even entire states were built on white desires for segregation—a fact unbeknownst to most Americans given that this history is rarely, if ever, taught in schools. Oregon, for example, was originally founded as a "white utopia." In 1844, before it was a recognized state, Black people were ordered to leave the territory or face whipping every six months until they complied. When granted statehood in 1859, the Oregon Constitution explicitly prohibited Black people from living, working, or owning property there, and for nearly 70 years (until 1926), it was illegal for Black people to move into the state. The impact of this history is evident today. Oregon remains overwhelmingly white (it was only about 2 percent Black in 2018) (Brown 2017; Novack 2015; U.S. Census Bureau 2018). Other states implemented similar laws at one time or another—including Illinois, Ohio, Michigan, Indiana, and California (Loewen 2018).

Present-Day Discrimination

Historical factors are powerful drivers in explaining today's racial segregation, but so too is present-day discrimination. Housing discrimination is alive and well roughly 50 years after housing discrimination was outlawed with the passage of the Fair Housing Act of 1968. The most blatant forms of housing discrimination have declined over time (such as landlords openly saying, "I don't rent to your kind"), but experimental studies, such as paired tests, show that subtler forms of discrimination persist. In paired tests, researchers typically send two people (one white and one nonwhite) who are otherwise identical (e.g., they are matched on financial qualifications, dress, and educational level) in search of housing. Claudia Aranda, a senior research associate in Urban's Metropolitan Housing and Communities Policy Center, has supervised more than 14,000 of these studies in over 44 metropolitan areas and repeatedly finds unequal treatment of racial groups by landlords and real estate agents (Aranda 2019). A 2012 study by the U.S. Department of Housing and Urban Development (HUD), for example, found that landlords showed Black, Latinx, and Asian American testers fewer rental units than white testers. Real estate agents showed similar patterns with homebuyers—white testers were shown nearly 18 percent more homes than Black testers and nearly 19 percent more homes than Asian American testers (Turner et al. 2013). This type of discrimination limits housing options for minorities, and because it is nearly impossible to detect, it typically goes unseen and unreported.

Housing discrimination is also evident in *racial steering*, a practice by which real estate agents "steer" prospective homebuyers toward or away from certain neighborhoods based on the buyer's race. Studies show that whites are more often shown homes in middle-class/affluent, predominantly white neighborhoods, and minorities are more often shown houses in high-minority, poorer neighborhoods—even when home seekers are matched on income (Turner et al. 2013). Acting as neighborhood gatekeepers, real estate agents perpetuate housing segregation, and, though illegal, the practice remains commonplace.

One study found that racial steering has not declined since stricter housing laws were passed in the late 1980s; if anything, the study's researchers claim that the practice has only increased—at least as of 2005 (Galster and Godfrey 2005). A 2016 undercover investigation of Long Island illustrates the persistence of racial steering: researchers found that when two testers (of different races but matched on gender, age, income, and housing preferences) approached the *same* real estate agents, they were treated very differently (Ferré-Sadurní 2019). Analyzing 240 hours of hidden video of interactions with nearly a hundred real estate agents, they found that people of color were treated unequally 40 percent of the time and frequently steered toward particular neighborhoods. For example, one agent told a Black homebuyer that houses in a predominantly white neighborhood were "too expensive" for him, although the agent showed the homes to a white buyer who had the same amount of money to spend. In another case, an agent warned a white client of gang violence in a high-minority neighborhood but told a Black client that residents were the "nicest people."

Social networks also preserve racial segregation. Sociologist Judith DeSena, author of *Protecting One's Turf* (2005), writes about several strategies white homeowners use to maintain white neighborhoods and communities. She studied segregated Greenpoint, New York, and found that whites kept the southern part of Greenpoint uniformly white by use of informal social networks. For example, white homeowners (1) limited information about available housing (they typically kept housing ads out of the paper and instead relied on word-of-mouth advertising to fellow whites) and (2) utilized informal coercion (they formed informal pacts with neighbors to rent or sell only to whites; those who did not comply were intimidated or confronted by neighbors). Surely, Greenpoint is not alone. Other communities across the nation likely use similar tactics to keep their communities white.

Moreover, even online social network platforms play a role in segregation. In 2019, HUD announced charges against Facebook for encouraging housing discrimination through the company's advertising platform (Aranda 2019). The company allowed advertisers to exclude certain races from even viewing their housing ads, thus restricting information about housing to specific racial groups. Twitter and Google were also under review that year for similar practices, illustrating, as Claudia Aranda writes, "how housing discrimination continues to evolve" (2019).

Further, gentrification also promotes racial segregation. *Gentrification* refers to the influx of middle- and upper-middle-class whites into high-minority, low-income urban areas in dire need of investment. At first glance, gentrification looks like a model of racial integration as different races converge together in a geographic space, but gentrification often displaces low-income minorities. As wealthy whites move in, housing prices rise; consequently, poor people of color are often "priced out" of the neighborhood and forced to relocate to other more affordable areas. Thus, the racially segregated landscape does not become more integrated but simply redistributes or shifts.

Further, when studying gentrification in Greenpoint, New York, Judith Desena found that even when living side by side, white and minority residents socially segregate (DeSena 2012). For example, she found that working-class minorities typically sent their children to local schools, while wealthier whites sent their children to prestigious public schools in Manhattan, progressive alternative schools, or homeschooled. Children of minority families also tended to engage in local activities (played in the streets, rode bikes, and generally uses the neighborhoods as a playground), while children of gentrifiers tended to participate in more organized activities outside the community. In short, DeSena found that these groups, though living in close proximity, formed their own social networks; as such, racial integration was minimal. More research is needed to see whether other gentrified communities follow a similar pattern.

Finally, social class is also a significant "residential separator" in the United States (DeSena 2012), as many families of color, because of limitations of income or creditworthiness, are unable to access middle-class white neighborhoods. However, even affluent Black families face considerable challenges moving into white communities (Eligon and Gebeloff 2016). As previously discussed, many Black families are steered away from white neighborhoods by real estate agents—even if they can afford the homes. Further, some move into white neighborhoods only to turn around and leave because of anti-Black hostilities and harassment. For instance, in 2015, a Black family in a predominantly white California neighborhood woke up to find that someone had intentionally torched their home (CBSLA 2015); in 2017, a Black family in Minnesota returned home to find intruders had spray-painted the words "Get Out" on their interior walls (Nasa and Glickhouse 2019); and in 2019, a Black family in Indiana was terrorized by a racist neighbor who repeatedly hurled threats and slurs and eventually stabbed their dog (Morgan-Smith 2019). Most incidents like these go unreported, though the Documenting Hate database cites thousands of similar cases of anti-Black harassment from 2016 to 2019 alone.

For other Black families, their moving in causes their white neighbors to flee to other suburbs or "exurban" areas even farther removed from cities—a phenomenon called *white flight* (Fischer 2008). As white families leave in large numbers, middle- and upper-middle-class Black families are eventually once again surrounded by Black neighbors as the neighborhood around them shifts from white to Black—sometimes in a matter of a few years. Because of these reasons, "affluent black families, freed from the restrictions of low income, often end up living in poor and segregated communities anyway" (Eligon and Gebeloff 2016).

In sum, housing segregation is more than the mere accumulation of people's desires and decisions to live with same-race others. While studies show that whites want to live together, this is not true of nonwhite racial groups, who more so desire racial integration. Historical and present-day discrimination against racial minorities better explain housing segregation today, and this is particularly important because racial segregation is not simply about whites and people of color living apart. It is about educational and job opportunities, access to doctors and grocery stores, quality of public services, the accumulation of family wealth, and the reproduction of inequality from generation to generation (for more on why racial segregation is problematic, refer to Q11).

Finally, it bears noting that while housing segregation remains high in the United States today, census data suggest that there has been some improvement since 2000. For example, the number of Americans living in integrated neighborhoods increased from 8 percent in 2000 to 12.6 percent in 2015 (Spader and Rieger 2017). Nonetheless, researchers Jonathan Spader and Shannon Rieger of the Joint Center for Housing Studies at Harvard University maintain that "integrated neighborhoods remain the exception rather than the rule in the United States" (Spader and Rieger 2017).

FURTHER READING

Aranda, Claudia L. 2019. "Housing Discrimination in America: Lessons from the Last Decade of Paired-Testing Research." Urban Institute, February 27.

Badger, Emily, and Darla Cameron. 2015. "How Railroads, Highways and Other Man-Made Lines Racially Divide America's Cities." *Washington Post*, July 16.

Baker, Elizabeth, and Matthew S. Schwartz. 2017. "In Detroit, a Colorful Mural Stands as a Reminder of the City's 'Segregation Wall.'" NPR, July 22.

Brown, DeNeen L. 2017. "When Portland Banned Blacks: Oregon's Shameful History as an 'All-White' State." *Washington Post*, June 7.

California Newsreel. 2003. "Race: The Power of an Illusion." PBS. Retrieved on November 23, 2020, at http://newsreel.org/video/race-the-power-of-an-illusion.

Census Reporter. 2019. "Forsyth County, Georgia." Retrieved on November 23, 2020, at https://censusreporter.org/profiles/05000US13117-forsyth-county-ga/.

CBSLA. 2015. "Was Black Family Targeted in 'Suspicious' Manhattan Beach Fire?" Retrieved on March 30, 2020, at https://losangeles.cbslocal.com/2015/02/05/suspicious-fire-under-investigation-in-manhattan-beach/.

DeSena, Judith N. 2005. *Protecting One's Turf*. Lanham, MD: University Press of America.

DeSena, Judith N. 2012. "Segregation Begins at Home: Gentrification and the Accomplishment of Boundary-Work." *Urbanities* 2(2). Retrieved on November 23, 2020, at http://www.anthrojournal-urbanities.com /wp-content/uploads/2015/11/Judith-N.-DeSena-Segregation-Begins -at-Home-2.pdf.

Documenting Hate. https://projects.propublica.org/graphics/hatecrimes.

Eligon, John, and Robert Gebeloff. 2016. "Affluent and Black, and Still Trapped by Segregation." *New York Times*, August 20.

Encyclopedia of Detroit. n.d. "Eight Mile Road." Detroit Historical Society. Retrieved on March 30, 2020, at https://detroithistorical.org/learn /encyclopedia-of-detroit/eight-mile-road.

Ferré-Sadurní, Luis. 2019. "What Happens When Black People Search for Suburban Homes." *New York Times*, November 18.

Fischer, Mary. 2008. "Shifting Geographies: Examining the Role of Suburbanization in Blacks' Declining Segregation." *Urban Affairs Review* 43(4): 475–496.

Galster, George, and Erin Godfrey. 2005. "By Words and Deeds: Racial Steering by Real Estate Agents in the U.S. in 2000." *Journal of the American Planning Association* 71(3): 251–268.

Galyean, Crystal. 2015. "Levittown: The Imperfect Rise of the American Suburbs." U.S. History Scene. Retrieved on March 30, 2020, at https:// ushistoryscene.com/article/levittown/.

Gross, Terry. 2017. "A 'Forgotten' History of How the U.S. Government Segregated America." NPR. Retrieved on November 23, 2020, at https://www.npr.org/2017/05/03/526655831/a-forgotten-history-of -how-the-u-s-government-segregated-america.

Halsey, Ashley, III. 2016. "A Crusade to Defeat the Legacy of Highways Rammed through Poor Neighborhoods." *Washington Post*, March 29.

Havekes, Esther, Michael Bader, and Maria Krysan. 2016. "Realizing Racial and Ethnic Neighborhood Preferences? Exploring the Mismatches between What People Want, Where They Search, and Where They Live." *Population Research and Policy Review* 35: 101–126.

Kamp, Allen R. 1987. "The History behind *Hansberry v. Lee*." *UC Davis Law Review* 20: 481–499.

Loewen, James W. 2018. *Sundown Towns: A Hidden Dimension of American Racism*. New York: The New Press.

McCrary, Lacy. 1997. "Trauma of Levittown Integration." *Baltimore Sun*, August 21.

McIntosh, Kriston, Emily Moss, Ryan Nunn, and Jay Shambaugh. 2020. "Examining the Black-White Wealth Gap." Brookings, February 27.

Morgan-Smith, Kia. 2019. "Black Family Terrorized by Racist Neighbor Who Stabbed Their Dog 'The KKK Is Coming.'" TheGrio, January 29.

Nasa, Rahima, and Rachel Glickhouse. 2019. "'Get Out': Black Families Harassed in Their Own Homes." Pro Publica, January 7.

Nodjimbadem, Katie. 2017. "The Racial Segregation of American Cities Was Anything but Accidental." *Smithsonian*, May 30.

Novack, Matt. 2015. "Oregon Was Founded as a Racist Utopia." Huff-Post, January 22.

Phillips, Patrick. 2017. "Charlottesville Was Not a Surprise." Slate, August 19.

Rose, Julie. 2010. "Hidden in Old Home Deeds, A Segregationist Past." NPR, February 6.

Rothstein, Richard. 2017. *The Color of Law: A Forgotten History of How Our Government Segregated America*. New York: Liveright Publishing Corporation.

Seattle Civil Rights & Labor History Project. n.d. "Racial Restrictive Covenants." University of Washington. Retrieved on March 30, 2020, at http://depts.washington.edu/civilr/covenants.htm.

Silver, Christopher. 1997. "The Racial Origins of Zoning in American Cities." Pp. 23–42 in *Urban Planning and the African American Community: In the Shadows*, edited by June Manning Thomas and Marsha Ritzdorf. Thousand Oaks, CA: Sage.

Spader, Jonathan, and Shannon Rieger. 2017. "Are Integrated Neighborhoods Becoming More Common in the United States?" Joint Center for Housing Studies of Harvard University, September 19.

Turner, Margery Austin, Rob Santos, Diane K. Levy, Doug Wissoker, Claudia Aranda, Rob Pitingolo, and the Urban Institute. 2013. "Housing Discrimination against Racial and Ethnic Minorities 2012." U.S. Department of Housing and Urban Development. Retrieved on November 23, 2020, at https://www.urban.org/research/publication /housing-discrimination-against-racial-and-ethnic-minorities-2012 -full-report.

Q13. DID *BROWN V. BOARD OF EDUCATION* (1954) END RACIAL SEGREGATION IN EDUCATION?

Answer: No. *Brown v. Board of Education* (1954) was a landmark Supreme Court case that struck down school segregation in the United States; however, racial segregation in American public schools persists nearly 70 years later. The 1970s saw much improvement, but reversals of desegregation orders in the late 1980s and on as well as "white flight" from integrated communities have stalled or perhaps even worsened school segregation. Racial segregation in education is problematic not simply because students are educated in separate schools; there are stark funding disparities that translate to "separate and unequal" educations for white students and students of color. As such, different racial groups do not compete on a level playing field in American society.

The Facts: In *Brown v. Board of Education of Topeka* (1954), the U.S. Supreme Court justices ruled unanimously (9–0) that segregated public education in the United States is unconstitutional, dealing the first major blow to Jim Crow segregation in the United States. The court argued that "separate educational facilities were inherently unequal" and in direct violation of the Fourteenth Amendment to the U.S. Constitution, which affords citizens equal protection under the law. The class action suit was filed on behalf of Black parents and students in Kansas, South Carolina, Delaware, Virginia, and Washington, DC, though the ruling ultimately affected 17 states, all in the southeast. In a lesser known second ruling, *Brown II* (1955), the Supreme Court also ordered states to integrate "with all deliberate speed."

They did not. White Southerners vociferously and sometimes violently protested school desegregation. To avoid integrating public schools, some officials opted instead to shut them altogether. The governor of Virginia, for example, closed all public schools in several counties; the schools in Prince Edward County, Virginia, remained closed for five years. White parents also pulled their children out of public schools across the South and enrolled them in thousands of "segregation academies" (or "seg academies")—all-white private schools that sprouted in southern states in the wake of *Brown* (as private schools were exempt from the ruling). Some southern states even provided white parents with tuition grants to pay for this alternative, all-white private education. By contrast, no alternative education emerged for Black students. Additionally, some white townspeople went so far as to force African Americans out of their communities to avoid school integration, including in Sheridan, Arkansas, and Highland Park and University Park, Texas. Black populations in at least five Kentucky and Tennessee counties also "fell precipitously" around the time of the *Brown* decisions, suggesting that Black residents were forced out (Loewen 2018).

In other locations, white parents, students, and community members protested school integration by assembling in mobs and physically blocking Black students from entering schools, hurling threats and slurs, and even engaging in violent acts. For example, in Little Rock, Arkansas,

President Dwight Eisenhower deployed federal army troops in 1957 to escort nine Black students into the local high school after they were repeatedly blocked from entry and physically threatened by white mobs. The troops provided protection for Black students for the entire school year—until local officials ordered the school closed the following year to halt further integration.

In 1960 (six years after the *Brown* ruling), six-year-old Ruby Bridges was the first Black student to integrate her all-white elementary school in New Orleans. On the first day of school, the first grader was escorted to school by four federal marshals (and every day for the remainder of the year), and as she ascended the front steps of the school that first day, New Orleans erupted into citywide riots. Most white parents pulled their children from the elementary school; by the end of the week, only children from three white families remained. Only one teacher was willing to teach Bridges, and for the remainder of the year, she taught the first grader in a class of one. Two years later, the integration of the University of Mississippi by James Meredith, an African American, led to similar protests. A mob of white students and even the governor of the state physically blocked Meredith from enrolling at the all-white institution. To ensure compliance with federal law, President John F. Kennedy ordered in approximately 31,000 federal troops. Students responded by rioting through the night, leaving hundreds injured and two people dead. These are but a few of many examples of white protests of school integration throughout the 1950s and 1960s.

Though the Supreme Court justices required integration "with all deliberate speed," little changed until 1968—nearly 15 years after the *Brown* decision. That year, the U.S. Supreme Court ruled that school districts had to adopt concrete plans to achieve racial integration. In 1971, just three years later, the court ruled in favor of busing—a practice in which students, Black and white, were transported to schools (often outside their districts) to promote racial integration. Though busing was successful in some districts, others vehemently and sometimes violently resisted, even in districts outside the South. In the mid-1970s, for example, the Boston Public School System was ordered by the court to implement busing to integrate city schools. In response, many white parents pulled their children from Boston schools, and some violently protested the order, even attacking buses carrying Black children to white schools (Browne-Marshall 2019).

Nonetheless, despite these protests, data show that school segregation "declined substantially" from the late 1960s until about 1980 as a result of busing and other desegregation measures (Reardon and Owens 2014).

Moreover, studies indicate that increased integration during these years was beneficial to both Black and white students. High school graduate rates and standardized test scores improved for Black students. Desegregation during this time also led to higher incomes, reduced odds of poverty and criminality, increased chances of working white-collar jobs, and resulted in better health outcomes for Black students later in life. Studies show that school integration also reduced racial prejudice among whites (Boddie and Parker 2018; Johnson 2019; Reardon and Owens 2014).

Despite the many benefits of school integration, however, scholars argue that, since 1980, school segregation has, at best, remained stagnant or, at worst, intensified over time (Reardon and Owens 2014). Georgetown University law professor Sheryll Cashin maintains that "school segregation levels are about where they were in 1968" (Cashin 2018), and Berkeley professor of public policy Rucker C. Johnson notes that half of U.S. schoolchildren attend schools where "more than three-quarters of their peers are of the same race" (Johnson 2019).

There are at least two key explanations for contemporary school segregation. First, the late 1980s, 1990s, and 2000s saw repeated court reversals of desegregation orders across the nation, thus making school integration difficult, if not impossible, to achieve. A key setback came in 2007 when the U.S. Supreme Court prohibited the use of race in school admissions as a tool of integration, thus crippling desegregation efforts in American schools and, according to some critics, virtually reversing *Brown* (Nazaryan 2017).

Second, school segregation is directly related to housing segregation (for more on housing segregation today, see Q11). Students typically attend schools in the communities where they live; hence, persistent residential segregation across the nation contributes to racial segregation in public schools. Studies further show that *white flight* (the movement of whites to other districts to avoid integrated neighborhoods and schools), in addition to whites leaving the public school system for private schools, also explain segregated schools in the twenty-first-century (Reardon and Owens 2014).

Importantly, school integration is much more than having students of color sitting next to white students in classrooms. It is about money, resources, and opportunities. Public schools are commonly funded by local property taxes, which is problematic in a society where race and class are closely intertwined. Given that communities tend to be segregated by race (and, as such, often by social class as well), white communities tend to have a greater tax base and hence more money to fund their public schools as compared to communities of color, especially those that are predominantly Black and Latinx. For example, 2008–2009 data of American schools analyzed by the Center for American Progress (2012) show that schools nationwide typically spent $334 less on students of color than on white students. The disparity was even more pronounced in segregated schools: schools with 90 percent or more students of color spent $733 less per student per year than schools with 90 percent or more white students. In some states, the discrepancy was significantly higher. California, for example, spent $4,380 less per student at 90 percent minority schools than schools that are 90 percent white.

Moreover, as the number of students of color in a school increased, the amount of money spent on each student went down. An increase in 10 percent of students of color was associated with a national average decrease in spending of $75 per student. In some states, these numbers were even more staggering. For example, an increase in 10 percent of students of color in a school was associated with $762 less spent per student in Vermont, $582 less in New Hampshire, $298 less in Nebraska, and $257 less in Nevada. Thirteen states showed no significant spending differences based on the racial composition of their schools, and 12 states showed increases in spending as the percentage of nonwhite students in schools increased. However, in 24 states accounting for 63 percent of all students of color in the United States, an increase in the percentage of students of color was correlated with a decrease in dollars spent per student.

Uneven funding translates into wide disparities in American schools. Some examples include the following:

- *Teachers.* Teachers in predominantly minority schools tend to be lower paid and less experienced than those in predominantly white schools (U.S. Department of Education 2016). They also tend to be less qualified in terms of level of education, certification, and training in the fields that they teach. Teacher quality is important because research shows that racial disparities in standardized test scores are due, in part, to the qualifications of their teachers (Darling-Hammond 1998).
- *Counselors.* One in five American schools have no school counselors, and this is particularly problematic for students of color. According to data by the U.S. Department of Education (2016), 1.6 million American children (usually Black, Latinx, and Asian) attended schools with law enforcement officers but zero counselors. However, studies show that students who talk with their school counselor about future plans are more than three times likely to attend college than those who do not (Velez n.d.).

- *Curriculum.* High-minority schools offer fewer advanced placement (AP) and honors classes and a more limited curriculum. For example, schools with large numbers of Black and Latinx students are less likely to offer courses such as calculus, algebra II, chemistry, and physics (U.S. Department of Education 2016), which (with the exception of calculus) are necessary for college readiness.

- *Facilities.* Poor districts, which are mostly composed of children of color, are more likely than wealthy white districts to educate children in dilapidated schools that for some kids feel "more like a jail than a school" (Lartney 2017). Many schools lack funds to renovate aging schools (the average public school building in America was built in 1968), and this is problematic given that these students are educated in decaying schools. Many of these schools have been described as having peeling paint, flooded corridors, patched carpets, buckling ceilings, poor lighting, cracked blackboards, or uncomfortable temperatures. Some students also attend schools that lack functional sewage facilities, running water, and internet, and they spend much of their time in overcrowded classrooms without windows or ventilation (Kozol 1991; Filardo, Vincent, and Sullivan 2019). According to decades of research, the condition of schools affects teacher turnover, student morale and attendance, student and teacher health, and academic achievement (Filardo, Vincent, and Sullivan 2019). A 2017 analysis of five million student records from the Los Angeles Unified School District, for example, found increases in student attendance and standardized test scores when students were moved from overcrowded and dilapidated schools into newly constructed facilities (Lafortune and Schonholzer 2017).

- *Resources.* Students in high-minority schools are less likely than predominantly white schools to have computers/laptops, updated software programs, internet access, digital whiteboards, projectors, laboratory equipment, current (or enough) textbooks, and even robust libraries. Lack of textbooks is problematic given that standardized tests are often based on information in textbooks, as the companies that create standardized tests also publish the textbooks. According to Meredith Broussard, a New York University professor of data journalism, "Any teacher who wants his or her students to pass the [standardized] tests has to give out books from the Big Three publishers. If you look at a textbook from one of these companies and look at the standardized tests written by the same company, even a third grader can see that many of the questions on the test are similar to questions in the book" (Broussard 2014). Access to books in school libraries is also problematic, with affluent, predominantly white schools typically having much larger and more current holdings of books and other library resources for students than schools in poor districts with high percentages of students of color.

Schools are a major driver of inequality, and they reproduce poverty generation after generation. Minority students that attend low-quality schools are more likely to see chronic absenteeism, higher high school dropout rates, lower college attendance, and dimmer futures than those attending wealthier schools. They are also comparatively more likely to end up in low-paying jobs with little way out of high-poverty communities. They then send their own children to similar failing neighborhood schools, whereby the cycle begins again. This is especially problematic for a society that prides itself on being an "equal opportunity for all" meritocracy. If our schools remain "separate and unequal," American children will never start from the same starting point, nor will they ever compete on a level playing field.

FURTHER READING

Boddie, Elise C., and Dennis D. Parker. 2018. "Linda Brown and the Unfinished Work of School Integration." *New York Times*, March 30.

Broussard, Meredith. 2014. "Why Poor Schools Can't Win at Standardized Testing." *The Atlantic*, July 15.

Browne-Marshall, Gloria J. 2019. "Busing Ended 20 Years Ago. Today Our Schools Are Segregated Once Again." *TIME*, September 11.

Cashin, Sheryll. 2018. "A Look at the State of School Integration 64 Years after Brown v. Board of Education." Interview with Sheryll Cashin by Audie Cornish. NPR, March 28. Retrieved on April 10, 2020, at https://www.npr.org/2018/03/28/597750714/a-look-at-the -state-of-school-integration-64-years-after-brown-v-board-of-educat.

Center for American Progress. 2012. "Students of Color Still Receiving Unequal Education." August 22. Retrieved on April 10, 2020, at https://www.americanprogress.org/issues/education-k-12/news/2012/08 /22/32862/students-of-color-still-receiving-unequal-education/.

Coleman, Arika L. 2018. "The County That Closed Its Public Schools Rather Than Desegregate after Brown v. Board of Education." *TIME*, May 16.

Darling-Hammond, Linda. 1998. "Unequal Opportunity: Race and Education." Brookings, March 1. Retrieved on April 10, 2020, at https:// www.brookings.edu/articles/unequal-opportunity-race-and-education/.

Filardo, Mary, Jeffrey M. Vincent, and Kevin J. Sullivan. 2019. "How Crumbling School Facilities Perpetuate Inequality." Phi Delta Kappa, April 29.

History.com editors. 2019. "James Meredith at Ole Miss." History, June 10. Retrieved on October 29, 2020, at https://www.history.com/topics /black-history/ole-miss-integration.

Johnson, Rucker C. 2019. "Why School Integration Works." *Washington Post*, May 16.

Kozol, Jonathan. 1991. *Savage Inequalities: Children in America's Schools.* New York: Crown Publishers.

Lafortune, Julia, and David Schonholzer. 2017. "Does New School Construction Impact Student Test Scores and Attendance?" California Policy Lab, Policy Brief, October. Retrieved on April 10, 2020, at https://www.capolicylab.org/wp-content/uploads/2017/10/Policy-Brief -Lafortune-Schoenholzer.pdf.

Lartney, James. 2017. "Two Schools in Mississippi—And a Lesson in Race and Inequality in America." *The Guardian*, August 2.

Loewen, James W. 2018. *Sundown Towns: A Hidden Dimension of American Racism.* New York: The New Press.

Nazaryan, Alexander. 2017. "Whites Only: School Segregation Is Black, from Birmingham to San Francisco." *Newsweek*, May 2.

Reardon, Sean F., and Ann Owens. 2014. "60 Years after Brown: Trends and Consequences of School Segregation." *Annual Review of Sociology* 40: 199–218.

U.S. Department of Education. 2016. *2013–2014 Civil Rights Data Collection: A First Look.* Retrieved on April 10, 2020, at https://www2.ed.gov /about/offices/list/ocr/docs/2013-14-first-look.pdf.

Velez, Erin Dunlop. n.d. "How Can High School Counseling Shape Students' Postsecondary Attendance?" National Association for College Admission Counseling. Retrieved on April 10, 2020, at https://www .nacacnet.org/globalassets/documents/publications/research/hsls-phase -iii.pdf.

Q14. IS EDUCATION THE KEY TO RACIAL EQUALITY IN AMERICA?

Answer: If *racial equality* is defined as equal socioeconomic status among all racial groups, then no. Education has the potential to benefit any nation by imparting knowledge and skills to its populace, though the American educational system persistently disadvantages people of color as compared to whites. Furthermore, systemic racial discrimination in hiring and promotion undermines the power of a college degree for many Americans of color.

The Facts: American educator Horace Mann, an advocate of public education in the nineteenth century, famously described *education* as the "great equalizer of the conditions of men." His words resonated in a meritocratic-minded society, and even today, many Americans perceive education to be the key to individual success and broader racial equality. American society repeatedly tells children of the importance of education, and public service announcements implore them to "Stay in school!" Though education can benefit any population and has great potential for achieving racial equality, there are several problems that prevent education from being a "great equalizer" in American society: (1) people of color are more likely than their white counterparts to bear the brunt of deep disparities in America's K-12 education, (2) they are more apt to be disadvantaged in college, and (3) they are more prone to suffer the downside (i.e., debt accumulation) and limitations of their college degrees. Hence, even when people of color attain equal levels of education to whites, they do not necessarily secure socioeconomic parity with whites.

Disparities in K-12 Education

First, as described in Q13, there exist profound disparities in American public education. Because public schools are typically funded by local property taxes, schools in middle-class and wealthy communities, which are often majority white, tend to be funded at higher rates than those in communities that are comparatively poorer. Poorer schools are typically found in high-minority inner cities, on Native American reservations, and in rural white areas, though minority children are affected at higher rates than their white counterparts. Uneven funding translates into wide educational disparities, and children in poorer districts are more likely than those in wealthier districts to have inexperienced and uncertified teachers, staff instability, crumbling and outmoded facilities, overcrowded classrooms, and lower-quality curriculum. They are also less likely to have access to challenging curricular material and engaging activities, counselors, enough/up-to-date instructional resources (e.g., computers, internet, textbooks, and science equipment), robust libraries, playgrounds, and so on (Darling-Hammond 2001; Kozol 1991). Students who attend underfunded and underperforming schools drop out at higher rates than those at well-funded high-resource schools. In fact, many of these poorly funded schools are "dropout factories," meaning that 60 percent or more of students drop out before graduation (Blair 2007). Though many factors related to poverty contribute to their high dropout rates, poor-quality schools cannot be overlooked as part of the problem.

Further, not only are students of color disproportionately disadvantaged by underfunded schools, but they also often receive different types of education than their white counterparts—even within the same schools—through a practice called *tracking*. Tracking is the process of grouping students by ability and assigning them to curricular tracks. Although tracking can be useful (such as allowing teachers to teach to students with similar abilities), studies show that the practice too often racially segregates students within schools and exacerbates racial inequalities. White and Asian students are more likely to be tracked into advanced courses, while Black, Latinx, and Native students are more often tracked into remedial and special education courses.

Tracking is often based on test scores or prior educational opportunities, but critics contend that it is also linked to different expectations that teachers hold for students depending on students' race. In fact, when controlling for test scores, studies have found that race and class have long influenced who is tracked into high school honors courses, vocational programs (Darling-Hammond 2001), and even gifted programs. For example, a 2016 study found that Black students were half as likely as white students to be selected for elementary school gifted programs, even though they had identical standardized test scores in reading and math. The study revealed that teachers played an important role as gatekeepers of these programs (Grissom and Redding 2016), illustrating that personal biases may keep some children of color out of advanced programs.

Teachers' expectations affect tracking and, hence, the types of education that students ultimately receive, but their expectations also influence students in other ways. A 2016 study found that "teacher expectations tend to line up with student outcomes" primarily because their expectations become self-fulfilling prophesies for students. For example, when students in the study were randomly assigned to teachers with high expectations as compared to those with comparatively lower expectations, researchers found that they were more likely to complete a college degree in the future (Papageorge and Gershenson 2016).

Teacher expectations can also influence student IQ. A classic study from the 1960s found that when teachers were told that certain students scored high on a "special test from Harvard," they interacted with them differently as compared to other students. Teachers were told the test predicted which children were about to experience a dramatic rise in IQ.

In reality, the test did no such thing, and the experimenter simply chose children at random. The researcher then followed the teachers and children for two years and found that when teachers believed children scored high on the test, it affected their "moment-to-moment interactions with the children . . . in a thousand almost invisible ways"; for example, they provided them more time to answer questions, smiled and nodded at them more, and gave them more feedback and approval. Not surprisingly, those children did see higher gains in their IQ, illustrating just how powerful teacher expectations can be for students (see Spiegel 2012). If teachers have lower expectations for Black, Latinx, and Native children as compared to white children (as studies suggest they do, especially if the teacher is white), these expectations will likely affect students in countless ways (Perry 2017).

Data also show that students are disciplined in American schools differently depending on their race, which has implications for their education and their future trajectories. Students of color, especially Black, Latinx, and Native American students, are punished more frequently and more severely than white students—even for similar offenses. They are more likely to be suspended, referred to police, and arrested and consequently miss school and instructional time in the classroom. This is true even for Black preschoolers, who even at three and four years old are suspended from preschool at about two times the rate of other children (Malik 2017).

A 2013 study led by Lance Hannon of Villanova University further found that suspension rates are even higher for Black children with dark skin. Analyzing national data, Hannon and his colleagues discovered that the odds of suspension were about three times higher for Black girls with the darkest skin tones compared to those with the lightest skin, even after controlling for their family's socioeconomic status, academic achievement, and frequency of delinquent activity (Hannon, DeFina, and Bruch 2013).

Scholars argue that these disparate punishments contribute to the "school-to-prison pipeline"—the disproportionate tendency of racial minorities to become incarcerated because of harsh school policies that overly penalize and often criminalize even minor transgressions (e.g., arguments/fights, smoking, vandalism, in-class cell phone usage, and dress code violations). In Arizona, for example, Native students comprise 8 percent of students but are 23 percent of those arrested (Blad and Harwin 2017). One grandfather, a plaintiff in a lawsuit against an Arizona elementary school, said his 11-year-old special needs grandson, who is Native American, was suspended from school, arrested, and prosecuted in federal court for pulling wires from a computer monitor (Wong 2017). In 2019, a charter school in Orlando made national headlines when a local police officer cuffed and arrested two Black children (ages six and eight) for misbehaving at school (Law 2019). Thus, many social justice activists, education researchers, and other critics contend that while students in middle-class and wealthy districts are typically groomed for college, students of color in poorer districts are primed for the criminal justice system. For more on the school-to-prison pipeline, see Q18.

College: An Uneven Playing Field

Even when poor students of color attend college, the playing field is far from equal. Stark funding disparities in American public schools and different K-12 educational experiences mean that even for students who stay in school, some will discover that their public schools did little to prepare them for college. Of all students accepted by American colleges in the 2014–2015 academic year, nearly a half million are estimated to have arrived unprepared for college-level work. "The numbers reveal a glaring gap in the nation's educational system," according to one analysis. "A high school diploma . . . doesn't guarantee that students are prepared for college courses" (Butrymowicz 2017). Black and Latinx students, for instance, are less likely to attend high schools that offer a college-prep curriculum (Quinton and National Journal 2014), and many of these high schools fail to offer basic courses necessary for college readiness, such as algebra II, chemistry, and physics (U.S. Department of Education 2016). To compensate, colleges often require that these students enroll in remedial college courses to bridge the gap, though students of color are disproportionately affected; an estimated 56 percent of Black students and 45 percent of Latinx students are enrolled in remedial college courses nationwide, as compared to 35 percent of white students (Jimenez et al. 2016). Even more problematic is that data show that students who enter college on a remedial track are more likely to drop out. Most students will see this as a personal failure, not fully considering how the cards were stacked against them from the start.

Moreover, according to Maria G. Rendon (2020), an assistant professor of urban planning and public policy at the University of California–Irvine, some college students "carry the burden of our vast inequalities." While middle- and upper-class students often "navigate college with ease," Rendon points out that lower-class students in her home state of California, many of whom are Latinx students arriving from the poorest communities, are distinctly disadvantaged. Many students struggle with spiraling tuition costs. Because of "sticker shock," many pass up elite private colleges for cheaper public colleges, arguably missing out on all the opportunities and benefits that top schools provide.

However, even public schools are far from inexpensive. According to *U.S. News & World Report*, tuition at an in-state public college was nearly 75 percent less than that of a private college, but it was still a little over $10,000 for the 2019–2020 academic year (Powell and Kerr 2019)—this price tag excludes housing, food, and miscellaneous school fees (e.g., textbooks, lab fees, and parking). Many middle- and upper-class students have parents who foot their tuition bills (sometimes even providing a stipend for additional expenses). Those from lower classes often must balance work and school to pay college costs, thus preventing them from focusing solely on their academic work and, for some, from attending school full time. Working while attending college (especially when it is for tuition and survival, not for "pocket money") undoubtedly also affects their ability to participate in extracurricular activities and unpaid internships—activities that could pad their resumes and widen their professional networks.

Many students also struggle with housing and food insecurity, especially those who already come from impoverished backgrounds. Homelessness is a growing problem among college students and affects approximately 18 percent of those attending two-year colleges and 14 percent of those at four-year colleges, according to a 2019 survey of nearly 86,000 students conducted by the Hope Center for College, Community, and Justice (Jones 2019; Goldrick-Rab et al. 2019). The problem is so dire that some schools have proposed opening campus parking lots to homeless students so they can safely sleep in their cars (Jones 2019). Further, food insecurity is an underappreciated problem for millions of college students around the country. According to Christopher Nellum, a senior director of higher education research and policy at the Education Trust, two of every five students attending public universities in California experience food insecurity, which can affect their academic performance (Williams 2019). Nellum says that hunger means "sitting in a classroom hoping no one hears your stomach growl," but it also means "spending time worrying about where to get food for the next week rather than studying for next week's exam" (Williams 2019). The same is true for students who constantly worry about housing, transportation, or obligations at home (e.g., parents who rely on them to contribute money to the household). Clearly, all of these additional pressures make it harder for them to graduate let alone post the sort of academic honors or top grades that can aid their future job prospects.

Limitations of a College Degree for Americans of Color: College Debt and Workplace Discrimination

Finally, a college degree does not hold the same value for everyone. Though a college degree can translate into increased yearly earnings, this must be weighed against (1) the debt incurred and (2) future job prospects. First, American colleges are notoriously expensive, and the brunt of college debt is not carried equally; Black, Latinx, and Native American students carry higher debt burdens than white and Asian students (Pallardy 2019). For example, a 2019 study by Jason N. Houle, an assistant professor of sociology at Dartmouth College, and Fenaba R. Addo, an assistant professor of consumer science at the University of Wisconsin-Madison, found that Blacks held 186 percent more debt than whites 15 years after graduation, primarily because they are more likely to come from financially disadvantaged households (and hence take out more loans to pay for college), are more likely to leave college without a degree (as previously explained), are more likely to attend for-profit colleges (which often leave students with high debt and little education to show for it), and are less likely to be financially sound in young adulthood as compared to their white counterparts (which affects their ability to repay their loans) (Houle and Addo 2019). According to Houle and Addo, "racial inequalities in student debt may contribute to the fragility of the next generation of the black middle class" (2019: 573), thus challenging the notion that education is the path to upward mobility and key to racial equality for all.

Second, research shows that people of color continue to face workplace discrimination in the United States, which can blunt the power of their college degrees. For example, data show that a college degree makes a big difference in the employment prospects of Black men. However, study after study also confirms that racial discrimination in employment persists. A 2014 study, for instance, found that Black men need more education than white men to gain employment. Specifically, researchers found that Black male college graduates have about the same employment prospects as white males who have completed some college but have no degree (Barthel 2014; O'Sullivan, Mugglestone, and Allison 2014). Janelle Jones and John Schmitt of the Center for Economic and Policy Research further argue in a report titled *A College Degree Is No Guarantee* (2014) that the Great Recession of 2008 and its aftermath was difficult on all recent college graduates, but it was particularly difficult on recent Black graduates. They were more likely to be unemployed and underemployed (i.e., working in low-paying jobs that did not require a college degree) as compared to all other recent graduates. In 2013, for example, the unemployment rate of recent Black college graduates was 12.4 percent as compared to only 5.6 percent for all recent college graduates. Further, 55.9 percent of recent Black graduates were underemployed as compared to 45 percent of all recent college grads. The authors attribute these racial disparities to persistent discrimination in employment. For additional examples of racial discrimination in the workplace, see Q15.

In sum, education has great potential to bring about racial equality in the United States. However, for every American to reap the benefits of education, much work needs to be done to reduce disparities in K-12 education, to equalize opportunities at college, and to ensure that a college degree holds the same benefit for all. Otherwise, the American educational system may do little more than reproduce current racial inequalities in the United States.

FURTHER READING

Barthel, Margaret. 2014. "Black Men Need More Education Than White Men to Get Jobs." *The Atlantic*, August 10.

Blad, Evie, and Alex Harwin. 2017. "Black Students More Likely to Be Arrested at School." Education Week, January 24.

Blair, Kristen. 2007. "'Dropout Factories' and Assembly-Line Education." *Carolina Journal*, November 1.

Butrymowicz, Sarah. 2017. "Most Colleges Enroll Students Who Aren't Prepared for Higher Education." *PBS NewsHour*, January 13.

Darling-Hammond, L. 2001. "Inequality in Teaching and Schooling: How Opportunity Is Rationed to Students of Color in America". Pp. 208–233 in *The Right Thing to Do, the Smart Thing to Do: Enhancing Diversity in the Health Professions, Summary of the Symposium on Diversity in Health Professions in Honor of Herbert W. Nickens, M.D. Institute of Medicine*. Washington, DC: National Academy Press.

Duncan, Arne. 2018. "Education: The "Great Equalizer." *Encyclopaedia Britannica*. Retrieved on April 14, 2020, at https://www.britannica.com/topic/Education-The-Great-Equalizer-2119678.

Goldrick-Rab, Sara, Christine Baker-Smith, Vanessa Coca, Elizabeth Looker, and Tiffani Williams. 2019. *College and University Basic Needs Insecurity: A National #RealCollege Survey Report*. n.p.: The Hope Center. Retrieved on August 16, 2020, at https://hope4college.com/wp-content/uploads/2019/04/HOPE_realcollege_National_report_digital.pdf.

Grissom, Jason A., and Christopher Redding. 2016. "Discretion and Disproportionality: Explaining the Underrepresentation of High-Achieving

Students of Color in Gifted Programs." *American Educational Research Association Open* 2(1): 1–25.

Hannon, Lance, Robert DeFina, and Sarah Bruch. 2013. The Relationship between Skin Tone and School Suspension for African Americans." *Race and Social Problems* 5: 281–295.

Houle, Jason N., and Fenaba R. Addo. 2019. "Racial Disparities in Student Debt and the Reproduction of the Fragile Middle Class." *Sociology of Race and Ethnicity* 5(4): 562–577.

Jimenez, Laura, Scott Sargrad, Jessica Morales, and Maggie Thompson. 2016. "Remedial Education: The Cost of Catching Up." Center for American Progress, September 28.

Jones, Charisse. 2019. "Homeless in College: Students Sleep in Cars, on Couches When They Have Nowhere Else to Go." *USA Today*, June 10.

Jones, Janelle, and John Schmitt. 2014. *A College Degree Is No Guarantee.* Washington, DC: Center for Economic and Policy Research. Retrieved on April 15, 2020, at https://www.cepr.net/documents/black-coll-grads-2014-05.pdf.

Kozol, Jonathan. 1991. *Savage Inequalities: Children in America's Schools.* New York: Crown Publishers.

Law, Tara. 2019. "Two Children, Ages 6 and 8, Were Arrested at School in Florida. Police Say the Officer Acted without Permission." *TIME*, September 22.

Malik, Rasheed. 2017. "New Data Reveal 250 Preschoolers Are Suspended or Expelled Every Day." Center for American Progress, November 6.

O'Sullivan, Rory, Konrad Mugglestone, and Tom Allison. 2014. *Closing the Race Gap: Alleviating Young African American Unemployment through Education.* Washington, DC: Young Invincibles. Retrieved on July 3, 2020, at https://d3n8a8pro7vhmx.cloudfront.net/yicare/pages/141/attachments/original/1403804069/Closing_the_Race_Gap_Ntnl_6.25.14.pdf.

Pallardy, Richard. 2019. "Racial Disparities in Student Loan Debt." Savingsforcollge.com, August 27.

Papageorge, Nicholas, and Seth Gershenson. 2016. "Do Teacher Expectations Matter?" Brookings, September 16.

Perry, Andre. 2017. "What's Wrong with White Teachers?" The Hechinger Report, May 1.

Powell, Farran, and Emma Kerr. 2019. "See the Average College Tuition in 2019–2020." *U.S. News & World Report*, September 19.

Quinton, Sophie, and National Journal. 2014. "The Race Gap in High School Honors Classes." *The Atlantic*, December 11.

Rendon, Maria G. 2020. "For Latinos, a College Degree Doesn't Guarantee Entrance into the Middle Class." *Orange County Register*, February 20. Retrieved on November 25, 2020, at https://www.ocregister.com/2020/02/20/for-latinos-a-college-degree-doesnt-guarantee-entrance-to-the-middle-class/.

Spiegel, Alix. 2012. "Teachers' Expectations Can Influence How Students Perform." NPR, September 17. Retrieved on November 25, 2020, at https://www.npr.org/sections/health-shots/2012/09/18/161159263/teachers-expectations-can-influence-how-students-perform.

U.S. Department of Education. 2016. *2013–2014 Civil Rights Data Collection: A First Look.* Washington, DC: U.S. Department of Education. Retrieved on April 10, 2020, at https://www2.ed.gov/about/offices/list/ocr/docs/2013-14-first-look.pdf.

Williams, Joseph P. 2019. "Fighting Food Insecurity on College Campuses." *U.S. News & World Report*, February 4.

Wong, Alia. 2017. "The Longstanding Crisis Facing Tribal Schools." *The Atlantic*, January 12.

Q15. DO ALL RACES HAVE EQUAL OPPORTUNITY IN THE AMERICAN WORKPLACE TODAY?

Answer: No. Research suggests that inequality persists in the American workplace in the twenty-first century. According to a growing number of studies, Americans of color, especially Black Americans, are regularly disadvantaged as compared to white Americans when it comes to employment, especially regarding hiring, wages, and evaluations on the job. Moreover, though some companies describe themselves as "equal opportunity employers" or tout affirmative action policies and programs, the reality remains that white Americans are the most privileged racial group when it comes to employment and work, even in cases when they are not the most qualified candidates or most proficient employees.

The Facts: In 2014, José Zamora applied to as many jobs posted on Craigslist as he could—he estimates somewhere between 50 to 100 a day for months. There were no replies—no e-mails from employers or phone calls inviting him in for an interview. Frustrated by the lack of response, Zamora decided to try a new strategy: he altered his name on his resume by simply dropping one letter (the *s*) in his first name to see whether employers might respond differently. After changing his name to Joe, Zamora found that he was suddenly flooded with inquiries from prospective employers who now wanted to meet with him. He said, "That's when all the responses started coming in. That's when all the replies and e-mails. . . . 'The position is open,' 'We want to meet with you,' 'Call us back.'" He added, "I was applying for the same exact jobs, the exact same resume, the exact same experience—just a different name" (Taube 2014). Is his experience typical?

Experimental studies, field studies, and employment data reveal that Zamora's experience is likely no anomaly; discrimination persists in the workplace even in the twenty-first century. One's race affects whether employers call applicants to interview, whether they hire them, how much they pay, and even how they are evaluated on the job.

For example, race affects whether applicants receive callbacks for interviews:

- A 2004 study, in which researchers sent out nearly 5,000 resumes to 1,300 job ads in Boston and Chicago, found that job applicants with "Black-sounding" names (such as Lakisha or Jamal) were 50 percent less likely to get called back for interviews than those with "white-sounding" names (such as Emily or Greg)—despite having similar qualifications. They further found that having a white name is like having an extra eight years of job experience. The study also discovered that improving one's qualifications benefited whites more than Blacks. Researchers created both high- and low-quality resumes and found that when they compared the high-quality resumes sent to employers, white applicants were *even more* advantaged (more likely to get callbacks) over their similarly qualified Black counterparts (Bertrand and Mullainathan 2004).
- A study in 2016, however, potentially challenges the above results. Like the 2004 study, this study examined bias by varying names on resumes. Unlike the earlier study, however, the 2016 study added Hispanic names along with those of Black and white applicants. Researchers sent nearly 9,000 resumes to online job postings in seven U.S. cities. Unlike the 2004 study, they found *no* difference in callbacks by race, though the authors of the study admit that perhaps the names used in the study were weak indicators of race. One of the study's authors noted that 90 percent of people with the surname "Washington" and 75 percent of those with "Jefferson" are Black, but he admits that "maybe no one knows that." Even the first names used in the study were perhaps problematic: Megan and Brian were used for white candidates and Chloe and Ryan for Black candidates—hardly clear indicators of race. According to

Northwestern University professor David Figlio, "If I got a resume in the mail for Chloe Washington or Ryan Jefferson it would be hard for me to imagine that I would have interpreted that differently from Megan Anderson or Bryan Thompson" (Elejalde-Ruiz 2016).

Thus, though some hailed the study's findings as evidence that racial bias is a problem of the past, the study's results are arguably not an accurate indicator of present-day racial bias in hiring practices. Nonetheless, it is promising that they found that resumes with Hispanic names (e.g., Isabella and Carlos as first names and Garcia and Hernandez as surnames) were not any less likely to receive callbacks for interviews.

Even when white applicants have criminal records, they are still advantaged over Black applicants:

- A 2003 study found that having a criminal record affects one's job prospects, but, importantly, race mattered more than criminal record. Employers were more likely to call whites *with* criminal records (17 percent were offered an interview) than Blacks *without* criminal records (14 percent). Hence, all else being equal, Black applicants with clean records were still disadvantaged as compared to whites with criminal histories (Pager 2003).

Race also matters when it comes to hiring and pay:

- A 2010 study paired people of different races who had similar credentials and sent them to apply as servers to upscale restaurants in New York City. People of color were only 54 percent as likely to be hired as whites. Furthermore, when they were hired, nonwhite employees were paid 12 percent less than their white counterparts (Bendick, Rodriguez, and Jayaraman 2010).
- A 2012 study also found that, even with the same qualifications, Black applicants received fewer job offers than whites (and even fewer callbacks) in Milwaukee. They matched applicants on physical appearance (height, weight, attractiveness), verbal skills, and interactional styles (level of eye contact, demeanor, and verbosity). They also provided them nearly identical fictional resumes, with the same educational attainment, work experience, and even neighborhood of residence. Whites received callbacks or job offers in 34 percent of cases, whereas Blacks only received them in 14 percent of

cases. The authors found similar patterns in New York City: whites received callbacks or job offers in 31 percent of cases, as compared to 25 percent of cases for Latinxs and only 15 percent of cases for Blacks. The authors further found that when interviewed, employers often expressed prejudicial attitudes about applicants of color even when they claimed that race did not matter to them when making hiring decisions (Pager and Western 2012; see also Pager, Western, and Bonikowski 2009).

- A 2014 study found that Black men need more education than white men to get jobs. Black male college graduates have about the same employment prospects as white males with some college education but no degree (Barthel 2014).
- A 2014 analysis found that "a college degree is no guarantee" for Black men. Looking at employment data in the aftermath of the 2008 Great Recession, researchers found that of all recent college graduates, Black graduates were hit hardest. Five years after the Great Recession, for example, recent Black graduates were most likely to be unemployed; their unemployment rate was 12.4 percent as compared to only 5.6 percent for all recent college graduates. They were also most likely to be underemployed; 55.9 percent of recent Black graduates were underemployed as compared to 45 percent of all recent college grads. The authors attributed these racial disparities to persistent discrimination in employment (Jones and Schmitt 2014).
- A 2019 study looked at faculty perceptions and hireability of post-doctoral candidates who differed by race and gender. Faculty at eight universities were asked to read one of eight curricula vitae (CVs), each depicting a hypothetical job candidate applying to a postdoctoral research position in physics or biology. All CVs were identical in quality, except for the applicant's name, which was chosen to signify gender and race. For example, the name "Shanice Banks" was chosen to represent a Black female; examples of other names in the study include "Maria Rodriguez" (Latina), "Claire Miller" (white woman), and "Wang Li" (Asian male). Regarding race, researchers found that physics faculty rated Asian and white candidates as more competent and hirable than Black and Latinx candidates, and those in biology rated Asian candidates as more competent and hirable than Black candidates and as more hirable than Latinx candidates. The study's authors argued that the results indicate that racial biases contribute to the underrepresentation of Blacks and Latinxs in STEM fields (Eaton et al. 2020).

Studies also show that there is value when people of color "whiten" their resumes, further revealing that race matters in employment:

- A 2016 study found that when Black and Asian applicants "whit-ened" their resumes, they were more likely to receive callbacks for interviews. They whitened their resumes by anglifying their names and omitting experiences that might signal minority status (e.g., omitting work experience in Chinatown or membership in a Black student organization). A quarter of Black candidates with whitened resumes received callbacks as compared to only 10 percent who left their resumes unwhitened, and 21 percent of Asians received callbacks with whitened resumes as compared to 11.5 percent with nonwhitened resumes. Further, more than a third (36 percent) of all applicants in the sample admitted that they routinely whitened their resumes (Kang et al. 2016). José Zamora's story (discussed at the beginning of this entry) is an example of this phenomenon.

Race also affects how people are evaluated on the job:

- A 2007 study of the NBA found that white referees were more likely to call personal fouls on Black rather than white players, and this had an impact on the probability of a majority Black team winning a basketball game when officiated by mostly white referees (Price and Wolfers 2007). A 2013 follow-up study found that when referees were made aware of the original findings from the 2007 study, the bias disappeared (Pope, Price, and Wolfers 2013).
- A 2014 study found that partners at law firms rated legal briefings differently depending on the perceived race of the author. Though the fabricated briefings were identical, law partners rated them lower when they were told they were written by Black authors (3.2 out of 5) as compared to when they were told they were written by white authors (4.1 out of 5). When they were under the impression that the author was Black, they were also more likely to point out spell-ing, grammar, and technical errors than when they believed the brief was authored by a white person (Reeves 2014).

Taken collectively, these studies reveal that opportunities in the work-place are far from equal. Sociologists Devah Pager and Bruce Western (2012) argue that because most contemporary discrimination is subtle, it typically leaves minority applicants completely unaware of the ways in which they are differentially treated. They have no way of knowing the qualifications of other applicants, they have little information about the needs of the employer or how they came to their decisions, and they have no access to employment data that can tell them whether their racial group was treated statistically differently. Consequently, workplace discrimination typically goes unnoticed and unreported.

Moreover, when a 2019 Pew Research poll asked Americans whether "Blacks are treated less fairly than whites in hiring, pay, and promotion," most Black Americans (82 percent) agreed. By contrast, only 44 percent of white Americans agreed, illustrating that perceptions of discrimination in the American workplace differ greatly by race (Horowitz, Brown, and Cox 2019). Further, many white Americans firmly believe that it is they who are most discriminated against (Gonyea 2017), often pointing to affirmative action programs as evidence of "reverse discrimination." Though there certainly are cases (or perhaps particular industries, such as government jobs) in which Black applicants or other applicants of color may land jobs over white applicants because of affirmative action policies intended to expand opportunities for people of color, the reality is that the job market, taken as a whole, advantages whites above and beyond all other racial groups. The research described above shows that even with affirmative action programs, persistent discrimination ensures that whites remain the most advantaged racial group in the American workplace—even when they are not the most qualified candidates.

FURTHER READING

Barthel, Margaret. 2014. "Black Men Need More Education Than White Men to Get Jobs." *The Atlantic*, August 10.

Bendick, Marc, Jr., Rekha Eanni Rodriguez, and Sarumathi Jayaraman. 2010. "Employment Discrimination in Upscale Restaurants: Evidence from Matched Pair Testing." *Social Science Journal* 47: 802–818.

Bertrand, Marianne, and Sendhil Mullainathan. 2004. "Are Emily and Greg More Employable Than Lakisha and Jamal? A Field Experiment on Labor Market Discrimination." *American Economic Review* 94(4): 991–1013.

Eaton, Asia A., Jessica F. Saunders, Ryan K. Jacobson, and Keon West. 2020. "How Gender and Race Stereotypes Impact the Advancement of Scholars in STEM: Professors' Biased Evaluations of Physics and Biology Post-Doctoral Candidates." *Sex Roles* 82: 127–141.

Elejalde-Ruiz, Alexia. 2016. "Hiring Bias Study: Resumes with Black, White, and Hispanic Names Treated the Same." *Chicago Tribune*, May 4.

Gonyea, Don. 2017. "Majority of White Americans Say They Believe Whites Face Discrimination." NPR, October 24.

Horowitz, Juliana Menasce, Anna Brown, and Kiana Cox. 2019. "Race in America 2019." Pew Research Center, April 9.

Jones, Janelle and John Schmitt. 2014. *A College Degree Is No Guarantee.* Washington, DC: Center for Economic and Policy Research. Retrieved on April 15, 2020, at https://www.cepr.net/documents/black-coll-grads -2014-05.pdf.

Kang, Sonia K., Katherine A. DeCelles, Andras Tilcsik, and Sora Jun. 2016. "Whitened Resumes: Race and Self-Presentation in the Labor Market." *Administrative Science Quarterly* 61(3): 469–502.

Pager, Devah. 2003. "The Mark of a Criminal Record." *American Journal of Sociology* 108(5): 937–975.

Pager, Devah, and Bruce Western. 2012. "Identifying Discrimination at Work: The Use of Field Experiments." *Journal of Social Issues* 68(2): 221–237.

Pager, Devah, Bruce Western, and Bart Bonikowski. 2009. "Discrimination in a Low-Wage Labor Market: A Field Experiment." *American Sociological Review* 74(5): 777–799.

Pope, Devin G., Joseph Price, and Justin Wolfers. 2013. *Awareness Reduces Racial Bias.* NBER Working Paper Series. Cambridge, MA: National Bureau Of Economic Research. Retrieved on April 15, 2020, at https:// www.nber.org/papers/w19765.pdf.

Price, Joseph, and Justin Wolfers. 2007. "Racial Discrimination among NBA Referees." NBER Working Paper Series. Cambridge, MA: National Bureau Of Economic Research. Retrieved on April 15, 2020, at https://www.nber.org/papers/w13206.pdf.

Reeves, Arin N. 2014. *Written in Black & White: Exploring Confirmation Bias in Racialized Perceptions of Writing Skills.* Yellow Paper Series. Chicago: Nextions.

Taube, Aaron. 2014. "How One Man Turned His Fruitless Job Search around by Changing His Name." Business Insider, September 4.

Q16. DOES RACIAL BIAS NEGATIVELY AFFECT THE HEALTH OF AMERICANS OF COLOR?

Answer: Yes. People of color in the United States generally have worse health outcomes than white Americans, and researchers point to a number of factors to explain the racial disparities. Among these factors is systemic racial bias. Systemic racial bias affects the health of people of color via chronic stress due to discrimination, bias and unequal care in the American health-care system, heightened exposure to harmful toxins, and even housing discrimination.

The Facts: Data show that people of color in the United States experience more illness, worse medical outcomes, premature death, and higher rates of mortality as compared to white Americans (Tello 2017). Researchers have identified a number of factors that help to explain racial disparities in health, including (but not limited to) differences in wealth/income, education, access to health insurance and medical care, quality of medical care, and even ethnic/racial culture (see Q4 for further discussion of some of these factors). Researchers also point to systemic racial bias as important in explaining the uneven health outcomes between white and nonwhite Americans. In particular, racial bias affects the health of people of color in at least four ways: (1) via chronic stress due to discrimination; (2) through systemic bias and unequal care in the American health-care system; (3) by means of disproportionate exposure to harmful toxins as a result of environmental racism; and (4) as a consequence of decades of housing discrimination due to redlining.

Chronic Stress Due to Discrimination

According to a growing body of research, exposure to discrimination is a risk factor for many ailments, including mental health disorders (e.g., depression and anxiety), frequent sickness, chronic disease, poor birth outcomes, premature aging, diabetes, high blood pressure, and heart disease (Trent, Dooley, and Douge 2019; Wan 2019). To explain the link between discrimination and negative health outcomes, researchers argue that chronic stress from recurrent exposure to discrimination leads to elevated levels of stress hormones, such as cortisol. When activated for long periods, these hormones can cause significant wear and tear on the body and lead to subsequent health problems.

Illustrating the causality between discrimination and health, a 2006 study found a higher rate of poor birth outcomes (i.e., preterm births and low birth weights) among babies born to Arab American women in California in the six months following the September 11, 2001, terrorist attacks as compared to the six months prior to the attacks. The study's author argues that "chronic exposures to stressors" such as harassment, violence, and workplace discrimination experienced by the women or the community as a whole in the months immediately following the attacks likely explain the different birth outcomes before and after 9/11 (Lauderdale 2006, 198). Other studies similarly link preterm birth and low birth weight among babies of Black and Latinx mothers to maternal stress caused by racial discrimination (see Trent, Dooley, and Douge 2019; Wan 2019).

Harvard professor David Williams argues that it is not only the big experiences of discrimination that affect health (such as heightened harassment after 9/11) but also the "day-to-day little indignities" regularly experienced by people of color in America, such as being treated disrespectfully, repeatedly receiving poor service at restaurants and stores, or working with a biased boss or coworkers (Martin 2017). For example, researchers have linked the persistent day-to-day discrimination experienced by African Americans to the development of coronary heart disease (Martin 2017), high blood pressure (Hicken et al. 2014), and even accelerated aging.

Regarding the latter, a longitudinal study that followed African American adults for 25 years found a link between discrimination and rapid aging (Chae et al. 2020). In particular, researchers examined aging at the cellular level and discovered that increased experiences with discrimination among African Americans led to more rapid shortening of telomeres (those pieces of DNA that protect cells) as compared to African Americans with fewer experiences of discrimination; this is important because the shortening of telomeres has been linked with increased susceptibility to and faster progression of aging-related illness and disease. Anthony D. Ong, of Cornell University, and his colleagues similarly found a connection between day-to-day discrimination and a number of poor health outcomes. Using a survey to gauge experiences of discrimination and blood tests to measure risk for disease, they observed that African American adults who reported high levels of everyday discrimination (such as being called names, insulted, threatened, or harassed) had elevated risk for heart disease, diabetes, inflammation, and nerve problems (Ong et al. 2017).

Studies also reveal negative health effects of discrimination for children of color. An analysis of more than 1,300 studies on children's health found that children who experienced racial discrimination showed an increased likelihood of substance abuse, obesity, susceptibility to sickness, and premature aging (Carter et al. 2019; Heard-Garris et al. 2018; Wan 2019). A review of 121 studies further found that children who experienced discrimination were significantly more likely to experience mental health problems such as depression and anxiety as compared to those who did not experience discrimination (Carter et al. 2019; Priest et al. 2013). Even "secondhand exposure" to discrimination—for example, that which is experienced by their parents and friends—had negative consequences for children (Heard-Garris et al. 2018). The authors of the study argue that even indirect exposure to discrimination can be distressing for children and increase their risk of depression and anxiety.

Systemic Bias and Unequal Care in the American
Health-Care System

Disparate health outcomes among white Americans and racial minorities are also rooted in systemic bias and unequal care in the American health-care system. Monique Tello of Harvard Medical School argues that health-care workers, including physicians, may not be explicitly biased, but some nonetheless hold subconscious prejudices that affect how they interact with and care for their patients (2017).

For example, a study of nearly 200 physicians looked at how race affected their perceptions of patients (van Ryn and Burke 2000). Researchers asked physicians (who were mostly white) to rate their patients (who were either Black or white) on a number of characteristics, and they found that patient race mattered. Physicians rated Black patients as less intelligent, less educated, more likely to abuse drugs and alcohol, more likely to fail to comply with medical advice, more likely to lack social support, and less likely to participate in cardiac rehabilitation than white patients. One possible explanation is that physician perception is based on *true* differences between Blacks and whites rather than their own stereotypical racial biases, though the authors of the study point out that some of their perceptions are difficult to accept as accurate. For instance, physicians rated Black patients as "significantly less educated" than white patients, even though the authors controlled for education (in other words, physicians believed this to be true even when Black and white patients had similar levels of education). Furthermore, physicians were more likely to report that they could see themselves being friends with their white patients as compared to their Black patients, which may affect how they interact with and care for Black versus white patients.

Further, research shows that racial stereotypes held by medical professionals can directly affect patient care. A 2016 study found that personal biases of medical students and physicians affected pain assessments and treatment recommendations for Black and white patients (Hoffman et al. 2016). They asked more than 400 medical students and physician residents to rate the extent to which they believed that Black and white bodies are biologically different from each other (as measured by their responses to 15 statements). Some of these statements, all false, included the following:

- Whites have larger brains than Blacks.
- Blacks' nerve endings are less sensitive than whites'.
- Whites have a more efficient respiratory system than Blacks.

- Blacks have denser, stronger bones than whites.
- Black people's blood coagulates more quickly than whites'.

Researchers found that half of all medical students and physicians in the study endorsed at least one false belief about African Americans, illustrating that even highly educated medical professionals are not immune to racial bias and misinformation. Further, they found that the more false beliefs about Black bodies that study participants endorsed, the more likely they were to underestimate the pain that Black patients experienced. This is particularly important because they were then less likely to recommend adequate pain management treatment for Black patients as compared to white patients. These findings mirror other studies that also show that if patients are Black, their pain will likely be underestimated and undertreated than if they are white (see Anderson, Green, and Payne 2009; Cintron and Morrison 2006; Green et al. 2003; Staton et al. 2007).

This is true even for Black children. In a study of nearly one million children diagnosed with appendicitis, Black children were less likely than white children to receive appropriate pain medication, and they were less likely to receive any pain medication at all (Goyal et al. 2015). In another study, Black children were less likely than white children to be prescribed narcotic medication for postoperative pain (Sabin and Greenwald 2012).

Research also reveals racial disparities in other types of medical treatment. For example, physicians are less likely to recommend cardiac catheterization for Black patients who exhibit signs of coronary heart disease than white patients who present with similar symptoms—which may have life or death consequences for cardiac patients (Schulman et al. 1999). Studies also show that physicians interact and communicate differently with Black versus white patients. Regarding their Black patients, physicians spend less time (Johnson et al. 2004), more often dominate medical conversations, and less often involve them in their own medical decisions as compared to white patients (Johns Hopkins Medicine 2012). Moreover, data from the Centers for Disease Control and Prevention (CDC) show that Black newborns are two times more likely to die than their white counterparts (Driscoll and Ely 2020). A number of factors likely contribute to this disparity (including poverty, access to health care, and education), though a 2020 study by researchers at George Mason University found that the race of the physician also greatly impacts mortality rates for Black newborns. They analyzed data from nearly two million births in Florida that occurred from 1992 to 2015 and found that when Black newborns were treated by Black physicians, their mortality rate was cut in half (as compared to Black newborns cared for by white physicians) (Greenwood et al. 2020). The authors of the study do not provide an explanation, though previous research shows that physician bias contributes to racial disparities in health. As such, they write that "it gives warrant for hospitals and other care organizations to invest in efforts to reduce such biases and explore their connection to institutional racism" (Greenwood et al. 2020, 6–7). The aforementioned studies suggest that Black patients often receive poorer medical care as compared to their white counterparts, and this differential treatment likely has tangible consequences for the health and lives of Black Americans and other people of color in the United States.

Environmental Racism and Disproportionate Exposure to Harmful Toxins

Data also show that people of color are more likely than their white counterparts to be exposed to environmental toxins—from noxious gases emitted from factory smokestacks to poisonous chemicals dumped in local water supplies to hazardous waste material submerged in the soil—and this exposure has harmful effects on health, such as increasing risk for cancers, lung conditions, cardiac problems, and premature death (among others). A growing body of research shows that polluters (such as factories, landfills, and toxic waste facilities) are disproportionately located in minority communities, including in Black and Hispanic neighborhoods and on Native American reservations—a phenomenon termed *environmental racism*. For example, according to one source, "Native tribes across the American West have been and continue to be subjected to significant amounts of radioactive and otherwise hazardous waste as a result of living near nuclear test sites, uranium mines, power plants and toxic waste dumps" ("Reservations about Toxic Waste" 2010). As such, Native peoples living on reservations are more likely than the average American to live precariously close to noxious industries and toxic waste. Companies often prey on impoverished tribes by offering them millions of dollars to take their harmful waste, and this can be particularly attractive to poor Native communities with few options to generate revenue. Depositing this waste on reservations is further problematic because this land is not subject to the same regulations and environmental protections as U.S. land ("Reservations about Toxic Waste" 2010).

Sociologist Robert Bullard, who is described in the field as the "father of environmental justice," points to additional examples of environmental racism in the United States (Bullard 2019; for more see Bullard, Johnson, and Torres 2011):

- African Americans are nearly 80 percent more likely than whites to live where industrial pollution poses the greatest health danger.
- The percentage of African Americans living near the nation's most dangerous chemical plants is 75 percent greater than for the United States as a whole, and the percentage for Latinxs is 60 percent greater.
- People of color breathe nearly 40 percent more polluted air than whites.
- Nearly 70 percent of African Americans live within 30 miles of a dirty coal-fired power plant as compared to 56 percent of whites. Residents living near dirty coal plants are more likely to suffer from respiratory illnesses than those living farther away.
- People of color make up over half of the residents who are at greatest cancer risk from oil refinery pollution.
- More than three-quarters of Americans who live within three miles of the top twelve "dirtiest" coal power plants are people of color.

Some critics claim that these racial disparities can simply be explained by social class. According to this argument, people of color are more likely than whites to live near polluters because they are more likely to be poor and hence live in undesirable communities. Indeed, in the case of Native Americans living on reservations, poverty undoubtedly plays a role in their exposure to toxins (as described earlier). However, based on decades of research, Bullard finds race to be a more important factor than socio-economic status, and he argues that discrimination plays a crucial role in the geographic distribution of factories, garbage dumps, and toxic waste facilities (see also Newkirk 2018). He writes, "Race is still more potent than income in predicting the distribution of pollution and polluting facilities. Even money does not insulate some Americans from pollution and environmental racism. African American households with incomes between $50,000 to $60,000 live in neighborhoods that are more polluted than the average neighborhood in which white households with incomes below $10,000 live" (Bullard 2019).

As such, Americans of color, regardless of social class, are more likely than white Americans to live near polluters and hence are more prone to diseases and disorders related to toxic exposure. Groups most affected by environmental racism are African Americans, Hispanic Americans, and Native Americans, while whites remain the least affected.

Housing Discrimination Due to Redlining

Finally, decades of systemic housing discrimination in the United States, via redlining, has had a profound effect on the health of people of color, especially Black Americans. Redlining refers to the twentieth-century practice by the U.S. government and that of private banks of denying home and business loans to those living in high-minority areas (communities were redlined simply because of the racial background of residents—see Q12 for more on redlining). A growing body of research shows that those who live in previously redlined areas have, on average, shorter life spans than those living in nonredlined areas, even within the same cities. For example, researchers from the National Community Reinvestment Coalition, the University of Richmond, and the University of Wisconsin-Milwaukee analyzed historical redlined areas across 142 U.S. cities and found that residents in those communities have shorter life spans and higher rates of chronic diseases such as asthma, diabetes, hypertension, kidney disease, and obesity. One study also found links between redlined communities in New York City and preterm births and late-stage cancer diagnoses (Godoy 2020).

Lisa Cooper, a physician and professor at Johns Hopkins Bloomberg School of Public Health, points out that people often think of health as the result of individual choices (e.g., diet and exercise), but she argues that lack of choices as the result of racist policies also explains health (Godoy 2020). For instance, when banks systematically denied loans in these communities, it led to several problems that had direct effects on the health of people of color—these problems persist even today (Godoy 2020). Some examples include:

- While white families, who were granted home loans, were building intergenerational wealth through home equity throughout the mid- to late twentieth century, people of color in redlined areas were denied this opportunity and, as such, poverty became increasingly concentrated in these communities. Poverty is linked to several factors affecting health such as lack of medical insurance, reduced access to quality medical care, limited leisure time for exercise, and insufficient access to food (including healthy food options because of cost).
- Loan denials in redlined areas made it difficult, if not impossible, for residents to buy or refinance their homes. Systematic lack of investment over time meant that many homes fell into disrepair, leading to preventable health hazards such as mold and lead paint.
- Little bank investment in redlined areas led to little, if any, access to community parks, green spaces, and other places to exercise.

- Without bank investment, communities declined with time as poverty increased. As a result, retailers, including grocery stores, left redlined areas (often based on their calculated decisions that they would not receive a return on their investment). This has meant less access to healthy and affordable food options for residents.

In 2019, Milwaukee County, Wisconsin, declared racism a "public health crisis." Whether other jurisdictions follow suit remains to be seen, though the effects of prejudice, discrimination, and racism on the health of Americans of color certainly cannot be overstated—from chronic stress due to racism to uneven care in the American health-care system to disproportionate exposure to harmful toxins to the modern-day consequences of redlining. Researchers, community activists, lawmakers, and others have expressed hope that identifying racism as a public health crisis will bring needed attention and potential solutions to a pervasive, though often hidden, problem.

FURTHER READING

Anderson, K. O., C. R. Green, and R. Payne. 2009. "Racial and Ethnic Disparities in Pain: Causes and Consequences of Unequal Care." *Journal of Pain* 10(12): 1187–1204.

Bullard, Robert. 2019. "African Americans on the Frontline Fighting for Environmental Justice." February 22. Retrieved on February 19, 2020, at https://drrobertbullard.com/african-americans-on-the-front line-fighting-for-environmental-justice/.

Bullard, Robert D., Glenn S. Johnson, and Angel O. Torres. 2011. *Environmental Health and Racial Equity in the United States.* Washington, DC: American Public Health Association.

Carter, Sierra E., Mei Ling Ong, Ronald L. Simons, Frederick X. Gibbons, Man Kit Lei, and Steven R. H. Beach. 2019. "The Effect of Early Discrimination on Accelerated Aging among African Americans." *Health Psychology* 38(11): 1010–1013.

Chae, David H., Connor D. Martz, Tiffany Yip, Thomas E. Fuller-Rowell, Karen A. Matthews, Erica C. Spears, Yijie Wang, Natalie Slopen, Nancy E. Adler, Jue Lin, Gene H. Brody, Eli Puterman, and Elissa S. Epel. 2020. "Racial Discrimination and Telemere Shortening among African Americans: The Coronary Artery Risk Development in Young Adults (CARDIA) Study." *Health Psychology* 39(3): 209–219.

Cintron, A., and R. S. Morrison. 2006. "Pain and Ethnicity in the United States: A Systemic Review." *Journal of Palliative Medicine* 9(6): 1454–1473.

Driscoll, Anne K., and Danielle M. Ely. 2020. "Effects of Changes in Maternal Age Distribution and Maternal Age-Specific Infant Mortality Rates on Infant Mortality Trends: United States, 2000–2017." *National Vital Statistics Report* 69(5): 1–18.

Godoy, Maria. 2020. "In U.S. Cities, The Health Effects of Past Housing Discrimination Are Plain to See." NPR, November 19. Retrieved on December 8, 2020, at https://www.npr.org/sections/health-shots/2020/11/19/911909187/in-u-s-cities-the-health-effects-of-past-housing-discrimination-are-plain-to-see.

Goyal, M. K., N. Kuppermann, S. D. Cleary, S. J. Teach, and J. M. Chamberlain. 2015. "Racial Disparities in Pain Management of Children with Appendicitis in Emergency Departments." *JAMA Pediatrics* 169(11): 996–1002.

Green, Carmen R., Karen O. Anderson, Tamara A. Baker, Lisa C. Campbell, Sheila Decker, Roger B. Fillingim, Donna A. Kalauokalani, Kathryn E. Lasch, Cynthia Myers, Raymond C. Tait, Knox H. Todd, and April H. Vallerand. 2003. "The Unequal Burden of Pain: Confronting Racial and Ethnic Disparities in Pain." *Pain Medicine* 4(3): 277–294.

Greenwood, Brad N., Rachel R. Hardeman, Laura Huang, and Aaron Sojourner. 2020. "Physician-Patient Racial Concordance and Disparities in Birthing Mortality for Newborns." *Proceedings of the National Academy of Sciences of the United States of America* 117(35): 21194–21200. https://doi.org/10.1073/pnas.1913405117.

Heard-Garris, N. J., M. Cale, L. Camaj, M. C. Hamati, and T. P. Dominguez. 2018. "Transmitting Trauma: A Systematic Review of Vicarious Racism and Child Health." *Social Science & Medicine* 199: 230–240.

Hicken, Margaret T., Hedwig Lee, Jeffrey Morenoff, J. S. House, and David R. Williams. 2014. "Racial/Ethnic Disparities in Hypertension Prevalence: Reconsidering the Role of Chronic Stress." *American Journal of Public Health* 104(1): 117–123.

Hoffman, Kelly M., Sophie Trawalter, Jordan R. Axt, and M. Norman Oliver. 2016. "Racial Bias in Pain Assessments and Treatment Recommendations, and False Beliefs about Biological Differences between Blacks and Whites." *Psychological and Cognitive Sciences* 113(16): 4296–4301.

Johns Hopkins Medicine. 2012. "Study: 'Unconscious' Racial Bias among Doctors Linked to Poor Communication with Patients, Dissatisfaction with Care." The Lund Report, March 16. Retrieved on February 19, 2020, at https://www.thelundreport.org/content/study-unconscious-racial-bias-among-doctors-linked-poor-communication-patients.

Johnson, R. I., D. L. Roter, N. R. Powe, and L. A. Cooper. 2004. "Patient Race/Ethnicity and Quality of Patient-Physician Communication during Medical Visits." *American Journal of Public Health* 94(12): 2084–2090.

Lauderdale, Diane S. 2006. "Birth Outcomes for Arabic-Named Women in California before and after September 11." *Demography* 43(1): 185–201.

Martin, Michel. 2017. "Racism Is Literally Bad for Your Health." NPR, October 28. Retrieved on February 19, 2020, at https://www.npr.org /2017/10/28/560444290/racism-is-literally-bad-for-your-health.

Newkirk, Vann R., II. 2018. "Trump's EPA Concludes Environmental Racism Is Real." *The Atlantic*, February 28.

Ong, A. D., D. R. Williams, U. Nwizu, and T. L. Gruenewald. 2017. "Everyday Unfair Treatment and Multisystem Biological Dysregulation in African American Adults." *Cultural Diversity and Ethnic Minority Psychology* 23(1): 27–35.

Priest, Naomi, Yin Paradies, Brigid Trenerry, Many Truong, Saffron Karlsen, and Yvonne Kelly. 2013. "A Systematic Review of Studies Examining the Relationship between Reported Racism and Health and Wellbeing for Children and Young People." *Social Science & Medicine* 95: 115–127.

Sabin, Janice A., and Anthony G. Greenwald. 2012. "The Influence of Implicit Bias on Treatment Recommendations for 4 Common Pediatric Conditions: Pain, Urinary Tract Infection, Attention Deficit Hyperactivity Disorder, and Asthma." *American Journal of Public Health* 102(5): 988–995.

Schulman, Kevin A., Jesse A. Berlin, William Harless, Jon F. Kerner, Shyrl Sistrunk, Bernard J. Gersh, Ross Dube, Christopher K. Taleghani, Jennifer E. Burke, Sankey Williams, John M. Eisenberg, William Ayers, and Jose J. Escarce. 1999. "The Effect of Race and Sex on Physicians' Recommendations for Cardiac Catheterization." *New England Journal of Medicine* 340(8): 618–626.

"Reservations about Toxic Waste: Native American Tribes Encouraged to Turn Down Lucrative Hazardous Disposal Deals." *Scientific American*, March 31, 2010. Retrieved on December 10, 2020, at https://www .scientificamerican.com/article/earth-talk-reservations-about-toxic -waste/.

Staton, Lisa J., Mukta Panda, Ian Chen, Inginia Genao, James Kurz, Mark Pasanen, Alex J. Mechaber, Madhusudan Menon, Jane O'Rorke, JoAnn Wood, Eric Rosenberg, Charles Faeslis, Tim Carey, Diane Calleson, and Sam Cykert. 2007. "When Race Matters: Disagreement in Pain Perception between Patients and Their Physicians in Primary Care." *Journal of the National Medical Association* 99(5): 532–538.

Tello, Monique. 2017. "Racism and Discrimination in Healthcare: Providers and Patients." *Harvard Health Publishing*, January 16. Retrieved

on November 25, 2020, at https://www.health.harvard.edu/blog/racism
-discrimination-health-care-providers-patients-2017011611015.
Trent, Maria, Danielle G. Dooley, and Jacqueline Douge. 2019. "The
    Impact of Racism on Child and Adolescent Health." *Pediatrics* 144(2).
    Retrieved on November 25, 2020, at https://pediatrics.aappublications
    .org/content/144/2/e20191765.
van Ryn, Michelle, and Jane Burke. 2000. "The Effect of Patient Race and
    Socio-Economic Status on Physicians' Perceptions of Patients." *Social
    Science & Medicine* 50(6): 813–828.
Wan, William. 2019. "Racism Has Devastating Effects on Children's
    Health, Pediatricians Warn." *Washington Post*, August 2.

Q17. DOES RACIAL INEQUALITY EXIST IN BANKING AND LENDING?

Answer: Yes. People of color, especially Black Americans, are disproportionately disadvantaged in banking and lending as compared to their white counterparts. This differential treatment has had a tangible impact on their wealth accumulation and partially accounts for the gap in wealth between whites and people of color in the United States.

The Facts: In 2018, an African American woman named Clarice Middleton walked into an upscale-area Atlanta bank to cash a $200 check. Three bank employees closely scrutinized her check and identification and refused to look at the additional proof of ID that she offered. One employee then accused her of trying to cash a fraudulent check and proceeded to call 911. An officer arrived on the scene, determined that the check was authentic, and departed. The incident, however, left Middleton visibly shaken and upset (Flitter 2020).

Middleton's experience is not an outlier. Other African Americans recount similar stories of discrimination while banking—a phenomenon increasingly labeled on social media with the hashtag #BankingWhileBlack. They describe interactions with tellers and bank managers who treat them with suspicion and disrespect, closely inspect their IDs, question their checks and motives, turn them away, and, at times, call police—all while they are attempting to make legitimate transactions (Flitter 2020).

Studies also show that when examining banking and lending practices more broadly, deep racial inequalities exist in the United States. For example, a 2018 study by professors Jacob Faber and Terri Friedline, of New York University and the University of Kansas, respectively, found a number of "racialized costs of banking" in the United States (Faber and Friedline 2018). Some of the study's key findings include the following:

- Banks typically charge people of color more than their white counterparts for opening checking accounts. For instance, the minimum opening deposit is nearly $81 in majority Black neighborhoods, but it is only $68.50 in majority white neighborhoods.
- It is cheaper for those in white neighborhoods to maintain their checking accounts (a minimum of about $625 must remain in their accounts to avoid bank fees) than for those residing in majority Black neighborhoods (about $871) or those in majority Latinx neighborhoods (about $749). This means that those living in majority Black or Latinx communities must keep more of their earnings in their checking accounts than those living in majority white areas; consequently, a greater proportion of their earnings cannot be accessed.
- Banks tend to open and operate the majority of their branches in middle- and upper-class white communities, creating "banking deserts" in low-income and nonwhite communities. Consequently, people of color living in poorer areas with few white residents must travel farther to find a banking facility or instead rely on more expensive services, such as payday lenders, check cashing stores, and other nonbank services that typically proliferate in these communities. This is especially problematic for impoverished Americans without cars or other motorized transportation. According to the study's authors: "Brick-and-mortar bank branches still matter for accessing credit to build wealth. Without a bank branch in their community, households have limited access to safer and more affordable [banking services]." Furthermore, they point out that: "Residents lose access to small business loans and mortgages . . . hindering the investment and entrepreneurship needed to drive local economic growth" (Friedline and Despard 2016).

Though Faber and Friedline (2018) primarily focus on neighborhood and community banks, they assert that large national banks are also discriminatory. They point out that several national banks have been sued for widespread discriminatory practices against people of color, such as allegedly opening accounts and lines of credit without their knowledge, illegally charging fees for dormant accounts they did not even know they possessed, automatically closing accounts when they exhibited signs of fraudulent activity (instead of first conducting investigations as legally required), and charging them comparatively higher interest rates than their white counterparts. Accordingly, the study's researchers argue that national and local banks "engage in racially discriminatory practices that effectively siphon wealth out of communities of color through the very financial products and services that are considered to be tools for wealth and investment" (Faber and Friedline 2018, 10).

Research also shows that it pays to be white when it comes to lending—particularly when Americans apply for home, car, and business loans. As compared to people of color (especially African Americans), they are more likely to be granted loans, offered lower interest rates, given better customer service, and offered more information from loan officers—at times regardless of creditworthiness. The following sections provide examples.

Mortgage Loans

- A 2016 study found differential treatment by mortgage loan originators (MLOs)—the primary point people that homeowners typically deal with when applying for mortgages (they are the original lenders, and they work with other mortgage professionals, such as underwriters and loan processors, to advise prospective homebuyers and guide loans through to closing). MLOs were more likely to respond to e-mails from prospective borrowers with white-sounding names than those with Black-sounding names. They also found that the effect of having a Black-sounding name on how MLOs responded to prospective borrowers was equivalent to having a credit score that is 71 points lower (Hanson et al. 2016).
- A 2018 study of 31 million mortgage applications in 2015 and 2016 found that people of color, especially African Americans and Latinxs, were denied conventional mortgage loans at much higher rates than whites—even when they had the same level of income. Banks often point to the comparatively lower credit scores of people of color to explain the disparities, though because this information is not publicly available (because lenders refuse to report credit score data to the government), there is no way to know for sure (Glantz and Martinez 2018).
- In 2019, the real estate company Clever analyzed 1.7 million mortgage applications from 2016 and found that Black applicants were denied home loans at twice the rate of white applicants, even when controlling for income. Furthermore, more than half of Black applicants (52 percent) were given no reason for why their loans were denied (this was the highest percentage for any racial group). The authors of the study called for more transparency in mortgage lending (Tekin 2019).

Car Loans

- In 2015, popular auto lender Honda was penalized by the U.S. Department of Justice and the Consumer Financial Protection Bureau for charging higher interest rates on car loans and higher dealer markups for Black, Asian, and Latinx customers as compared to white customers—regardless of consumer creditworthiness. This discriminatory practice meant that minority borrowers consistently paid more for their auto loans as compared to whites (Consumer Financial Protection Bureau 2015). Studies also show that racial minorities regularly face discrimination by car dealerships; they are charged more for their cars, pressured to buy add-on products (sometimes falsely told that these additions are required), and, according to an attorney for the National Consumer Law Center (NCLC), charged "hundreds and even thousands of dollars more to finance a car" (Valladares 2019).

- A 2015 analysis by the NCLC found racial disparities in auto dealer loan rates in every region of the country and in every single state where data was provided. Analyzing loans by Honda, GMAC, and Ford, researchers found that Blacks consistently paid more than whites—anywhere from 95 to 496 percent more—for their auto loans. For example, at GMAC in Wisconsin, the markup loan rate for whites was $144 and $714 for Blacks. At Honda in Florida, whites paid a $669 loan markup rate, and Blacks paid $1,063. The NCLC filed suit against offending auto finance companies and banks, alleging that for more than 75 years, they had "maintained policies which permit car dealers to 'mark-up' the finance rates on loans based on subjective criteria unrelated to creditworthiness." The auto companies and bank lenders settled their cases, and, collectively, the settlements were valued at more than $100 million.

- In 2018, an investigation by the National Fair Housing Alliance sent white and nonwhite "testers" to car dealerships in Virginia. The nonwhite tester was more qualified than the white tester, but more than 60 percent of the time, the nonwhite person was given more costly loan options—meaning the nonwhite tester would pay, on average, $2,662 more over the length of the loan. Despite the fact that discriminatory practices in auto lending are illegal, in 2018, Congress eased watchdog measures put in place under the Obama administration to combat racial discrimination in the United States (Nova 2018).

Small Business Loans

- A 2019 study by the National Community Reinvestment Coalition sent white, Black, and Hispanic "testers" to Los Angeles–area banks to see how they were treated when applying for small business loans. The testers had identical business profiles and credit histories, but the Black and Hispanic testers had slightly better incomes, assets, and credit scores than their white counterparts. The study revealed that despite their advantaged positions, Black and Hispanic testers faced more scrutiny and worse customer service than less qualified white testers. For example, Black and Hispanic applicants were given less information about the loans and were asked more questions about their loan eligibility. Further, 17 percent of Blacks and 12 percent of Hispanics were asked to provide their personal W-2 forms, though not a single white tester was asked for the document. Black testers were the only group asked about their educational level. Loan officers were also more likely to provide information about loans to whites than Blacks or Hispanics (Jan 2019).

Consequences of Racial Disparities in Lending Practices

As of 2016, the average wealth of white families was 10 times that of Black families in the United States (Moise 2019)—see figure 17.1 for a comparison of median household wealth by race. Much of this wealth gap stems from different rates of home ownership and the accumulation of home equity over time. According to Princeton sociologist Dalton Conley, "The majority of Americans hold most of their wealth in the form of home equity. So that's their nest egg. That's how they can finance the education of their offspring, that's how they can . . . save up for retirement. It's their savings bank. They're living in their savings bank" (Conley 2003). However, American lenders have a long history of denying home loans to people of color, especially African Americans (through a practice called *redlining*—see Q12), and studies suggest the practice of denying loans to people of color persists. As whites obtain mortgage loans, buy homes, and build equity, they continue to build wealth, though the same opportunities are not always afforded to people of color, even when they have similar incomes. Furthermore, less access to business loans further hurts African Americans' ability to build wealth, as they are more likely than white Americans to be shut out of small business ownership.

White Americans also benefit from increased access to banks, less expensive bank services, increased access to their money, and lower interest loans on homes and cars. A study conducted by consulting firm

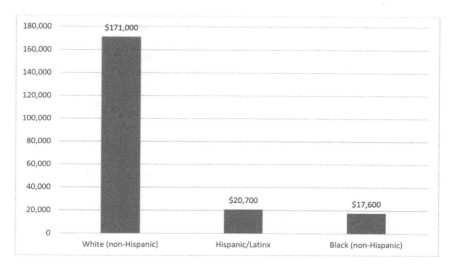

Figure 17.1. Median Household Wealth in the United States by Race (2016).

(*Source*: Federal Reserve, Survey of Consumer Finances https://www.statista.com /statistics/639650/median-household-wealth/)

McKinsey and Company estimated that increased access to banking services alone could save the average Black American up to $40,000 over their lifetime (Moise 2019). Moreover, while inequality in banking and lending often goes unnoticed (especially by those who most benefit from their uneven practices), discrimination and inequality persist, disproportionately hitting people of color in their wallets. The McKinsey report notes, however, that addressing these inequalities and closing the Black-white wealth gap will benefit all Americans, not just Black Americans. They argue, for example, that raising Black wealth by equalizing opportunities in banking and lending could increase the nation's overall gross domestic product (GDP) by 6 percent through increased investments and consumer consumption.

FURTHER READING

Conley, Dalton. 2003. "Race: The Power of an Illusion: Background Readings: Interview with Dalton Conley." California Newsreel. PBS. https://www.pbs.org/race/000_About/002_04-background-03-03.htm.
Consumer Financial Protection Bureau. 2015. "CFPB and DOJ Reach Resolution with Honda to Address Discriminatory Auto Loan Pricing."

July 14. Retrieved on February 26, 2020, at https://www.consumer
finance.gov/about-us/newsroom/cfpb-and-doj-reach-resolution-with
-honda-to-address-discriminatory-auto-loan-pricing/.

Faber, Jacob, and Terri Friedline. 2018. "The Racialized Costs of Banking."
New America. Retrieved on July10, 2020, at https://d1y8sb8igg2f8e
.cloudfront.net/documents/The_Racialized_Costs_of_Banking_2018
-06-20_205129.pdf.

Flitter, Emily. 2020. "'Banking while Black': How Cashing a Check Can
Be a Minefield." *New York Times*, June 18.

Friedline, Terri, and Mathieu Despard. 2016. "Life in a Banking Desert."
The Atlantic, March 13.

Glantz, Aaron, and Emmanuel Martinez. 2018. "Modern-Day Redlining:
How Banks Block People of Color from Homeownership." *Chicago Tribune*, February 17.

Hanson, Andrew, Zackary Hawley, Hal Martin, and Bo Liu. 2016. "Discrimination in Mortgage Lending: Evidence from a Correspondence
Experiment." *Journal of Urban Economics* 92: 48–65.

Jan, Tracy. 2019. "Banking while Black: Minority Business Owners with
Better Credit Scores Than White Counterparts Face Worse Treatment
and More Scrutiny." *Washington Post*, September 10.

Moise, Imani. 2019. "American Americans Underserved by US Banks:
Study." Reuters, August 13.

National Consumer Law Center. 2015. "Racial Disparities in Auto Loan
Markups State-by-State Data." June. https://www.nclc.org/images/pdf
/car_sales/ib-auto-dealers-racial_disparites.pdf.

Nova, Annie. 2018. "Congress Eases Rules against Racial Discrimination
in the Auto Loan Market." CNBC, May 9.

Tekin, Eylul. 2019. "Exploring Racial Discrimination in Mortgage Lending: A Call for Greater Transparency." Clever, June 25. Retrieved
on July 13, 2020, at https://listwithclever.com/real-estate-blog/racial
-discrimination-in-mortgage-lending/.

Valladares, Mayra Rodriguez. 2019. "As Auto Lending Delinquencies Rise,
Discrimination is Even More Dangerous to the Economy." *Forbes*, May
1. Retrieved on November 25, 2020, at https://www.forbes.com/sites
/mayrarodriguezvalladares/2019/05/01/as-auto-lending-delinquencies
-rise-discrimination-is-even-more-dangerous-to-the-economy/?sh
=7f388fe370e3.

4

❖❖❖

Crime and Criminal Justice

In 2009, after arriving home from an overseas trip to China, Henry Louis Gates Jr., a prominent African American Harvard history professor and filmmaker, found the front door of his Cambridge, Massachusetts, home jammed. With the help of his cab driver, he was able to force the door open, though not before a neighbor called police. It was early afternoon, and the caller, a white woman, told police she was suspicious after seeing two Black men on the porch, one of whom was (as the police report claimed) "wedging his shoulder into the door as if he was trying to force entry." Cambridge police soon arrived on the scene, knocked on Gates's door, and asked him to step outside. The officer, Sergeant Joseph Crowley, told the near 60-year-old historian that he was investigating a possible burglary.

Though the full story of what happened that July afternoon is disputed, what is clear is that Gates was arrested and handcuffed on his own front porch (the officer had alleged that he was belligerent when asked to produce identification, though Gates disputes this). He was then transported in a squad car to police headquarters, where he was subsequently booked on charges of disorderly conduct. The charges were later dropped; however, his encounter with police gained national attention and even drew the attention of then president Barack Obama, who, when asked by a reporter about the incident, said, "What I think we know separate and apart from this incident is that there's a long history in this country of African Americans and Latinos being stopped by law enforcement disproportionately. That's just a fact." Others further pointed out that had Gates been white, perhaps his neighbor would have never called police in the first place. Societal stereotypes about Black men and crime may have impelled her to call police when she saw two Black men jiggling the door of the home. Moreover, in 2020, more than a decade after Henry Louis Gates Jr.'s arrest by police at his own home, former attorney general Jeff Sessions reflected on the incident by simply referring to the Harvard professor as "some criminal."

Drawing on available data and empirical research, this chapter examines claims of racial bias in the American criminal justice system as well as racial stereotypes—particularly those that link people of color, especially Black Americans, with crime. The first three questions focus exclusively on the criminal justice system in the United States. Question 18 asks, "Are the majority of inmates in American prisons African American?" This entry examines the data on American prisons and offers explanations for the high rate of Black incarceration. Question 19 then builds on one of these explanations—systemic racism in criminal justice—and asks, "Is the American criminal justice system racially biased?" A growing body of research examines whether Blacks and whites are treated differently in the criminal justice system—for example, in interactions with police officers, use of force by police, arrest rates, convictions, and sentencing. Extending the discussion of use of force by police, Question 20 asks, "Are African Americans more likely than white Americans to be killed by police?" This entry relies on national data of fatal police shootings and explores (using available empirical data) two competing explanations for racial disparities in use of lethal force by police. One claims that Black people are more likely to be armed and resist arrest than whites, thus necessitating higher rates of deadly force by officers. Another explanation blames the racial disparity on police bias, alleging that many officers (both white and nonwhite) harbor explicit and implicit biases against people of color—particularly toward African Americans.

The final three questions of this chapter explore common beliefs regarding people of color and crime. Question 21 asks, "Is it true that there are more Black men in prison than in college?" This entry draws on prison statistics and college enrollment data in the United States to investigate this frequently quoted and often unquestioned "fact." Question 22, "Do African Americans suffer from 'Black-on-Black' crime?," draws on homicide data to examine whether African Americans uniquely suffer from same-race violent crime. This chapter compares intraracial violent crime among African Americans and among whites, and it also addresses stereotypes that link Blackness with innate violent tendencies.

Finally, Question 23 shifts attention to the media and asks, "Is the American media racially biased in its coverage of crime?" This question looks at whether alleged crimes are disproportionately reported in news media depending on whether the perpetrator is white or nonwhite, and whether white and nonwhite suspects are differently portrayed.

Q18. ARE THE MAJORITY OF INMATES IN AMERICAN PRISONS AFRICAN AMERICAN?

Answer: No. African Americans make up less than half of the American prison population (40 percent in 2010). However, there are more Black inmates in American prisons than inmates of any other racial group. Their raw numbers are close to those of white Americans, though they have the highest rate of incarceration of any race or ethnic group in the United States, followed by American Indians/Alaska Natives, Latinxs, and whites. To explain their high rate of imprisonment, researchers point to systemic disparities in the criminal justice system (including the consequences of the "War on Drugs"), uneven punishment in American schools, and poverty.

The Facts: African Americans make up about 40 percent of the prison population, and the remaining inmates are white (39 percent), Latinx (19 percent), Native American (1 percent), and other groups (1 percent). See figure 18.1 for a breakdown of racial and ethnic groups in American correctional facilities based on 2010 census data.

Although African Americans do not make up the majority of all inmates, there are more African Americans in American prisons than any other racial or ethnic group. According to the Pew Research Center, in 2018, state and federal prisons held about 465,200 Black inmates as compared to 430,500 white inmates (the next highest number of those incarcerated) (Gramlich 2020). Black Americans are also incarcerated at much higher rates than all other racial groups in the United States, followed by American Indians/Alaska Natives, Latinxs, and then whites. See figure 18.2 for incarceration rates in the United States by race based on 2010 census data (note: data from the 2010 census is the most comprehensive data as of 2020).

Asian American/Pacific Islanders (AAPI) are not included in this data (as they are typically lumped in with other groups as "Other" in prison data), but they, too, are affected. During the 1990s, the AAPI prison population grew faster than the overall prison population; it swelled 250 percent

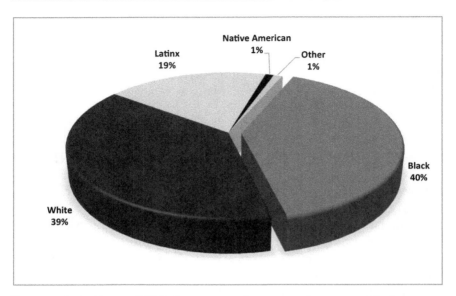

Figure 18.1. Race of U.S. Inmates in American Prisons and Jails.
(*Source*: US Census 2010, Sawyer and Wagner [2020])

as compared to the overall prison population, which grew by 77 percent
(Wang 2015; Lum 2018). Southeast Asian Americans (e.g., Cambodians, Laotians, and Vietnamese) and Pacific Islanders are more frequently
arrested and incarcerated as compared to other Asian ethnic groups (Wang
2015)—which is perhaps not surprising given that they are more prone to
poverty. In areas with high concentrations of AAPIs, these patterns are
evident. In the San Francisco Bay area in the 1990s, for example, Laotians
and Vietnamese were among the most arrested groups. Difficult circumstances have led some of these Asian ethnics, who arrived as impoverished refugees in the 1970s and 1980s, "down a rough path"—one that
included gangs, organized crime, drug dealing, theft, and armed robbery
(Yam 2018).

The data clearly show, however, that African Americans are incarcerated at the highest rate—but why? Scholars point to three key
explanations.

Disparities in Criminal Justice and the War on Drugs

Researchers find disparities in how Blacks and whites are treated at all
levels of the criminal justice system—from stops to arrests to sentencing.

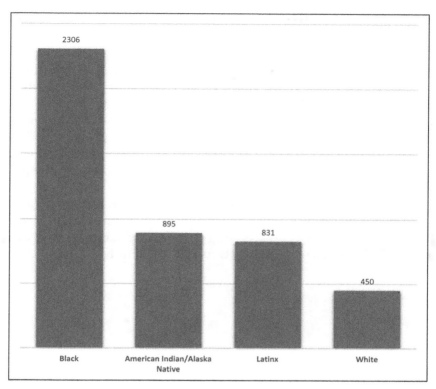

Figure 18.2. United States Incarceration Rates by Race, 2010 (Number of people incarcerated per 100,000 people in that group).
(*Source*: Reproduced from Wagner [2014])

For example, Bill Quigley (2016), a law professor at Loyola University, argues that Black Americans are more likely than whites to be stopped and searched by police when walking on the street or driving cars, even when there is no indication of a crime. When committing the same infractions, Black motorists are also more likely to be ticketed than their white counterparts. Most of those ticketed face fines, not jail time, though poor people in some cities who fail to pay their fines are sentenced to jail. For example, in 2015, civil rights attorneys sued the city of Ferguson, Missouri, for jailing the poor when they could not afford to pay their traffic tickets; the attorneys alleged that the city was using its jails as a modern-day "debtor's prison" (Shapiro 2015). Further, even when engaging in similar crimes, Blacks are more likely than whites to be arrested and convicted, and they receive longer sentences. A report by the U.S. Sentencing Commission, for instance, found that Black men who commit the same crimes as white men receive federal prison sentences that are, on average, 20 percent longer (Ingraham 2014).

Black men are also disproportionately incarcerated in American prisons. This reality is, in part, a consequence of the federal "War on Drugs," an evolving set of antidrug law enforcement policies and initiatives that began in 1968 under the Richard Nixon administration. Tougher drug laws, greater policing for drug crimes, and increased prosecutions of drug-related offenses in a concerted effort to be "tough on crime" led to skyrocketing rates of incarceration—a fivefold increase since the early 1970s (Moore and Elkavich 2008). See figure 18.3 for the number of people incarcerated for drug offenses in 1980 as compared to 2017. The numbers ballooned, though not simply because of an uptick in drug crimes; there had been a fervent increase in policing and prosecution. In fact, there are more people behind bars for drug offenses today than there were in 1980 for *all* crimes combined (Dimon 2014). Further, most of those

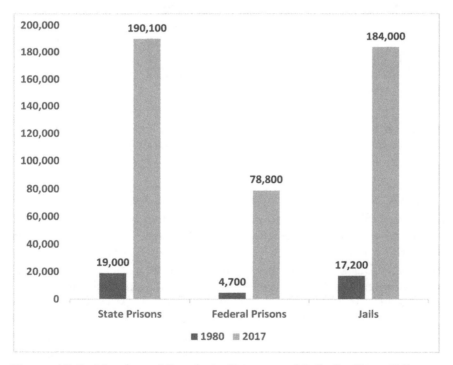

Figure 18.3. Number of People in Prisons and Jails for Drug Offenses, 1980 and 2017.

(*Source:* Reproduced with permission from The Sentencing Project, https://www.sentencingproject.org/criminal-justice-facts/)

incarcerated as a result of the War on Drugs were and are primarily low-level, nonviolent drug offenders.

Moreover, Black Americans have been more affected by the War on Drugs than any other racial group. For instance, data show that even though Black Americans are not more likely to do drugs than other racial groups, they are more likely to be arrested for drug use. For example, data from 2010 to 2018 showed that Blacks and whites used marijuana at similar rates, but Blacks were nearly four times more likely than whites to be arrested for marijuana possession (ACLU 2020). Data from both the *National Longitudinal Survey of Youth* and the *National Survey of Drug Use and Health* further reveal that white youths are more likely to sell drugs than their Black counterparts. Given the higher rate of drug dealing by whites combined with their larger population size, one would assume that more whites than Blacks would be arrested for selling drugs, but data show that Blacks are far more likely to be arrested for doing so (Alexander 2012; Ingraham 2014; Rothwell 2014).

The disparities are explained by researchers Lisa D. Moore and Amy Elkavich: "Drug use in suburban areas goes unchecked and underreported, while people of color are profiled in urban areas as potential drug users and dealers" (2008, 783). As such, Black people living in urban areas bear the brunt of the War on Drugs, while whites in suburban and rural communities, where drug use and sale is just as (or even more) prevalent, typically avoid arrest and prosecution. Officer decisions regarding whom to stop and search are heavily influenced by location. At first blush, this might appear to be a race-neutral policing strategy, but urban ghettos are composed mostly of Black and brown Americans; thus, when police disproportionately target these areas, there is nothing race neutral about their decisions to do so. According to Michelle Alexander, civil rights lawyer and author of the best-selling book *The New Jim Crow*, police often rely on racial stereotypes when deciding whom to stop and search, and she points out that "a young black male wearing baggy pants, standing in front of his high school surrounded by a group of similarly dressed friends, may be stopped and searched because police believe he 'looks like' a drug dealer." Meanwhile, "a young white male wearing baggy pants, standing in front of his high school and surrounded by his friends, might well be ignored by police officers" (Alexander 2012, 221). National data (as previously described) suggest that the white student is more likely to deal drugs, though data also indicate that the Black student will be the one who police stop and search.

When it comes to incarceration, Blacks and whites are again treated differently. Whites generally use drugs at about the same rate as Blacks, but because of their larger population size in the United States, there are significantly more white than Black drug users. Inmate demographics, however, fail to reflect this; about three-fourths of all those incarcerated in American prisons for drug offenses are Black or Latinx (Alexander 2012). Nationwide, Black men are also incarcerated for drug infractions at 13 times the rate of white men, and in 10 states, the rates were 26 to 57 times higher (according to data from the early 2000s) (Moore and Elkavich 2008). This is particularly important because inmates convicted of drug offenses make up a substantial proportion of the American prison population. They constitute about 20 percent of all those incarcerated in American prisons and jails (Sawyer and Wagner 2020), but in federal prisons alone, drug offenses are the primary conviction for nearly half of all inmates (King et al. 2015).

The overincarceration of Black men also perpetuates the stereotype that drugs are primarily a Black, not white, problem; however, the data consistently reveal otherwise. For instance, deaths due to drug overdose rose more than 5,000 percent from 1980 to 2014 in Appalachia. Opioid abuse has also disproportionately ravaged white communities nationwide since the 1990s, especially in places such as West Virginia, Kentucky, Ohio, Indiana, and Oklahoma (Levy 2018). Researcher Anjali Om of the Virginia Commonwealth University argues that because the face of the epidemic is white (nearly 90 percent of opioid addicts are white), the response has been far different than that toward earlier drug epidemics (Om 2018)—such as the crack epidemic of the 1980s, which disproportionately affected urban Black communities.

Rather than apprehend white drug abusers and toss them in prison, white drug use is more often framed as an issue of public health. President Donald Trump, for example, declared the opioid epidemic a "public health crisis" in 2018, politicians have made emotional speeches advocating for government funding of drug treatment facilities and programs, and the media have largely reported on the crisis with a general attitude of "sensitivity and empathy," which Om characterizes as clear evidence of a "racial double standard" (Om 2018, 615). The crack epidemic was never treated as an issue of public health, nor as a crisis that demanded federal funding for public health resources to help Black Americans; instead, it was handled as an issue of criminal justice, as Black people were arrested and incarcerated in unprecedented numbers.

The policies born from the War on Drugs had and continue to have an enormous impact on the overincarceration of African Americans in American prisons. However, this is far from the only example of their differential treatment in the criminal justice system. For more information on racial disparities throughout the criminal justice system and their disproportionate impact on African Americans, see Q19.

School-to-Prison Pipeline

To further explain the disproportionate incarceration of African Americans in U.S. prisons, scholars point to K-12 education and the different experiences afforded to Black children as compared to their white counterparts, particularly regarding punishment. Black students are disciplined more frequently and more severely at school, even when committing the *same infractions* as white students. This uneven punishment increases their contact with the criminal justice system and raises their chances of incarceration as adults. Scholars term the path from school punishment to eventual incarceration the "school-to-prison pipeline."

As compared to their white peers, studies show that Black students are more likely to be suspended, referred to police, and even arrested. Regarding out-of-school suspensions, for instance, data from the Department of Education show that 1 out of every 6 Black students is suspended at least once in K-12 as compared to 1 in 20 white students (Losen and Gillespie 2012). Even Black preschoolers are more likely to be suspended than white preschoolers; they constitute 19 percent of preschoolers, but nearly half of all out-of-school suspensions. These suspensions mostly involve four-year-old children, raising questions about how children are punished before they even reach kindergarten (U.S. Department of Education 2016). Critics of preschool suspensions often ask: What merits suspension (and lost days of school) for a four-year-old child? And why are Black children disproportionately affected?

Teacher bias may partially explain these racial disparities. A Yale study that used cutting-edge eye tracking technology analyzed the eye gazes of more than 130 early education teachers as they watched preschoolers play. They found that teachers more closely watched Black boys as compared to other groups (Black girls, white girls, and white boys)—perhaps because they expected them to misbehave. Moreover, when asked which children most required their attention, most (42 percent) pointed to Black boys; by comparison, the remaining teachers indicated white boys (34 percent), white girls (13 percent), or Black girls (10 percent). The study's authors theorized that closer surveillance of Black boys increases the likelihood of teachers spotting their misbehaviors over those of other groups (Gilliam et al. 2016).

In another study, nearly 200 teachers were asked to read a story about a misbehaving student and recommend punishment. The researchers presented a scenario of a boy misbehaving in class—though some teachers read about a boy named "Jake" or "Greg" (stereotypical white names), and others read about "Darnell" or "Deshawn" (stereotypical Black names). Teachers disciplined both boys the same, but when presented with a second infraction, teachers typically punished the Black boy more harshly. They also reported that they were more likely to see the Black boy than the white boy as a "troublemaker," more likely to see his behavior as indicative of a pattern, and more likely to imagine themselves suspending him in the future (Okonofua and Eberhardt 2015). Moreover, although this study did not examine whether there were differences in how teachers responded to the student based on their own race (as most teachers in the study were white), the former study did compare both Black and white teachers. Surprisingly, they found that compared to white teachers, Black teachers *more* closely watched Black boys. Given the small sample size of the Yale study, however, more research is needed to ascertain whether Black and white teachers react differently to Black students—especially to Black boys.

Black students are also more likely than white students to be referred to police by schools and arrested. As such, they are more likely to find their school misbehavior criminalized, which can disrupt and completely "derail" their lives (Blad and Harwin 2017). Their disparate treatment may occur for two reasons. First, Black students are more likely than white students to attend schools with police presence. According to Allison Brown, the executive director of the Communities for Just Schools Fund, Black and brown communities, and by extension their schools, are routinely overpoliced; as a consequence, police "often criminalize behavior they wouldn't in other places"—including misbehaviors such as using a cell phone in class, vandalism, smoking, and truancy (Blad and Harwin 2017). Former U.S. attorney general Eric Holder criticized this overcriminalization of school misbehavior, arguing that "a routine school disciplinary infraction should land a student in the principal's office, not in a police precinct" ("Black Preschoolers" 2014). Second, the behavior of Black boys may be more often criminalized because they are frequently "perceived as older than they are" ("Black Preschoolers" 2014). A 2014 study led by Phillip Goff of the University of California-Los Angeles asked people to look at photographs of children (ages 10 and older who were white, Latinx, or Black) to assess their ages and rate their innocence (Goff et al. 2014; "Black Preschoolers" 2014). On average, the participants, who were mostly white women, overestimated the ages of Black children by 4.5 years, and they repeatedly rated them as less innocent than white and Latinx children.

Because infractions by Black children are more often criminalized, they are funneled at higher rates into the American criminal justice system. Police are more likely to be called, and these students are more likely to enter the criminal justice system—though the juvenile system. Thus, Black Americans are more likely than white Americans to be channeled into the criminal justice system *even as children*—though the misbehavior is often the same. For more on the school-to-prison pipeline, see Q14.

Poverty

Finally, no discussion of incarceration can ignore the effects of poverty. A 2018 report by the Brookings Institute showed a clear relationship between poverty and incarceration. Boys who grew up in families in the bottom 10th percentile of income are 20 times more likely to go to prison than boys born to the wealthiest families (Looney and Turner 2018). Based on this data, it is not surprising that African Americans (and even Native Americans) have high rates of incarceration in the United States; they have high rates of poverty. Even some Asian American ethnic groups with high rates of poverty have higher rates of incarceration in the United States than wealthier Asian American ethnics.

This poverty-prison correlation is evident outside of the United States as well. Aboriginal people and Torres Straight Islanders are disproportionately incarcerated in Australia, as are Maoris in New Zealand and Indigenous people in Canada—these Indigenous groups also experience high rates of poverty in their respective nations (in addition to systemic discrimination throughout each country's criminal justice system). See figure 18.4 for the representation of each Indigenous group in their nation's total population versus their representation in the prison system.

To explain the poverty-prison correlation, researchers point to money. Money can buy access to good schools, postsecondary education, nice neighborhoods, and myriad other advantages and opportunities. By contrast, those living in poverty without viable opportunities may look to unlawful avenues to attain money and status. Indeed, studies show that extremely disadvantaged neighborhoods experience higher rates of crime—regardless of racial composition (The Sentencing Project 2013). Hence, those living in impoverished communities, regardless of race, increase their chances of contact with the criminal justice system and subsequent incarceration.

Moreover, mental illness plagues the American prison system. As state psychiatric institutions began to close across the nation in the 1960s, many Americans had fewer and fewer places to seek help. According

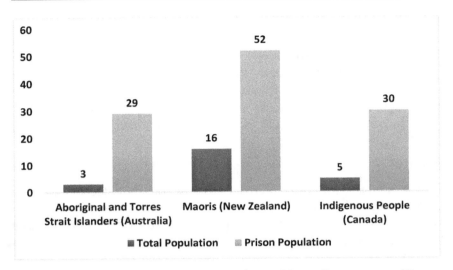

Figure 18.4. Percentage of Total Population Versus Percentage of Prison Population, Australia, New Zealand, Canada, 2020.

(*Sources*: Ara Poutama Aotearoa Department of Corrections, Prison Facts and Statistics, 2020, https://www.corrections.govt.nz/resources/statistics/quarterly _prison_statistics/prison_stats_june_2020#total; Australian Bureau of Statistics, Prisoners in Australia, 2020, https://www.abs.gov.au/statistics/people/crime-and -justice/prisoners-australia/latest-release#:~:text=The%20Aboriginal%20 and%20Torres%20Strait,up%2029%25%20of%20all%20prisoners; IWGIA, The Indigenous World, 2020, https://www.iwgia.org/en/australia/3642-iw-2020 -australia.html#:~:text=Aboriginal%20and%20Torres%20Strait%20 Islander,3.3%20%25%20of%20the%20nation%E2%80%99s%20population; Government of Canada, Office of the Correctional Investigator, 2020, https:// www.oci-bec.gc.ca/cnt/comm/press/press20200121-eng.aspx.)

to the Center for Prisoner Health and Human Rights, a shortage of community-based treatment options led to a dramatic increase in the incarceration of people with mental illness. Correctional facilities in New York, Los Angeles, and Chicago currently act as the three biggest psychiatric facilities in the United States, and data from 2005 to 2006 reveal that *more than half* of jail and prison inmates nationwide met professional criteria for mental illness. Moreover, data show that people with mental illness are 4.5 times more likely to be arrested than the general public ("Incarceration and Mental Health" n.d.). Those who are poor are most affected because they are less likely to have health insurance and access to professional treatment. Consequently, they frequently end up warehoused in American prisons.

Finally, Quigley (2016) argues that poverty also affects one's legal defense in the criminal justice system; in other words, it clearly affects whether someone gets a fair shake in the system. According to a 2013 report to the United Nation's Human Rights Committee, "The United States in effect operates two distinct criminal justice systems: one for wealthy people and another for poor people and minorities" (The Sentencing Project 2013, 1). For example, poor people are less able to post bond and are therefore more likely to languish in jail awaiting some resolution to their case. Poor people are also more likely than wealthier people to never see a lawyer (yes, *never*, because though Americans have a right to a public defender, public defenders are often underfunded). If they do have access to a public defender, they are typically represented by those who are overworked and underpaid. Many, if not most, of these public defenders simultaneously juggle more than a hundred cases (or several hundred); hence, impoverished defendants have little chance of legal representation by someone invested in their case. For example, a 2019 *New York Times* story followed Jack Talaska, a public defender in Louisiana with nearly 200 clients. He was not alone. During that time, there were two dozen other public defenders in the state handling even more clients, and one had 413 (Oppel and Patel 2019). Because there is little personal focus on their cases, poor people are more likely to plead guilty, accept plea bargains, and go to prison without a trial. According to the Pew Research Center, for example, trials in the federal criminal justice system are "relatively rare," and in 2018, only about 2 percent of those imprisoned in federal prisons ever received a trial (Gramlich 2019b).

Deep systemic problems drive Black incarceration in the United States. Unequal treatment throughout the criminal justice system, disproportionate arrests and prosecutions as a direct consequence of the War on Drugs, overcriminalization of school misbehavior, and high rates of poverty all help to explain the overrepresentation of African Americans in U.S. prisons. According to a report by the Sentencing Project (2013), if the current trends continue, one in three Black males will go to prison in their lifetime. The report's authors conclude that "it is time for the United States to take affirmative steps to eliminate racial disparities in its criminal justice system" (The Sentencing Project 2013). Some of their recommendations include scaling back the War on Drugs, fully funding indigent defense agencies to ensure even the most impoverished defendants have access to appropriate legal defense, ending racial profiling of people of color by officers, and implementing antibias training at all levels of the criminal justice system—including for police officers, public defenders, prosecutors, judges, and jury members.

FURTHER READING

Alexander, Michelle. 2012. "The New Jim Crow." Pp. 217–225 in *Rethinking the Color Line: Readings in Race and Ethnicity*, edited by Charles A. Gallagher. New York: McGraw Hill.

American Civil Liberties Union (ACLU). 2020. "A Tale of Two Countries: Racially Targeted Arrests in the Era of Marijuana Reform." Retrieved on November 26, 2020, at https://www.aclu.org/report/tale -two-countries-racially-targeted-arrests-era-marijuana-reform.

"Black Preschoolers Far More Likely to Be Suspended." 2014. NPR, Code Switch, March 21.

Blad, Evie, and Alex Harwin. 2017. "Black Students More Likely to Be Arrested at School." Education Week, January 24.

Dimon, Laura. 2014. "19 Actual Statistics about America's Prison System." Mic, April 3. Retrieved on April 25, 2020, at https://www.mic.com /articles/86519/19-actual-statistics-about-america-s-prison-system.

Gilliam, Walter S., Angela N. Maupin, Chin R. Reyes, Maria Accavitri, and Frederick Shic. 2016. "Do Early Educators' Implicit Biases Regarding Sex and Race Relate to Behavior Expectations and Recommendations of Preschool Expulsions and Suspensions?" Yale Child Study Center, September 28.

Goff, Phillip Atiba, Matthew Christian Jackson, Brooke Allison Lewis Di Leone, Carmen Marie Culotta, and Natalie Ann DiTomasso. 2014. "The Essence of Innocence: Consequences of Dehumanizing Black Children." *Interpersonal Relations and Group Processes* 106(4): 526–545.

Gramlich, John. 2019a. "The Gap between the Number of Blacks and Whites in Prison is Shrinking." Pew Research Center, April 30.

Gramlich, John. 2019b. "Only 2% of Federal Criminal Defendants Go to Trial, and Most Who Do Are Found Guilty." Pew Research Center, June 11.

Gramlich, John. 2020. "Black Imprisonment Rate in the U.S. Has Fallen by a Third since 2006." Pew Research Center, May 6. https://www .pewresearch.org/fact-tank/2020/05/06/share-of-black-white-hispanic -americans-in-prison-2018-vs-2006/.

"Incarceration and Mental Health." n.d. Center for Prisoner Health and Human Rights. Retrieved on April 26, 2020, at https://www .prisonerhealth.org/educational-resources/factsheets-2/incarceration -and-mental-health/.

Ingraham, Christopher. 2014. "White People Are More Likely to Deal Drugs, but Black People Are More Likely to Get Arrested for It." *Washington Post*, September 30.

King, Ryan, Bryce Peterson, Brian Elderbroom, and Samuel A. Taxy. 2015. "How to Reduce the Federal Prison Population." Urban Institute. Retrieved on April 25, 2020, at http://apps.urban.org/features /reducing-federal-mass-incarceration/.

Levy, Gabrielle. 2018. "Deaths Blamed on Drug Use Soar 600 Percent from 1980–2014." *US News and World Report*, March 16.

Looney, Adam, and Nicholas Turner. 2018. "Work and Opportunity before and after Incarceration." Brookings, March 14.

Losen, Daniel J., and Jonathan Gillespie 2012. "Opportunities Suspended: The Disparate Impact of Disciplinary Exclusion from School." The Civil Rights Project, August 7. Retrieved on April 25, 2020, at https://civilrightsproject.ucla.edu/resources/projects/center-for-civil -rights-remedies/school-to-prison-folder/federal-reports/upcoming-ccrr -research.

Lum, Lydia. 2018. "Group Addresses Incarceration among Asian Americans, Pacific Islanders." Diverse: Issues in Higher Education, May 1.

Moore, Lisa D., and Amy Elkavich. 2008. "Who's Using and Who's Doing Time." *American Journal of Public Health* 98(5): 782–786.

Nellis, Ashley. 2016. "The Color of Justice: Racial and Ethnic Disparity in State Prisons." The Sentencing Project, June 14. https://www .sentencingproject.org/publications/color-of-justice-racial-and-ethnic -disparity-in-state-prisons/.

Okonofua, Jason A., and Jennifer L. Eberhardt. 2015. "Two Strikes: Race and the Disciplining of Young Students." *Psychological Science* 26(5): 617–624.

Om, Anjali. 2018. "The Opioid Crisis in Black and White: The Role of Race in Our Nation's Recent Drug Epidemic." *Journal of Public Health* 40(4): 614–615.

Oppel, Richard A., Jr., and Jugal K. Patel. 2019. "No Time." *New York Times*, January 31.

Quigley, Bill. 2016. "40 Reasons Why Our Jails Are Full of Black and Poor People." HuffPost, January 2.

"Report: The War on Marijuana in Black and White." ACLU. Retrieved on October 11, 2019, at https://www.aclu.org/report/report-war -marijuana-black-and-white?redirect=criminal-law-reform/war -marijuana-black-and-white.

Rothwell, Jonathan. 2014. "How the War on Drugs Damages Black Social Mobility." Brookings, September 30.

Sawyer, Wendy, and Peter Wagner. 2020. "Mass Incarceration: The Whole Pie 2020." Prison Policy Initiative. Retrieved on April 25, 2020, at https://www.prisonpolicy.org/reports/pie2020.html.

The Sentencing Project. 2013. *Report of the Sentencing Project to the United Nations Human Rights Committee.* Retrieved on June 15, 2020, at https://www.sentencingproject.org/wp-content/uploads/2015/12/Race-and-Justice-Shadow-Report-ICCPR.pdf.

Shapiro, Joseph. 2015. "Civil Rights Attorneys Sue Ferguson over 'Debtors Prisons.'" NPR, Code Switch, February 8.

U.S. Department of Education. 2016. *2013–2014 Civil Rights Data Collection: A First Look.* Retrieved on April 10, 2020, at https://www2.ed.gov/about/offices/list/ocr/docs/2013-14-first-look.pdf.

Wagner, Peter. 2014. "Our Best Data Visualizations in 2014." Prison Policy Initiative, December 29. Retrieved on June 30, 2020, at https://www.prisonpolicy.org/blog/2014/12/29/data2014/.

Wang, Frances Kai-Hwa. 2015. "New Report Discusses Impact of Mass Incarceration on AAPI Community." NBC News, December 8.

Yam, Kimberley. 2018. "The Forgotten Asian Refugees Fed into the US Prison System." HuffPost, January 29.

Q19. IS THE AMERICAN CRIMINAL JUSTICE SYSTEM RACIALLY BIASED?

Answer: Yes. Mounting empirical evidence points to a criminal justice system that is racially biased. Black and white Americans are treated differently at different levels of the criminal justice system, and this has important implications for the relationship that African Americans have with the criminal justice system in the United States and with those who police their communities. Studies further reveal that among African Americans, those with darker skin and Afrocentric features are treated worse than those with comparatively lighter skin and features deemed less Afrocentric.

The Facts: In 2016, a white former Stanford University student-athlete named Brock Turner was convicted of raping an unconscious woman behind a fraternity house dumpster. A jury subsequently found him guilty of three felony counts of sexual assault, but even though he potentially faced a 14-year prison sentence, the judge sentenced Turner to a mere six months. A public uproar ensued, with some calling the sentence "a slap on the wrist," and others publicly calling for the judge's dismissal. Much of the condemnation of the judge's decision focused on the belief that the light sentence conveyed the impression that rape and sexual assault are not serious crimes. Others, however, said that it underscored the racial inequality embedded in the American criminal justice system, pointing to similar cases involving Black men serving considerably longer sentences. The same year, media outlets also highlighted the case of Brian Banks, a Black man who served five years in prison for what would eventually prove to be a wrongful rape conviction. Facing 41 years in prison, he was advised by his lawyer to take a plea bargain and avoid trial because it was a better option "than a young black kid facing an all-white jury" (Gupta 2016; Stack 2016).

A 2019 Pew Research Center survey reveals that nearly 90 percent of Black adults believe that Blacks are treated less fairly by the American criminal justice system than whites; white adults, by contrast, are much less likely to perceive racial bias against Black Americans in the criminal justice system (only 61 percent of whites agree) (Gramlich 2019). Though the topic is polarizing and beliefs about the fairness of the criminal justice system are influenced by one's race, study after study show that the institution is, in fact, racially biased against people of color—especially against African Americans.

Black people have a long history of discriminatory treatment in the American criminal justice system. Following the Civil War, African Americans in the South faced "unique forms of policing, sentencing, and confinement" by whites who wanted to restrict their newfound freedoms and exploit their labor postslavery (Hinton, Henderson, and Reed 2018, 2). Black Codes, for example, were Southern state laws passed in the year immediately after slavery was abolished. These laws functioned to control the behavior of African Americans and keep them in a subservient position in Southern society. Black Codes prevented Black people from voting, owning weapons, walking at night, keeping a "disorderly house," testifying against a white person, or assembling in groups. In most Southern states, Black people could also face arrest if they were unemployed or failed to provide proof that they had a white employer. Any violation of these laws resulted in hefty fines, imprisonment, or forced labor through a private system of "convict leasing" that allowed for their virtual reenslavement for minor transgressions.

Laws in the Northeast, Midwest, and West also disproportionately imprisoned African Americans for offenses such as disorderly conduct, keeping and visiting disorderly houses, drunkenness, and minor violations of city ordinances. Their high rate of imprisonment, a direct result of these racist laws, was then touted by whites as "proof" that Black people were inherently criminal—a stereotype that persists today (Hinton, Henderson, and Reed 2018).

Though states have long since repealed these blatantly discriminatory laws, racism persists in the modern criminal justice system. African Americans face bias at all levels; the following examples are based on available empirical data:

Bias in Police Treatment

- An analysis of road stops (via video data from officers' body cameras) by researchers at Stanford University exposed wide racial disparities in how police interact with Black and white drivers. They analyzed 981 police stops by the Oakland, California, Police Department in April 2014 and found that officers spoke less respectfully to African Americans as compared to whites, regardless of the severity of the infraction, the location of the stop, the outcome of the stop, and even the race of the officer. For example, officers were more likely to address white drivers with respectful titles (such as sir or ma'am), while they more often addressed Black drivers by their first names. They were also more likely to use respectful phrases with whites (such as "drive safe, please" and "sorry to stop you") and less respectful phrases with Blacks (such as "hands on the wheel") (Voigt et al. 2017).

- Police are more likely to stop and search African Americans without cause than whites—a practice commonly referred to as *racial profiling*. Data show that only about 3 percent of these stops produce any evidence of a crime; thus, the overwhelming majority of people racially profiled, most of whom are people of color, are not breaking the law (97 percent) (Balko 2019). Data further indicate that though Blacks are disproportionately profiled by police, they typically have lower "hit" rates as compared to whites. For example, New York City officers disproportionately targeted people of color during the tenure of the city's "stop-and-frisk" program. This program operated from the late 1990s until it formally ended in 2014. It authorized officers to stop anyone they deemed suspicious and search for illegal contraband, such as drugs and weapons. The city's own report on the practice revealed that stops of whites were twice as likely to result in discovery of weapons than stops of Blacks. Further, Blacks were only two-thirds as likely as whites to be carrying something illegal (Bump 2016).

  In Chicago, a 2016 report found that Black drivers were searched four times as often as white drivers, yet the Chicago Police Department's own data show that contraband was found on white drivers twice as often as Black drivers (Makarechi 2016). Another study based on data from 2014 found that police also disproportionately stopped and searched Black people in San Francisco, yet a review of the practice revealed that contraband on Blacks was discovered at less than half the rate of contraband on whites (33 percent vs. 74.7 percent, respectively). In 2015, whites were found to be carrying contraband at twice the rate of Blacks when searched (*Blue Ribbon Panel* 2016; as cited in Makarechi 2016). Other cities mirror these patterns (for additional examples, see Balko 2019; Hinton, Henderson, and Reed 2018; Makarechi 2016).

Whites arguably have significantly higher "hit" rates than Blacks because police are more likely to stop them when they have reason to suspect a crime. African Americans, on the other hand, are stopped when police have reason to suspect criminal conduct but they are also often stopped simply because of their skin color.

Bias in Use of Force by Police

- A 2018 analysis of 6,000 use-of-force cases in seven U.S. cities found that white officers used greater force on Black suspects than white suspects, even when both Black and white suspects offered similar levels of resistance toward police. Black officers, by contrast, used comparable force against Black and white suspects (Paoline, Gau, and Terrill 2018).
- A 2019 Harvard study analyzed police records in New York and found that police were more likely to use force (nonlethal) on Black and Hispanic people than on whites (e.g., push subjects to the ground, shove them against walls, draw and point their weapons, and use pepper spray or batons), regardless of how civilians acted toward police officers and even if officers described the civilians as "perfectly compliant" with their questions and instructions (Fryer 2019).
- Data from 2013 to 2019 show that African Americans are 2.5 to 3 times more likely than whites to be shot and killed by police. They are also less likely than whites to pose an imminent threat to officers (i.e., less likely to be armed) at the time of the shooting (Makarechi 2016). A separate study that analyzed nearly a thousand fatal shootings in 2015 found a similar pattern; of those shot and killed by police, Blacks were more than twice as likely than whites to be unarmed (for a more in-depth discussion of disparate rates of fatal police shootings, see Q20).

Bias in Arrests

- Studies repeatedly show that police are more likely to arrest Blacks than whites for similar crimes. A meta-analysis of 23 studies conducted between 1977 and 2004 found that this was true even when controlling for the suspect's prior record (Hinton, Henderson, and Reed 2018).
- An analysis from 2010 to 2018 found that despite the fact that Blacks and whites use marijuana at similar rates, Black people were nearly four times more likely to be arrested for marijuana possession than whites (ACLU 2020). In some states, the disparity is significantly higher. The study found that in New York, for example, police arrest Blacks on low-level marijuana charges at eight times the rate of whites, though people in both Black and white neighborhoods called police about suspected marijuana use at the same rate. According to a *New York Times* analysis and interviews with defendants, police, and lawyers, there is "uneven enforcement" of drug laws: "In some neighborhoods, officers [were] expected to be assertive on the streets, seize on the smell of marijuana, and stop people who are smoking. In others, people smoke in public without fear" of officers (Mueller, Gebeloff, and Chinoy 2018).

Bias in Convictions

- Black people are more likely than whites to be wrongfully convicted of crimes. This is supported by data by the National Registry of Exonerations as of October 2016, which showed that nearly half of all exonerations involve African Americans. Black people are three and half times more likely than whites to be wrongfully convicted of sexual assault, seven times more likely to be wrongfully convicted of murder, and 12 times more likely to be wrongfully convicted of a drug-related offense. According to authors of the National Registry of Exonerations report *Race and Wrongful Convictions in the United States*, wrongful convictions of African Americans may be explained by eyewitness misidentification, overpolicing of African Americans and African American communities, misconduct by police and prosecutors, and conscious and subconscious bias throughout the entire criminal justice system (Gross, Possley, and Stephens 2017).

Bias in Sentencing

- Black men who commit the same crimes as white men receive federal prison sentences that are, on average, nearly 20 percent longer, according to a 2017 report on sentencing disparities from the U.S. Sentencing Commission (USSC). This disparity persists even after controlling for factors such as the defendant's prior criminal history and whether he was in possession of a weapon (Ingraham 2017).

- Blacks are more likely to receive prison sentences (and longer sentences) than whites for similar drug-related offenses. For example, from 1986 to 2010, crack cocaine users (who are typically Black) received much harsher sentences than powder cocaine users (who are mostly white), even though crack cocaine and powder cocaine are two forms of the same drug. In particular, federal law (termed the "100-to-1" rule) imposed an automatic 10-year sentence for anyone caught with 50 grams of crack (about 0.11 lbs, or the weight of a candy bar), though the same sentence was only given to those caught with 5,000 grams of powder cocaine (about 11 lbs, or enough to fill a suitcase). This also meant that Black Americans imprisoned for nonviolent crack cocaine offenses were serving just as much time as whites who were in for violent offenses (ACLU n.d.; "100-to-1 Rule" 2017).

Bias in Capital Punishment

- When it comes to the death penalty, it is unclear whether prosecutors more often seek the death penalty for Black defendants than white defendants based on the available data. However, prosecutors are more likely to seek the death penalty (and the death penalty is more likely to be handed down) if victims are white rather than Black. Studies show that this disparate pattern is evident in places such as Texas, Delaware, North Carolina, Florida, Illinois, Georgia, Maryland, Indiana, New Jersey, Virginia, Utah, and Washington State (this list is not exhaustive). In some states, the racial disparity is especially alarming. A 2016 study, for example, found that in Louisiana, killers of white victims were 14 times more likely to be executed than those who killed Blacks (Balko 2019). Undoubtedly, this discrepancy calls into question the value that these states place on Black versus white lives.
- Data further show that both the races of the alleged perpetrator and victim matter. A 2013 report to the United Nations Human Rights Committee by the Washington, DC–based advocacy group The Sentencing Project, for example, noted that since 1976, Black defendants with white victims were executed 13 times more than white defendants with Black victims.

These examples provide a mere snapshot of the different ways in which anti-Black bias permeates the American criminal justice system. Further problematic are the blatant disparities that exist in the treatment of African Americans depending on skin shade and facial features. A growing number of studies show that African Americans with darker skin and Afrocentric features (e.g., wide nose, coarse hair, and full lips) are treated more harshly in the criminal justice system than those with lighter skin and those who look less Afrocentric—a pattern most likely explained by the explicit and implicit biases of judges and jurors. Some examples include the following (as reviewed in Bennett and Plaut 2018):

- A study of inmates in Florida found that the stronger one's Afrocentric features, the longer the prison sentence. The researchers even found that white offenders with Afrocentric features received longer sentences than white offenders with less Afrocentric features.
- An examination of Black inmates in Mississippi found that the darker one's skin tone, the longer the prison sentence.
- An analysis of more than 12,000 cases of Black women imprisoned in North Carolina found that lighter-skinned women received more lenient sentences and served 11 percent less time than women with darker skin tones.
- A study of death penalty cases in Philadelphia found that Black defendants perceived to be more stereotypically Black in appearance were more than twice as likely to receive the death penalty as compared to those who were perceived as less stereotypically Black in appearance. However, this was only true for cases where the murder victim was white, not Black.
- A study in Georgia found that dark- and medium-skinned Blacks received sentences that were nearly 5 percent longer than whites, though light-skinned Blacks did not receive statistically different sentences than whites.

The underlying reasons for this disproportionality are complex, though a long history of systemic racial bias in the criminal justice system cannot be ignored. As a result, many African Americans have little confidence in the criminal justice system or in police. According to a 2017 survey asking Americans to rate police officers on a "feeling thermometer" from zero (the most negative rating) to 100 (the most positive rating), whites rated them a 72, but Blacks rated them much lower at 47 (Gramlich 2019). Another poll (conducted in 2017 by National Public Radio, Robert Wood Johnson Foundation, and Harvard) found that half of all African

Americans experienced discrimination when interacting with police, and nearly a third said that they had avoided calling the police when in need (Milano 2017). Clearly, racial bias in the criminal justice system is real for African Americans and has tangible consequences for how Black Americans view the police with whom they interact; it also affects their trust in the broader criminal justice system.

FURTHER READING

ACLU. n.d. "Fair Sentencing Act." Retrieved on October 11, 2019, at https://www.aclu.org/issues/criminal-law-reform/drug-law-reform/fair -sentencing-act.

ACLU. 2020. American Civil Liberties Union (ACLU). 2020. "A Tale of Two Countries: Racially Targeted Arrests in the Era of Marijuana Reform." Retrieved on November 26, 2020, at https://www.aclu.org /report/tale-two-countries-racially-targeted-arrests-era-marijuana -reform.

Balko, Radley. 2019. "There's Overwhelming Evidence That the Criminal-Justice System Is Racist. Here's the Proof." *Washington Post*, April 10.

Bennett, Mark W., and Victoria C. Plaut. 2018. "Looking Criminal and the Presumption of Dangerousness: Afrocentric Features, Skin Tone, and Criminal Justice." *UC Davis Law Review* 51(3): 745–803.

"The Blue Ribbon Panel on Transparency, Accountability, and Fairness in Law Enforcement." July 2016. Retrieved on November 26, 2020, at https://sfblueribbonpanel.com/brp-full-report.

Bump, Philip. 2016. "The Facts about Stop-and-Frisk in New York City." *Washington Post*, September 26.

Federal Bureau of Prisons. 2019. "Inmate Race." Retrieved on October 11, 2019, at https://www.bop.gov/about/statistics/statistics_inmate_race .jsp.

Fryer, Roland G., Jr. 2019. "An Empirical Analysis of Racial Differences in Police Use of Force." *Journal of Political Economy* 127(3): 1210–1261.

Gramlich, John. 2019. "From Police to Parole, Black and White Americans Differ Widely in Their Views of the Criminal Justice System." FactTank: News in the Numbers. Pew Research Center, May 21. Retrieved on October 11, 2019, at https://www.pewresearch.org/fact -tank/2019/05/21/from-police-to-parole-black-and-white-americans -differ-widely-in-their-views-of-criminal-justice-system/.

Gross, Samuel R., Maurice Possley, and Klara Stephens. 2017. "Race and Wrongful Convictions in the United States." National Registry

of Exonerations. Retrieved on October 11, 2019, at http://www.law
.umich.edu/special/exoneration/Documents/Race_and_Wrongful
_Convictions.pdf.

Gupta, Prachi. 2016. "The Stanford Rape Case Illustrates the Toxicity of
White Male Privilege." *Cosmopolitan*, June 7.

Hinton, Elizabeth, LeShae Henderson, and Cindy Reed. 2018. "An
Unjust Burden: The Disparate Treatment of Black Americans in the
Criminal Justice System." Vera Institute of Justice. Retrieved on October 11, 2019, at https://www.vera.org/downloads/publications/for-the
-record-unjust-burden-racial-disparities.pdf.

Ingraham, Christopher. 2017. "Black Men Sentenced to More Time for
Committing the Same Exact Crime as a White Person, Study Finds."
Washington Post, November 16.

Makarechi, Kia. 2016. "What the Data Really Says about Police and
Racial Bias." *Vanity Fair*, July 14.

Milano, Brett. 2017. "Racial Discrimination Still Rules, Poll Says." *Harvard Gazette*, October 30.

Mueller, Benjamin, Robert Gebeloff, and Sahil Chinoy. 2018. "Surest
Way to Face Marijuana Charges in New York: Be Black or Hispanic."
New York Times, May 13.

Mustard, David. 2001. "Racial, Ethnic, and Gender Disparities in Sentencing: Evidence from the Federal Courts." *Journal of Law and Economics* 44: 285–314.

"100-to-1 Rule." 2017. *New York Times*, November 15.

Paoline, Eugene A., III, Jacinta M. Gau, and William Terrill. 2018. "Race
and the Police Use of Force Encounter in the United States." *British
Journal of Criminology* 58(1): 54–74.

Quigley, Bill. 2016. "40 Reasons Why Our Jails Are Full of Black and
Poor People." HuffPost, June 2.

The Sentencing Project. 2013. *Report of the Sentencing Project to the United
Nations Human Rights Committee*. Washington, DC: The Sentencing
Project. Retrieved on June 18, 2020, at https://www.sentencingproj
ect.org/wp-content/uploads/2015/12/Race-and-Justice-Shadow-Report
-ICCPR.pdf.

Stack, Liam. 2016. "Light Sentence for Brock Turner in Stanford Rape
Case Draws Outrage." *New York Times*, June 6.

Voigt, Rob, Nicholas P. Camp, VinodKumar Prabhakaran, Williaml L.
Hamilton, Rebecca C. Hetey, Camilla M. Griffiths, David Jurgens,
Dan Jurafsky, and Jennifer L. Eberhardt. 2017. "Language from Police
Body Camera Footage Shows Racial Disparities in Officer Respect."
Psychological and Cognitive Sciences 114(25):6521–6526.

Q20. ARE AFRICAN AMERICANS MORE LIKELY THAN WHITE AMERICANS TO BE KILLED BY POLICE?

Answer: Yes. Data collected on fatal police shootings reveal that African Americans are approximately 2.5 to 3 times more likely than white Americans to be killed by police. One explanation for the racial disparity frequently used to defend police killings of African Americans is that they are more likely than whites to be armed and to resist arrest, thus necessitating violent force by police. A competing explanation centers on the racial biases of police officers and maintains that the explicit and implicit biases of officers affect the snap judgments they make about African Americans—including whether or not to shoot. Research provides support to the latter perspective, though the evidence is not conclusive.

The Facts: High-profile killings of unarmed Black people in the United States in the early twenty-first century have sparked a national debate on the use of police force on African Americans, in particular Black men. Some of these men have become household names: Eric Garner (who suffocated in an illegal chokehold by police in New York in 2014); Michael Brown (who was shot and killed by police in the streets of Ferguson, Missouri, in 2014); Tamir Rice (a 12-year-old who was shot by police in Cleveland, Ohio, in 2014 when officers allegedly mistook his toy gun for a real weapon); Freddie Gray (who died of a spinal cord injury while in police custody in Baltimore, Maryland, in 2015); Philando Castile (who was shot and killed by police in suburban Minnesota in 2016 during a routine traffic stop); Botham Jean (who was killed in his own apartment by an off-duty police officer in 2018); Elijah McClain (who died after an encounter with police in which he was injected with ketamine on a roadside in Aurora, Colorado, in 2019); and George Floyd (who died shortly after an officer pinned him to the ground with a knee to his neck for nearly nine minutes on a Minneapolis roadside in 2020). This list is not exhaustive, and their stories and those of others have raised questions about lethal police force and race: Are African Americans more likely than white Americans to be killed by police?

In 2016, former Arkansas governor Mike Huckabee appeared on cable news with a ready answer: "If we have a shooting, we end up assuming it had to be racial. . . . When in fact as we know . . . more white people have been shot by police officers this year than minorities" (as quoted in Lowery 2016). Is this true? Yes and no. In raw numbers, data show that more white Americans are shot and killed by police than Black Americans.

For example, in 2018, nearly a thousand people were shot and killed by police. Of those, 456 were white, and 228 were Black (based on the *Washington Post* database of fatal police shootings). However, it bears noting that there are nearly 160 million more white people than Black people in America (according to the 2010 U.S. Census) (Lowery 2016). If those numbers are adjusted for relative population size, data clearly show that Black Americans are more likely to be shot and killed by police. According to recorded police-involved deaths from 2013 to 2018, for instance, they were 2.5 times more likely than whites to be shot and killed by police (Edwards, Lee, and Esposito 2019). In 2019, they were three times more likely than whites to be killed by police according to data from Mapping Police Violence, a research collaborative that collects data on police shootings across the United States. See figure 20.1 for homicide rates by police for Blacks, Hispanics, and whites in the United States based on 2019 data.

There is a caveat. A 2019 Harvard study found blatant police bias against African Americans in incidents involving nonlethal force, though it surprisingly found no racial differences in officer-involved shootings when contextual factors were taken into account (such as whether the suspect was aggressive or had a weapon) (Fryer 2019). Though the study's results were widely publicized by the media, there are at least two problems with the study. First, the data largely come from Houston, Texas, and are therefore not nationally representative. Another study published in 2018 similarly found no racial bias in police shootings, but it was also limited to data from a single police department and not nationally representative (Worrall et al. 2018). Second, the author of the 2019 study concedes that

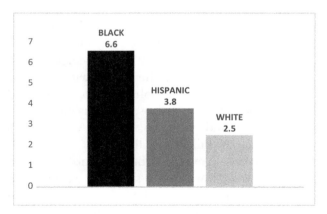

Figure 20.1. Homicide Rates (Per 1 Million People) by Police, 2019.
(*Source*: Mapping Police Violence, https://mappingpoliceviolence.org/home)

data are based on police reports, which only provide the perspective of officers (and not suspects); this is problematic according to the author of the study given that "there have been several high-profile cases of police storytelling that is not congruent with video evidence of the interaction" (Fryer 2019, 1218). He further adds that because the penalties for wrong-fully discharging one's weapon can be life changing, "the incentive to mis-represent contextual factors on police reports may be large" (Fryer 2019, 1222). As such, these data may be unreliable. Despite the findings of these regional studies, available national data (from both the *Washington Post's* database on fatal police shootings and Mapping Police Violence) show that Black Americans are killed by police at a significantly higher rate than their white counterparts.

But why is there racial disparity? There are at least two possible expla-nations. The first maintains that Black Americans are more likely to be killed by police because they are more apt to commit violent crime and hence, as the argument goes, are more likely to pose an imminent threat to officers. Indeed, data show that African Americans are more likely than white Americans to commit violent crime (see Q22 for a more in-depth discussion). Political commentator Heather MacDonald, author of *The War on Cops* (2016b), argues that "such a concentration of criminal violence in minority communities means that officers will be disproportionately confronting armed and often resisting suspects in those communities, raising officers' own risk of using lethal force" (Mac-donald 2016a). In other words, MacDonald argues that Black people are more likely to be killed because they are more likely to pose an immediate threat to officers.

Although this is a popular argument among some, many studies and available data contradict this assumption. For example, data from 2013 to 2019 revealed that when killed by police, Black people were 1.3 times more likely to be unarmed as compared to white people (Mapping Police Violence n.d.). In 2015 alone, unarmed Black Americans were 5 times more likely than unarmed white Americans to be shot and killed by police (Lowery 2016; Mapping Police Violence n.d.). A 2017 study fur-ther found that Blacks killed by police were less likely than whites killed by police to pose an imminent threat to the officers at the moment they were killed (Nix et al. 2017). The study's authors analyzed 990 fatal shoot-ings by police in 2015 and found that Blacks were killed at twice the rate of whites and were more than twice as likely as whites to have been unarmed when they were shot and killed by police (Nix et al. 2017). In other words, whites were more likely to be armed than Blacks, yet they were far less likely to die from their encounters with law enforcement.

This pattern persists even in cases of nonlethal police force. Economist Roland Fryer Jr. analyzed police records in New York and found that officers were approximately 53 percent more likely to use force on Blacks and Hispanics than on whites (force that included pushing subjects into walls or onto the ground, using batons and pepper spray, and drawing and pointing weapons), and he discovered that how civilians acted did not explain the racial disparity. For instance, when officers found contraband when frisking civilians, they were 21 percent more likely to use force against Blacks than whites, even when officers described civilians as "perfectly compliant" with their questions and instructions (see Ehrenfreund and Guo 2016).

A second argument suggests that police biases, both explicit and implicit, explain racial disparities in lethal force employed by officers. Explicit biases are those biases that are known to individuals, such as when officers are well aware that they are racially biased against people of color. In 2019, for example, investigative journalists discovered hundreds of law enforcement officers across the United States who were active members of overtly racist social media groups such as Ban the NAACP and Death to Islam Undercover (Harriot 2019). Prejudice exists in all segments of American society, and police officers are no exception. Certainly, however, not all officers are explicitly biased, though many may unknowingly hold implicit biases (as do many Americans).

In contrast to explicit biases, implicit biases are biases that operate outside of conscious control. They exist at the subconscious level and are unknown even to the people who hold them—even to "good" people who may pride themselves in being egalitarian and racially unbiased (for more on implicit bias, see Q33). Psychologist Katherine B. Spencer and her colleagues (2016) note that "it is important to bear in mind that police officers are normal human beings. . . . They are prone to make the same stereotype-biased judgements the rest of us are. Because they are often operating under conditions of uncertainty, high discretion, and stress and threat, the pervasive stereotypes linking Blacks and Latinos with violence, crime, and even specifically weapons are likely to cause them to make misattributions" of the intentions and behaviors of citizens.

Some white officers may harbor implicit biases toward Black Americans, though it is important to note that so, too, may officers of color. A 2019 study led by David J. Johnson at the University of Maryland examined data on fatal shootings that occurred in 2015 and found that white officers were not any more likely than nonwhite officers to shoot minority civilians (Johnson et al. 2019). Moreover, even African American officers are not immune from anti-Black stereotypes and bias against fellow

African Americans. Three of the six officers implicated in the 2015 death of Freddie Gray in Baltimore, for example, were Black. Charles Menifield, of Rutgers University, drawing on his own extensive research on use of deadly force by police, asserts that "white officers do not kill black suspects at a higher rate compared with nonwhite officers. . . . The killing of black suspects is a police problem, not a white police problem" (as cited in Jacobs 2018). The problem, according to Menifield, is much bigger than individual biases; it is rooted in institutionalized racism within many police departments across the nation.

Furthermore, explicit and implicit biases may affect the behavior of police officers, such as influencing snap judgments they make about citizens, how they interact with citizens and suspects, and even whether or not they draw and shoot their weapons. A 2010 report by New York State, for example, found that most of the 26 police offers killed by "friendly fire" in the previous three decades were officers of color. Ten were killed off-duty, and of those, nine were Black or Latinx. The report indicates that "racial bias, unconscious or otherwise, played a clear role," and they concluded that police officers made snap judgments that perhaps involved racial cues in assessing potential threat (as cited in Baker 2010). Further, a series of experimental studies used a simulated video game to gauge whether a suspect's race affected "shoot/don't shoot" decisions. They presented participants with Black and white suspects, each holding a gun or a non-threatening object (such as an aluminum can, a silver camera, a black cell phone, or a black wallet). They found that study participants shot armed targets more quickly if they were Black rather than white. They were also more likely to mistakenly shoot unarmed Black targets as compared to unarmed white targets, suggesting that personal biases can have real life or death consequences (Correll et al. 2002, 1325). Other simulated experiments have also found that study participants are quicker to shoot Black rather than white suspects (see James, James, and Vila 2016), and social psychologist Joshua Correll and his colleagues (2006) found that a neuro-physiological "threat" response in the brain was more pronounced when participants were faced with Black suspects as compared to white suspects.

The research on the impact of implicit bias, however, is mixed. A 2016 study, for example, found that participants, even those who tested high for implicit biases against African Americans, were three times less likely to shoot unarmed Black suspects than white unarmed suspects in video simulations. The authors of the study argue that study participants (who were police officers) may have been hesitant to shoot Black suspects in the simulation because of fears of societal backlash and criminal charges if they were to shoot African Americans in real life (James, James, and Vila

2016). It is also plausible that the officers were mindful of the purpose of the study, thus affecting the study's results. Nonetheless, the conflicting results of these simulation studies suggest that more research is needed.

In response to a series of shootings by police of unarmed Black men, the Black Lives Matter movement was created in 2013 by three Black women (Alicia Garza, Patrisse Cullors, and Opal Tometi). In 2014, then President Barack Obama established the 21st Century Task Force on Policing, which brought officers and activists together to make recommendations for policing reform in the United States. One recommendation was to implement implicit bias training for police officers, and some police departments have taken such steps; for example, in 2018, the New York Police Department initiated a training program on implicit bias for its officers (Baker 2018). Many departments have also added body cameras for increased accountability of officers, though a 2017 study suggests that body cameras may have little effect on police behavior. The 18-month study of 2,000 police officers found that officers wearing body cameras "used force and prompted civilian complaints at about the same rate as those who did not have them" (Ripley and Williams 2017). Nonetheless, while officer behavior may not change with cameras, the cameras do allow for documentation of interactions between police and civilians—as long as officers keep them turned on during encounters. For example, in the case of George Floyd, an unarmed African American man who died at the hands of Minneapolis police in 2020, police body camera footage allowed prosecutors get a full picture of his deadly arrest. The video showed him telling officers he was claustrophobic and begging them not to put him in the back of a squad car, volunteering to lie on the ground instead, and repeatedly telling officers the he could not breathe (Collins 2020). It also revealed that he was motionless and silent on the ground for nearly three minutes. Because officer and suspect accounts do not always match and because suspects are not always alive at the end of these encounters to tell their side of the story, body camera footage can be vital.

As a final point, though African Americans are killed by police at much higher rates than their white counterparts, other groups of color, such as Latinxs and Native Americans, are also disproportionately killed by police. In fact, according to data from the Centers for Disease Control and Prevention (CDC), Native Americans "are killed in police encounters at a higher rate than any other racial or ethnic group," including African Americans (Hansen 2017). Police shootings of Native Americans largely go unnoticed by the American public because of their relative invisibility in the United States (in part due to their small numbers; they make up less than 1 percent of the nation's population).

FURTHER READING

Baker, Al. 2010. "Bias Seen in 'Police-on-Police' Shootings." *New York Times*, May 27. Retrieved on September 11, 2019, at https://www.nytimes.com/2010/05/27/nyregion/27shoot.html.

Baker, Al. 2018. "Confronting Implicit Bias in the New York Police Department." *New York Times*, July 17. Retrieved on September 11, 2019, at https://www.nytimes.com/2018/07/15/nyregion/bias-training-police.html.

Collins, Jon. 2020. "Police Bodycam Video Shows George Floyd's Distress during Fatal Arrest." NPR, July 15.

Correll, Joshua, Bernadette Park, Charles Judd, and Bernd Wittenbrink. 2002. "The Police Officer's Dilemma: Using Ethnicity to Disambiguate Potentially Threatening Individuals." *Journal of Personality and Social Psychology* 83(6): 1314–1329.

Correll, Joshua, Geoffrey L. Urland, and Tiffany A. Ito. 2006. "Event-Related Potentials and the Decision to Shoot: The Role of Threat Perception and Cognitive Control." *Journal of Experimental Social Psychology* 42: 120–128.

Duster, Chandelis R. 2017. "Fatally Shot Black Americans Twice as Likely as Whites to Be Unarmed: Study." NBC, February 11. Retrieved on September 11, 2019, at https://www.nbcnews.com/news/nbcblk/afr-americans-fatally-shot-less-likely-be-armed-whites-n718666.

Edwards, Frank, Hedwig Lee, and Michael Esposito. 2019. "Risk of Being Killed by Police Use of Force in the United States by Age, Race-Ethnicity, and Sex." *Proceedings of the National Academy of Sciences of the United States of America* 116(34): 16793–16798.

Ehrenfreund, Max, and Jeff Guo. 2016. "How a Controversial Study Found That Police Are More Likely to Shoot Whites, Not Blacks." *Washington Post*, July 13. Retrieved on September 11, 2019, at https://www.washingtonpost.com/news/wonk/wp/2016/07/13/why-a-massive-new-study-on-police-shootings-of-whites-and-blacks-is-so-controversial/.

Fryer, Roland G., Jr. 2019. "An Empirical Analysis of Racial Differences in Police Use of Force." *Journal of Political Economy* 127(3): 1210–1261.

Hansen, Elise. 2017. "The Forgotten Minority in Police Shootings." CNN, November 10. Retrieved on September 11, 2019, at https://www.cnn.com/2017/11/10/us/native-lives-matter/index.html.

Harriot, Michael. 2019. "Report: Hundreds of Police Officers Belong to Racist Facebook Groups." The Root, June 15. Retrieved on September 11, 2019, at https://www.theroot.com/report-hundreds-of-police-officers-belong-to-racist-fa-1835542308.

Jacobs, Tom. 2018. "Black Cops Are Just as Likely as White Cops to Kill Black Suspects." *Pacific Standard*, August 9. Retrieved on November 21, 2019, at https://psmag.com/social-justice/black-cops-are-just-as -likely-as-whites-to-kill-black-suspects.

James, Lois, Stephen M. James, and Bryan J. Vila. 2016. "The Reverse Racism Effect: Are Cops More Hesitant to Shoot Black Than White Suspects?" *Criminology & Public Policy* 15(2): 457–479.

Johnson, David J., Trevor Tress, Nicole Burkel, Carley Taylor, and Joseph Cesario. 2019. "Officer Characteristics and Racial Disparities in Fatal Officer-Involved Shootings." *Psychological and Cognitive Sciences* 116(32): 15877–15882.

Lowery, Wesley. 2016. "Aren't More White People Than Black People Killed by Police? Yes, but No." *Washington Post*, June 11. Retrieved on September 11, 2019, at https://www.washingtonpost.com/news/post -nation/wp/2016/07/11/arent-more-white-people-than-black-people -killed-by-police-yes-but-no/.

MacDonald, Heather. 2016a. "The Myths of Black Lives Matter." *Washington Post*, February 11.

MacDonald, Heather. 2016b. *The War on Cops: How the New Attack on Law and Order Makes Everyone Less Safe*. New York: Encounter Books.

Mapping Police Violence. n.d. https://mappingpoliceviolence.org/.

Nix, Justin, Bradley A. Campbell, Edward H. Byers, and Geoffrey P. Alpert. 2017. "A Bird's Eye View of Civilians Killed by Police in 2015." *Criminology & Public Policy* 16(1): 309–340.

Ripley, Amanda, and Timothy Williams. 2017. "Body Cameras Have Little Effect on Police Behavior, Study Says." *New York Times*, October 20. Retrieved on September 11, 2019, at https://www.nytimes .com/2017/10/20/us/police-body-camera-study.html.

Spencer, Katherine B., Amanda K. Carbonneau, and Jack Glaser. 2016. "Implicit Bias and Policing." *Social and Personality Psychology Compass* 10(1): 50–63.

Worrall, John L., Stephen A. Bishopp, Scott C. Zinser, Andrew P. Wheeler, and Scott W. Phillips. 2018. "Exploring Bias in Police Shooting Decisions with Real Shoot/Don't Shoot Cases." *Crime & Delinquency* 64(9): 1171–1192.

Q21. IS IT TRUE THAT THERE ARE MORE BLACK MEN IN PRISON THAN IN COLLEGE?

Answer: No. Though the belief that there are more Black men in prison than in college has become a popular media soundbite, this is false.

According to college and prison data analyzed by Ivory Toldson of Howard University in 2013, there are more Black men in college (approximately 6.3 percent) than incarcerated (4.7 percent). Nonetheless, though
the statement is incorrect, Black incarceration remains disproportionately
high and cannot be ignored.

The Facts: Many activists, scholars, political pundits, and politicians
(both on the left and right of the political spectrum) have alleged that
there are more Black men in prison than in college. President Barack
Obama even repeated what many have assumed to be conventional wis-
dom when, as a presidential candidate in 2007, he told an NAACP audience, "We have more work to do when more young black men languish in
prison than attend colleges and universities across America" (Bouie 2013;
Toldson 2013a). The line has become such a popular media soundbite
that one scholar described it as "the most frequently quoted statistic about
black men in the United States"; however, the statement is false (Bouie
2013; Desmond-Harris 2015).

The belief originates from a 2002 Justice Policy Institute (JPI) report
titled "Cellblocks or Classrooms," in which the authors claimed that
nearly a third more Black men were incarcerated in prison than enrolled
in college (based on available postsecondary education statistics in 1999
and prison data from 2000). Though the JPI report was widely publicized,
Howard University professor Ivory Toldson (2013b) argued that the data
were incomplete and flawed. For instance, more than a thousand colleges
failed to report their head count of Black students, and some of these non-
reporting schools included large state universities and historically Black
colleges and universities (HBCUs); as such, the numbers of Black males
attending colleges and universities were widely underestimated. This is a
significant omission, with Toldson estimating that the JPI report missed
about 100,000 Black students (Stephenson 2013). Toldson further argues
that the numbers from the 2002 report are outdated (nearly 20 years old
at the time of this book's publication). This is problematic given that the
"more Black men in prison than college" mantra persists, and despite the
fact that enrollment for Black students, including Black males, in college
has steadily increased since 2000. According to the National Center for
Education Statistics (2020), college enrollment rates for African Americans aged 18 to 24, increased from 25 percent in 2000 to 33 percent
in 2018. This increase is due, in part, to better reporting of enrollment
numbers, social advancements, and the rise of community and for-profit
colleges that have attracted African American students (Toldson 2013b).

A final problem with the widely reported statistic is the college versus prison comparison itself. Journalist Jenee Desmond-Harris (2015),

who regularly covers stories on race, argues that comparing the two is an "apples-to-oranges" exercise because the college age of enrollment is typically narrow, though the incarceration age range is much broader. Janks Morton, the director of the film *What Black Men Think* (2007), similarly points out the absurdity in comparing rates of college attendance (which generally occurs from ages 18 to 24) to incarceration rates (the prison population's age range is 18 to 70 years and higher). The more appropriate comparison is to compare 18- to 24-year-old college students to 18- to 24-year-old inmates, and according to psychologist Michael Strambler (2007), there are indeed significantly more 18- to 24-year-old Black men in college than in prison. Further, in 2013, Toldson noted that there were approximately 18 million Black men in the United States aged 18 and older. He estimated that, of those, approximately 6.3 percent were in college and 4.7 in prison (Toldson 2013b). The remaining 89 percent included Black men who never attended college, those who had left school, and those who had already graduated.

Despite this evidence, the myth persists and has potentially harmful consequences for Black males. Black boys faced with the ominous statistic may underestimate their likelihood of one day attending college, which may affect their motivation in school and ultimate academic success. The widely cited claim may also shape the expectations that teachers and school administrators have for Black boys. Given that empirical studies consistently show that educators' expectations of students affect their success in school (see Q14), this may be especially problematic.

Finally, though there are indeed more Black men in college than in prison, this fact should not detract from the reality that the rate of incarceration among Black males in the United States remains disproportionately high. African Americans have the highest incarceration rate of any racial group in the nation, outpacing Native Americans/Alaska Natives, Latinxs, Asians, and whites (Wagner 2014). Though there was a 20 percent decline in the Black incarceration rate from 2007 to 2017 (Gramlich 2019), suggesting some progress, efforts should remain focused on understanding the effects of poverty and racial inequality on crime (for more on the high rate of Black incarceration, see Q18). More work is also needed to reduce social class and racial disparities in both education and the criminal justice system.

FURTHER READING

Bouie, Jamelle. 2013. "More Black Men in College Than in Prison." The American Prospect, February 28.

Desmond-Harris, Jenee. 2015. "The Myth That There Are More Black Men in Prison Than in College, Debunked in One Chart." Vox, February 12.

Gramlich, John. 2019. "The Gap between the Number of Blacks and Whites in Prison Is Shrinking." Pew Research Center, April 30.

Justice Policy Institute. 2002. "Cellblocks or Classrooms? The Funding of Higher Education and Corrections and Its Impact on African American Men." Retrieved on October 4, 2019, at http://www.justicepolicy .org/research/2046.

Morton, Janks, dir. 2007. *What Black Men Think.* iYAGO Entertainment Group. DVD.

National Center for Education Statistics. 2020. "College Enrollment Rates." Retrieved on June 30, 2020, at https://nces.ed.gov/programs /coe/pdf/coe_cpb.pdf.

Stephenson, Wesley. 2013. "Are There More US Black Men in Prison or College?" BBC Radio 4, March 17.

Strambler, Michael. 2007. "Are More Black Men Really in Jail Than in College?" *Baltimore Sun*, October 11.

Toldson, Ivory. 2013a. "Are There Really More Black Men in Prison Than College? Interview with Ivory Toldson." By Michael Martin. NPR, April 23. Retrieved on October 4, 2019, at https://www.npr.org /2013/04/23/178601467/are-there-really-more-black-men-in-prison -than-college.

Toldson, Ivory A. 2013b. "More Black Men in Jail than in College? Wrong." The Root, February 28.

Wagner, Peter. 2014. "Our Best Data Visualizations in 2014." Prison Policy Initiative. Retrieved on June 30, 2020, at https://www.prisonpolicy .org/blog/2014/12/29/data2014/.

Q22. DO AFRICAN AMERICANS SUFFER FROM "BLACK-ON-BLACK" CRIME?

Answer: Yes. However, the phrase "Black-on-Black" crime is misleading. Black-on-Black crime typically refers to violent crime that occurs within Black communities; this is typified by a Black assailant and a Black victim. Most Black victims of homicide are indeed killed by other Black people making this phrase factually correct, but white victims are most often killed by whites as well. Crime, particularly violent crime (such as murder or assault), generally occurs among those of the same race and often by someone known to the victim. Same-race crime is largely explained by persistent housing segregation in the United States (especially between whites and Blacks)—whites are likely to live and interact with other whites and Blacks with Blacks. As such, if they become victims of violent crime, they are likely to be murdered or assaulted by someone of their own racial group.

The Facts: According to crime data from the FBI, roughly 90 percent of Black victims of homicide in 2010 were killed by other Black people (DOJ and FBI 2010), suggesting that the Black community suffers from what some within and outside of the community have termed "Black-on-Black" crime. This phrase has often been used in politically and racially charged ways to suggest that Black Americans are uniquely afflicted by same-race violence.

Indeed, it is true that most Black victims are killed by other Black people but it is also true that most white victims are killed by other whites. In the same year that more than 90 percent of Black victims were killed by Black assailants, approximately 83 percent of whites were killed by other whites. The Bureau of Justice Statistics reports that, regardless of race, the majority of crimes are committed by a person of the same race as the victim (Neiwert 2017), though the media, political pundits, politicians, and other public figures rarely, if ever, talk about white-on-white, Asian-on-Asian, or Hispanic-on-Hispanic crime.

There are at least two explanations, both interconnected, underlying same-race crimes (e.g., Black-on-Black or white-on-white). First, most victims of violent crime personally know their assailants (Harriot 2017). For instance, according to 2010 FBI statistics, nearly 53 percent of victims in the United States knew their killers, and nearly half of those known assailants were family members (DOJ and FBI 2010). A 2018 report by the Violence Policy Center also found that most murdered females (93 percent) knew their male assailants—a friend, family member, coworker, neighbor, or, in most cases (63 percent of the time), an intimate partner.

Second, because the United States is deeply racially segregated, the people one knows are often of the same race. Census data from 2010 show that residential segregation is on the decline in the United States, though segregation remains high. White Americans tend to live with other white Americans, and one-third of African Americans live in hypersegregated urban centers (such as Chicago, Detroit, St. Louis, Birmingham, Baltimore, and Washington, DC—this list is not exhaustive) (Massey and Tannen 2015); this means that the average Black person residing in such cities lives in extreme residential segregation with little to no contact with other racial groups.

Moreover, the social networks of most Americans are mostly composed of people of the same racial group. One 2016 survey found that among white Americans, 91 percent of people in their social networks were white, while among African Americans, 83 percent were Black (Cox, Navarro-Rivera, and Jones 2016). Because the United States is starkly divided along racial lines, crimes typically involve people of the same race, especially when it comes to Blacks and whites. For this reason, a Black person who is murdered will likely be killed by another Black person. A white person who is murdered is likely going to die at the hands of another white person.

Gary Younge of *Nation* magazine calls the phrase "Black-on-Black" crime deceptive "nonsense," but he also acknowledges that "Black crime is a serious issue" (Younge 2014). A 2010 FBI report on homicides in the United States revealed that approximately half of all offenders and victims were Black. Given that Black Americans constitute only 13 percent of the American population, this is alarming.

The root causes of the proportionately higher rate of violent crime in Black communities are numerous. Researchers contend, for example, that Black Americans show higher rates of violent crime because they are more likely to live in poverty than most other racial groups in the United States. For example, in a 1996 study, Ohio State University researchers Lauren Krivo and Ruth Peterson found that violent crime (such as aggravated assault, rape, and homicide) is higher in extremely disadvantaged urban neighborhoods than elsewhere. They theorized that this may be due to community conditions that encourage violent behavior, such as a dearth of positive role models, a crime-ridden environment that encourages residents to use violence for self-defense and protection of their property, and high rates of joblessness that contribute to idleness and contact with less-than-desirable role models (among other explanations). Krivo and Peterson analyzed Black and white urban neighborhoods in Columbus, Ohio, and found that economic disadvantage explained much of the Black-white disparity in violent crime observed there: "Black urban neighborhoods do exhibit much higher crime rates than the typical white city neighborhood but this is largely because they are structurally more disadvantaged" (Krivo and Peterson 1996, 643). In fact, they found that when comparing Black and white neighborhoods of similar disadvantage in Columbus, violent crime rates were nearly identical in the majority of neighborhoods they compared.

Further, data from 2008 to 2012 collected by the U.S. Department of Justice (DOJ) revealed that people living in poor households had a higher rate of violent victimization as compared to those living in high-income households—regardless of race (Harrell et al. 2014). A 2009 study on violent crime across 79 American cities similarly found neighborhood disadvantage to be a powerful predictor of violent crime, regardless of its racial composition. In other words, as a neighborhood's disadvantage increased (as measured by percent of population living below the poverty line, percent unemployed, and percent of high school dropouts, among other indicators), violent crime increased in Black, Latinx, and white neighborhoods. However, the authors of the study note that when neighborhood disadvantage was controlled, rates of violent crime were still higher in Black communities as compared to white or Latinx communities (Krivo, Peterson, and Kuhl 2009). Peterson and Krivo (2010) suggest that this may be because Blacks more often live in segregated neighborhoods as compared to whites and Latinxs, and, as such, they tend to be comparatively more socially isolated from other racial groups (see Q11 and Q12 for more on housing segregation in the United States). Perhaps this leads to more deleterious living conditions, further contributing to violent crime in Black communities. More research is needed.

Furthermore, studies show a link between poverty and violent crime outside the United States. Violent crime is a problem around the world, and urban poverty is at least one explanatory factor. Patna, India, for example, was coined the "crime capital" of India in the 1990s because of its high rate of urban violence. According to a 2012 report by the Brooks World Poverty Institute of the University of Manchester, Patna's violent crime rate in slum areas is especially high and much higher than the rate found in middle- and upper-class areas of the city. The report found that nearly 80 percent of those living in the city's slums claimed that violence was "an overwhelming feature of their everyday lives," and violent crime, such as homicide, was linked to economic disadvantage—just as it is in the United States. For example, violence in Patna frequently stemmed from ongoing disputes over access to scarce resources, such as land, water, and basic sanitation staples (such as toilets) (Rodgers and Satija 2012).

In addition to poverty, studies in sociology, psychology, and criminology suggest a number of additional potential causes of violent crime. Yale scholar Mario Coccia (2017) looked at violent crime in 191 nations and argued that, after controlling for other variables, high levels of income inequality in a nation may also explain violent crime; perhaps experiencing poverty in an unequal society is a catalyst for hostility and aggression.

Like violent crime among African Americans, violent crime on Native American reservations is also disproportionate; the nation's 310 reservations have violent crime rates that are more than two and half times the national average (Williams 2012). As with African American communities struggling with high crime rates, these Native American communities suffer from higher rates of poverty and other markers of socioeconomic inequality than other racial groups. More generally, studies investigating potential causes of violent crime further point to the breakdown of the family, geographic and social isolation, and subcultural norms (not to be confused with so-called racial norms) of violence, and several of these factors are interrelated.

When studying violent crime, researchers must be able to identify causes of violence in Black and Indigenous communities given their proportionately high rates of violent crime, but they should also recognize that murder and assault occur across all racial groups and depend on place and time. In 2019, some of the most violent nations in the world were in Africa as well as in the Middle East and Latin America. Some parts of Africa, by contrast, showed relatively low rates of violence, such as Botswana, Malawi, and Ghana (World Population Review 2019). Further, according to a study that compared homicide rates by nation, 17 of the world's 20 most violent countries were not in Africa, but in Latin America (e.g., Mexico, Venezuela, Columbia, and Brazil) (World Population Review 2019), and in 2019, the murder capital of the world was Tijuana, Mexico ("50 of the Most Dangerous Cities" 2019).

Furthermore, no single racial group has a monopoly on violence. All racial groups have violent histories, including Europeans/whites. Consider the vast numbers of Native Americans killed across the nation in the nineteenth century. This "racial genocide," as historian Donald Fixico described it, stemmed from America's appetite for territorial expansion. This push for new land and resources, wrote Flexico, "led the U.S. government to authorize over 1,500 wars, attacks and raids on Indians, the most of any country in the world against its indigenous people. By the close of the Indian Wars in the late nineteenth century, fewer than 238,000 indigenous people remained, a sharp decline from the estimated 5 million to 15 million living in North America when Columbus arrived in 1492" (Fixico 2019). Consider also the near complete massacre of nearly every single Aboriginal person in Tasmania, Australia, in the early 1800s (only 3 Tasmanian Aboriginals of about 5,000 survived the British invasion; see Diamond 1992); the multicentury torture and murder of enslaved Africans in the United States, Brazil, and the Caribbean; violent expulsions of people of color from cities and towns across the United States throughout the Jim Crow era (for more, see Q12); widespread massacres of people of color in the United States (for two of many examples, see the massacres of Chinese immigrants in the late 1800s and those of African Americans in the first part of the twentieth century; see Q12); the brutal murder of millions of Jews in Europe in the 1930s and 1940s; and the 100-year history of lynching of African Americans that continued well into the 1960s.

Social scientists argue that no racial group is inherently prone to violence; rather, broader sociocontextual factors underlie their violent acts. For instance, white Americans used lynching as a method of social control in the United States—in particular, to instill fear in African American communities and keep them subjugated postslavery. Throughout the nineteenth and twentieth centuries, whites beat, drowned, set on fire, dismembered, castrated, dragged by horse or car, and hanged by rope Black men and, at times, Black women and even Black adolescents. Sometimes they did so for serious offenses, such as alleged murder or rape, and other times for petty crimes (such as theft). Others were murdered for being "uppity" to a white person, associating with a white woman, or merely whistling at a white woman (the latter was the case for 14-year-old Emmett Till, who was brutally beaten and drowned by white men in Mississippi in 1955 for that very reason). Further, lynching often occurred outside the legal system, as white mobs circumvented the law altogether (as in the case of Till) with impunity. These violent acts committed by whites, both within and outside the United States, are not evidence of any inborn temperament unique to the racial group; rather, they can be explained by the social circumstances of the time and whites' desire to preserve their elevated position in the social hierarchy.

Identifying the social causes of violence among humans (across racial groups, nations, and time) may help researchers understand violent acts more broadly and help to explain the disproportionate rate of violent crime within some segments of the African American community today, particularly among the most impoverished. Attention should be given to violence in these communities while simultaneously avoiding disingenuous phrases such as "Black-on-Black" crime and lazy stereotypes linking Blackness to innate violent tendencies. Contemporary data on violent crime indicate that same-race crime is not unique to African Americans. Further, while some segments of the African American community do exhibit high rates of violent crime, ample historical evidence and a growing number of studies indicate that violence is no more inherent to Black Americans as it is to other racial groups.

FURTHER READING

Coccia, Mario. 2017. "A Theory of General Causes of Violent Crime: Homicides, Income Inequality and Deficiencies of the Heat Hypothesis and of the Model of CLASH." *Aggression and Violent Behavior* 37: 190–200.

Cox, Daniel, Juhem Navarro-Rivera, and Robert P. Jones. 2016. "Race, Religion, and Political Affiliation of Americans' Core Social Networks." Public Religion Research Institute, August 3. Retrieved on February 21, 2019, at https://www.prri.org/research/poll-race-religion -politics-americans-social-networks/.

Diamond, Jared. 1992. *The Third Chimpanzee: The Evolution and Future of the Human Animal.* New York: HarperCollins.

"50 of the Most Dangerous Cities in the World." 2019. *USA Today.* Retrieved on January 17, 2019, at https://www.usatoday.com/picture -gallery/travel/news/2019/07/24/most-dangerous-cities-world-tijuana -caracas-cape-town/1813211001/.

Fixico, Donald L. 2019. "When Native Americans Were Slaughtered in the Name of 'Civilization.'" History.com, August 16. https://www .history.com/news/native-americans-genocide-united-states.

Harrell, Erika, Lyn Langton, Marcus Berzofsky, Lance Couzens, and Hope Smiley-McDonald. 2014. "Household Poverty and Nonfatal Violent Victimization, 2008–2012." U.S. Department of Justice, Bureau of Justice Statistics, November.

Harriot, Michael. 2017. "Why We Never Talk about Black-on-Black Crime: An Answer to White America's Most Pressing Question." The Root, October 3. Retrieved on February 21, 2019, at https:// www.theroot.com/why-we-never-talk-about-black-on-black-crime-an -answer-1819092337.

Krivo, Lauren J., and Ruth D. Peterson. 1996. "Extremely Disadvantaged Neighborhoods and Urban Crime." *Social Forces* 75(2): 619–650.

Krivo, Lauren J., Ruth D. Peterson, and Danielle C. Kuhl. 2009. "Segregation, Racial Structure, and Neighborhood Violent Crime." *American Journal of Sociology* 114(6): 1765–1802.

Loewen, James W. 2018. *Sundown Towns: A Hidden Dimension of American Racism.* New York: The New Press.

Massey, Douglas S., and Jonathan Tannen. 2015. "A Research Note on Trends in Black Hypersegregation." *Demography* 52(3): 1025–1034.

Neiwert, David. 2017. "White Supremacists' Favorite Myths about Black Crime Rates Takes Another Hit from BJS Study." Southern Poverty Law Center, October 23. Retrieved on February 21, 2019, at https:// www.splcenter.org/hatewatch/2017/10/23/white-supremacists-favorite -myths-about-black-crime-rates-take-another-hit-bjs-study.

Peterson, Ruth D., and Lauren J. Krivo. 2010. *Divergent Social Worlds: Neighborhood Crime and the Racial-Spatial Divide.* New York: Russell Sage Foundation.

Roberts, Sam. 2012. "Segregation Curtailed in U.S. Cities, Study Finds." *New York Times*, January 30. Retrieved on February 21, 2019, at https://

www.nytimes.com/2012/01/31/us/Segregation-Curtailed-in-US-Cities
-Study-Finds.html.

Robertson, Campbell. 2015. "History of Lynchings in the South Documents Nearly 4,000 Names." *New York Times*, February 10.

Rodgers, Dennis, and Shivani Satija. 2012. "Violence, Crime and Poverty in Patna, Bihar." *Brooks World Poverty Institute*. Issue 13 (April).
Retrieved on November 26, 2020, at http://hummedia.manchester.ac
.uk/institutes/gdi/publications/worldpoverty/Issue_13_Rodgers_Satija
.pdf.

U.S. Department of Justice (DOJ) and Federal Bureau of Investigation
(FBI). 2010. "Crime in the United States." Retrieved on February 21,
2019, at https://ucr.fbi.gov/crime-in-the-u.s/.

Violence Policy Center. 2018. "More Than 1,800 Women Murdered by
Men in One Year, New Study Finds." September 18. Retrieved on
February 21, 2019, at http://vpc.org/press/more-than-1800-women
-murdered-by-men-in-one-year-new-study-finds/.

Williams, Timothy. 2012. "Higher Crime, Fewer Charges on Indian
Land." *New York Times*. Retrieved on February 25, 2019, at https://www
.nytimes.com/2012/02/21/us/on-indian-reservations-higher-crime-and
-fewer-prosecutions.html.

Woody, Christopher. 2019. "These Were the 50 Most Violent Cities in
the World in 2018." Business Insider, March 2. Retrieved on January
10, 2020, at https://www.businessinsider.com/most-violent-cities-in
-the-world-in-2018-2019-3.

World Population Review. 2019. "Most Violent Countries 2020."
Retrieved on January 10, 2020, at http://worldpopulationreview.com
/countries/most-violent-countries/.

Younge, Gary. 2014. "About 'Black-on-Black Crime.'" The Nation,
December 9. Retrieved on February 21, 2019, at https://www.thenation
.com/article/about-black-black-crime/.

Q23. IS THE AMERICAN MEDIA RACIALLY BIASED IN ITS COVERAGE OF CRIME?

Answer: Yes. Studies of American news media reveal racial bias. When
watching or reading the news, many people assume that what they see
or read regarding crime is merely a straightforward retelling of the day's
new stories, but the reality is far different. For one, studies have found
that news outlets more often report on Black crime than crime committed by white people. As a consequence, they tend to overrepresent Black

suspects relative to their actual numbers of arrest while underrepresenting white suspects; thus, Americans are given the false impression that crime is mostly a Black problem. Furthermore, news media depict crime suspects very differently depending on their race. Numerous media studies have found that white suspects are more often humanized in news coverage, while nonwhite suspects are more frequently presented in dehumanized and stereotypical ways.

The Facts: Crime reports in local and national news are racially biased and tend to (1) emphasize Black rather than white crime and (2) unevenly portray white and nonwhite suspects.

Racially Imbalanced Crime Reporting

Studies reveal a racial imbalance regarding how crime stories are covered. A 2014 analysis of late-night news in New York City, for instance, found that news outlets more often reported on murders, thefts, and assaults when perpetrators were Black rather than white (Ghandnoosh 2014; Sun 2018). According to New York City Police Department statistics for a four-month period in 2014, African Americans were suspects in 54 percent of murders, 55 percent of thefts, and 49 percent of assaults. News coverage during this time, however, presented them in 74 percent of murder stories, 84 percent of theft stories, and 73 percent of assault stories. Consequently, they overrepresented alleged Black offenders relative to their number of actual arrests—a pattern observed beyond New York. For example, a two-year analysis (January 2015–December 2016) examined more than 800 local and national crime stories on major television networks (e.g., ABC, CBS, NBC, CNN, Fox News, and MSNBC), newspapers of national influence (e.g., *Washington Post, Wall Street Journal, New York Times*, and *USA Today*), Christian online news sites (e.g., Christianity Today and Christian Post), conservative websites (e.g., One News Now), and regional newspapers (e.g., *Baltimore Sun, Denver Post* and *Tampa Tribune*). The study revealed that Black Americans comprised 26 percent of all arrests in that two-year period (according to data by the FBI) but accounted for 37 percent of suspects covered by those media outlets. By contrast, whites made up most arrests (77 percent) according to the FBI but received only 28 percent of news coverage (Jan 2017; Dixon 2017) (see figure 23.1). This unequal reporting presents a distorted image of crime and gives Americans a false impression that crime is primarily committed by Black people.

Further, studies show that news media tend to focus on stories that involve Black perpetrators and white victims, though most crime,

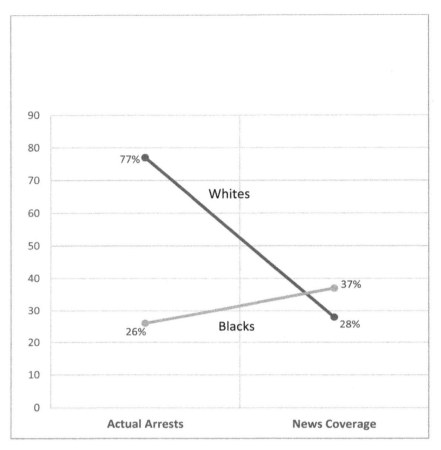

Figure 23.1. Actual Arrests vs. News Coverage, January 2015–December 2016.

(*Source*: This graph is constructed from data in Travis L. Dixon's "A Dangerous Distortion of Our Families." Color of Change and Family Story. Retrieved on May 3, 2020, at https://colorofchange.org/wp-content/uploads/2019/05/COC-FS-Families-Representation-Report_Full_121217.pdf.)

including violent crime, occurs *within* racial groups (i.e., Black-on-Black or white-on-white) (Ghandnoosh 2014; see also Q22). A 14-week analysis of crime news in Philadelphia conducted in 2014, for example, found that 42 percent of crimes reported on television involved whites who were victimized by Black perpetrators, though crime data during that period reveal that Black-on-white crime comprised only 10 percent of all crimes in the city during that time (Romer, Jamieson, and de

Coteau 1998; Ghandnoosh 2014). Researchers believe that this over-representation of whites as victims of Black crime likely contributes to anti-Black stereotypes and to white fears of victimization by Black Americans.

Uneven Depictions of White and Nonwhite Suspects

News media also depict white and nonwhite suspects in markedly different ways. Media reports are more likely to humanize white perpetrators while dehumanizing and stereotyping nonwhite perpetrators. For example, news media have considerable editorial discretion in using mugshots, which are photographs of suspects taken by police after an arrest. These photographs are not only typically unflattering, but they also carry with them an implied presumption of guilt.

Studies reveal that in reporting crime stories, newsrooms have historically broadcast the mugshots of Black suspects more frequently than those of white suspects (Sun 2018). A 2002 study of local news programming in Orlando, for example, found that ABC, CBS, and NBC affiliates aired mugshots for 42 percent of Black suspects as compared to just 22 percent of white suspects (Chiricos and Eschholz 2002).

The uneven use of mugshots in crime reporting is also illustrated in two crime stories reported by a single Iowa news outlet in 2015. Both were burglary reports, but one story involved three white men and the other four Black men. Though it was the same news station, the same crime, and even the same day, the Black suspects were pictured in their mugshots, and the white suspects (who also had mugshots) were presented in their well-groomed university yearbook photos, sporting suits and ties (Desmond-Harris 2015). Critics argue that the overuse of mugshots for people of color, especially for Black men, is dehumanizing and criminalizes alleged offenders before they have even been convicted of a crime. White suspects, on the other hand, benefit when news outlets opt not to display their less-than-flattering mugshots to the public.

Media also tend to humanize alleged white offenders in their news headlines and accompanying news report (Sun 2018)—even for those whose crimes are particularly abhorrent. When Brock Turner, a 19-year-old white college student, was arrested in 2015 for raping an unconscious woman behind a campus dumpster, reports repeatedly highlighted his Stanford swimming career, at times even publishing his swim times in the same stories that detailed his sexual assault. Some outlets also presented his smiling college photograph, not his disheveled mugshot, when providing visual content for the story.

Like Turner, other white perpetrators are similarly portrayed by the media in ways that personalize and humanize them. Reporter Sarah Ruiz-Grossman, for example, argued in 2017 that there was a "double standard" in how Stephen Paddock, a white man responsible for "the deadliest mass shooting in modern U.S. history" (he murdered nearly 60 people in a 2017 Las Vegas mass shooting), was portrayed by the media as compared to how they typically portray suspects who are Muslim or persons of color. She wrote, "As the news broke, major outlets across the country wrote headlines that humanized Paddock, pointing out that he was a country music fan, for example. They also portrayed his violent act as an anomaly, labeling him a 'lone wolf' who 'doesn't fit [the] mass shooter profile' rather than part of a systemic problem of violence by white men in this country. Past mass shooters who were nonwhite or Muslim have been depicted quite differently—and so have people of color who were *victims* of gun violence" (Ruiz-Grossman 2017). Regarding nonwhite victims of gun violence, for example, when Botham Jean, an unarmed African American man, was shot and killed in his own apartment by an off-duty white police officer (who allegedly mistook Jean's apartment for her own and presumed him to be an intruder), some media outlets reported on the marijuana that police purportedly found in his apartment after his death. University of Michigan professor Heather Thompson lambasted the media for its "blame the victim" approach. She pointed out: "There are many facts that one can report—we could have reported his religion, we could have reported how many times he was married. We could have reported on how many degrees he had" (Schladebeck 2018).Jean had been executed in his own living room while eating ice cream, though some news outlets still managed to focus on details unrelated to his death; their focus on marijuana, rather than the deadly actions of the officer, served to reify racial stereotypes about black men and criminality.

Additionally, white shooters are more likely than nonwhite shooters to be described in the media as mentally ill. A study of more than 400 news documents regarding nearly 220 mass shootings in the United States from 2013 to 2015, for instance, found that news media were nearly 20 times more likely to describe white shooters as mentally ill as compared to Black shooters. According to the study's authors, this sympathetic narrative diverts blame from white shooters by presenting them as unwitting victims of their mental illnesses (Duxbury, Frizzell, and Lindsay 2018). By contrast, Black shooters are far less likely to be described as mentally ill by news media and are instead more often characterized as inherently violent or simply labeled as "thugs," a racially pejorative word most often ascribed to young Black men. Muslim perpetrators of violent crime, regardless of race, are also rarely described as mentally ill in news reports but are typically stereotyped as "fanatics" and "terrorists," whose backstories and mental state are inconsequential and irrelevant (Ruiz-Grossman 2017; Sathish 2015). Given that there is no evidence to suggest that non-Muslim whites are more prone to mental illness than other groups, these divergent explanations are problematic.

An examination of news coverage of mass protests and riots further reveals racial bias. In response to public protest and riots over the death of Freddie Gray in 2015, ABC News invoked the word "thug" nearly 800 times in a single day (Greenwald and Jones 2016). Even President Obama called them "criminals and thugs who tore up the place," angering critics who argued that those who damaged property and looted stores were only a small fraction of Baltimore protesters (Jackson 2015). By contrast, white rioters are rarely, if ever, branded as "criminals" or "thugs"—even when white people engage in similar destructive and unlawful behavior. For example, when whites riot after professional sporting events (something not uncommon), the media never refers to them as "criminals" or "thugs"—even when they set fires, overturn cars, destroy property, and loot area businesses (to see firsthand how white rioters are portrayed in news stories, conduct an internet search of riots in Detroit in 1984 and 1990 after the city's professional sports teams won championships; riots in Denver in 1996, 1998, 1999, and 2001 after similar wins; riots in San Francisco when the Giants won in 2012, or riots in Huntington Beach following surf competitions in 1986 and 2013. There is no mention by media of "criminals," "thugs," or "thuggery.")

In 2011, students rioted in response to the ousting of football coach Joe Paterno at Penn State; he had been fired over allegations of child sexual abuse. The protesters, who were mostly white, were never referred to as "thugs" by media, even when they overturned a news van, clashed with police, and damaged school property to tune of nearly $200,000. And, in 2014, when crowds of white students and out-of-town visitors at the Keene State College Pumpkin Festival in New Hampshire rioted for no apparent reason and threw rocks and liquor bottles at officers, overturned and smashed cars, set multiple fires, destroyed public property, slashed tires, and broke into fistfights, they were never disparaged as inherently criminal or as "thugs" (Greenwald and Jones 2016); instead, they were characterized as "unruly" (CNN), as "rowdy" (*Boston Globe*), and as drunk "kids" (*New York Daily News*) who were merely "revelers" (*Los Angeles Times* and *TIME*) engaged in "revelry" (*New York Times*).

A poll conducted by the Pew Research Center in 2020, however, suggests some progress. Nearly 60 percent of Americans polled about the protests that took place across many American cities in the wake of the murder of George Floyd (including 72 percent of Black Americans) said that media coverage was "good" or "excellent" (Mitchell et al. 2020). University of Michigan researcher Michael T. Heaney, who studied media coverage of the protests, also noted that the coverage was "generally favorable," adding that this favorable reporting "has corresponded with shifts in white public opinion to support the Black Lives Matter movement and goals—in contrast to more critical white attitudes and news coverage from 2013 to 2016" (Heaney 2020).

Nonetheless, racially biased news reports that stereotype Americans of color remain the norm, which is perhaps unsurprising given that American mass media in the twenty-first century remains overwhelmingly white. In newsrooms across the nation, news executives, station managers and supervisors, producers, editors, and journalists are mostly white; together, they determine what stories are covered and how they are presented to American audiences. It would be naive to assume that their own racial biases, both explicit and implicit, have no influence on their reporting emphases or coverage priorities.

Understanding and challenging racial bias in news media is important because it has far-reaching implications for people of color. Studies show that biased crime reporting distorts people's perceptions of crime and who commits it. Because news media often provides the only information people have about crime (given that most will never experience it firsthand), it gives Americans the impression that crime is mostly a Black problem. Indeed, studies show that people tend to overestimate the proportion of crime committed by Black Americans. A 2002 study found that those surveyed (a racially diverse group of people) overestimated Black participation in crime by 11 percent (Ghandnoosh 2014). Though this overestimation is high, studies reveal that whites tend to overestimate Black crime at even higher rates. A 2010 survey, for example, asked white Americans to estimate the percentage of burglaries, illegal drug sales, and juvenile crime committed by Black Americans; they overestimated actual Black involvement in these crimes by about 20–30 percent (Ghandnoosh 2014).

As such, media bias reinforces stereotypes about people of color (e.g., they are inherently criminal and violent), increases fear and prejudice toward minorities (especially toward Black Americans and Muslims), and affects public opinions about policing and punishment. Regarding the latter, if Americans believe the falsehood that Black people commit most of the crimes in the United States, they are likely to support racially profiling Black drivers—on the assumption that they deserve closer scrutiny because "police will probably find something anyway" (see Q19 for more on racial profiling). They are also more likely to endorse heavy policing in Black communities and severe punishments for Black Americans who break the law—even for Black children who misbehave in school (see Q14 and Q18 for more on unequal punishment at school and implications for Black children). Even police, prosecutors, juries, judges, and policy makers are not immune to racial stereotypes disseminated by the media. This is perhaps apparent in the heavy-handed treatment of Blacks as compared to whites at all levels of the criminal justice system, including that of higher rates of police brutality, disproportionate arrests and incarceration, and lengthier prison sentences, even when both racial groups commit similar offenses (see Q19 for more on racial bias in the American criminal justice system).

FURTHER READING

Chiricos, Theodore, and Sarah Eschholz. 2002. "Race and Ethnic Typification in Crime and the Criminal Typification in Race and Ethnicity in Local Television News." *Journal of Research in Crime and Delinquency* 39(4): 400–420.

Desmond-Harris, Jenee. 2015. "These 2 Sets of Pictures Are Everything You Need to Know about Race, Crime, and Media Bias." Vox, April 1.

Dixon, Travis L. 2017. "A Dangerous Distortion of Our Families." Color of Change and Family Story. Retrieved on May 3, 2020, at https://colorofchange.org/wp-content/uploads/2019/05/COC-FS-Families-Representation-Report_Full_121217.pdf.

Duxbury, Scott W., Laura C. Frizzell, and Sade L. Lindsay. 2018. "Mental Illness, the Media, and the Moral Politics of Mass Violence: The Role of Race in Mass Shootings Coverage." *Journal of Research in Crime and Delinquency* 55(6): 766–797.

Ghandnoosh, Nazgol. 2014. "Race and Punishment: Racial Perceptions of Crime and Support for Punitive Policies." The Sentencing Project. Retrieved on May 3, 2020, at https://www.sentencingproject.org/wp-content/uploads/2015/11/Race-and-Punishment.pdf.

Greenwald, Robert, and Van Jones. 2016. "What Do You Call White Rioters? Anything but Thugs." HuffPost, June 16.

Heaney, Michael T. 2020. "The George Floyd Protests Generated More Media Coverage Than Any Protest in 50 Years." *Washington Post*, July 6.

Jackson, David. 2015. "Obama Stands by the Term 'Thugs,' White House Says." *USA Today*, April 29.

Jan, Tracy. 2017. "News Media Offers Consistently Warped Portrayals of Black Families, Study Finds." *Washington Post*, December 13.

Mitchell, Amy, Mark Jurkowitz, J. Baxter Oliphant, and Elisa Shearer. 2020. "Majority of Americans Say News Coverage of George Floyd Protests Has Been Good, Trump's Public Message Wrong." Pew Research Center, June 12.

Romer, Daniel, Kathleen H. Jamieson, and Nicole J. de Coteau. 1998. "The Treatment of Persons of Color in Local Television News." *Communication Research* 25(3): 286–305.

Ruiz-Grossman, Sarah. 2017. "The Double Standard in How the Media Is Portraying the Las Vegas Shooter." HuffPost, October 4.

Sathish, Madhuri. 2015. "Lafayette, Charleston, and the Hypocrisy of Only Humanizing White Shooters." Bustle, July 24.

Schladebeck, Jessica. 2018. "So What If Botham Jean Had 10.4 Grams of Marijuana in His Apartment?" New York Daily News, September 14. Retrieved on December 2, 2020, at https://www.nydailynews.com /news/ny-news-botham-jean-dallas-shooting-marijuana-irrelevant -20180914-story.html.

"South Caroline Student's Bomb Plot Foiled." 2008. CBS News, April 20. Retrieved on November 29, 2020, at https://www.cbsnews.com/news /south-carolina-students-bomb-plot-foiled/.

Sun, Elizabeth. 2018. "The Dangerous Racialization of Crime in US News Media." Center for American Progress, August 29. Retrieved on May 3, 2020, at https://www.americanprogress.org/issues/criminal-justice /news/2018/08/29/455313/dangerous-racialization-crime-u-s-news -media/.

5

◆⋅◆⋅◆

Social Policy

Social policies have generated, supported, and amplified racial inequality throughout American history. Some of the many examples of overtly discriminatory policies in the United States include the 250-year enslavement of people of African descent; the mass relocation of and systemic state-sponsored repression and violence against Native Americans in the nineteenth century; the forced repatriation of Mexican immigrants and American-born citizens of Mexican ancestry to Mexico; the incarceration of Japanese Americans (the majority of whom were U.S.-born American citizens) in internment camps during World War II; the segregation of African Americans in the first half of the twentieth century (in employment, schools, transportation, and public facilities); military policies that segregated ranks and limited opportunities for people of color; the disenfranchisement of Black voters and other people of color for most of American history; the forced sterilization of people of color (such as Native, Mexican, and Black Americans); zoning ordinances and restrictive covenants that limited housing options for people of color preventing them from accessing white communities; restrictive ordinances that banned African Americans (and sometimes other groups of color) from city/county/state limits; and the twentieth-century city-planning policies that ran highways through and destroyed Black communities and Black business districts in cities across the nation.

Even seemingly race-neutral public policies have excluded racial minorities, thereby disadvantaging them with far-reaching effects. For example, the Social Security Act of 1935, a national old-age pension system, excluded agricultural workers and domestic servants—occupations that were predominantly filled by African Americans. This provision alone excluded more than half of the African Americans in the labor force and over three-fifths of Black workers in the South from Social Security benefits. The Servicemen's Readjustment Act of 1944 (the G.I. Bill of Rights) was a generous benefit package for veterans that helped millions of Americans achieve upward socioeconomic mobility in the period after World War II. However, despite being the most comprehensive and racially inclusive public policy to that point in time, its benefits remained beyond the reach of most Black veterans because state and local government agencies were intent on maintaining Jim Crow segregation. The G.I. Bill widened an already vast racial gap during the period of postwar economic prosperity. As such, racial inequality in the United States was often perpetuated by design and through the administration of various social policies at the federal, state, and local levels. The long-term consequence has been that, even today, many of these social policies continue to benefit whites while disadvantaging people of color.

However, public policy can also play a critical role in the integration of racial minorities into society and aid in the alleviation of racial inequalities and disparities. Understanding the effects of past policies and practices that have systematically disadvantaged people of color is important for present-day efforts to create a racially just society.

This chapter considers key social policies in the United States and addresses some frequently asked questions—particularly in regard to immigration law, affirmative action policies, and social welfare programs. Americans often take pride in their immigrant history, and many proudly describe the United States as a "land of immigrants." Question 24, however, poses the question, "Has the United States always been open and welcoming to immigrants?" Question 25 asks, "Does affirmative action systematically disadvantage whites in employment and education?" Question 26 analyzes government data regarding welfare usage among Americans by race to consider, "Are most welfare recipients in America Black?" Finally, Question 27, "Do American Indians and Alaska Natives get college, health care, and housing for free?," investigates data regarding federal assistance for Native Americans.

Q24. HAS THE UNITED STATES ALWAYS BEEN OPEN AND WELCOMING TO IMMIGRANTS?

Answer: No. The United States is the leading immigrant-receiving country in the world and has a long history of incorporating newcomers from all corners of the globe into its social fabric. At the same time, however, the presence of new immigrants has almost always produced social anxiety, suspicion, and tension, which in turn has given rise to numerous legal restrictions on immigrant admissions. Once in the United States, immigrants—even legal ones—have frequently faced discrimination, exclusion, and native hostility.

Facts: The famous inscription on the Statue of Liberty offers the welcoming words: "Give me your tired, your poor, Your huddled masses yearning to breathe free." The phrase, from the poem "The New Colossus" (1883) by Jewish American author Emma Lazarus, arouses pride in many Americans for being part of a "nation of immigrants." In fact, immigrant heritage is considered by many to be an essential aspect of America's national identity. Popular representations of the United States as a "promised land" have lent credence to the belief that the country has been a haven in the world, openly welcoming all those that seek freedom, democracy, and opportunity.

The United States has a long history of accepting people from around the globe, which in turn has contributed to the nation's economic vitality and vibrant culture. Even so, fear and strong opposition to immigrants have also been part of the nation's history. American history has been marked at various times by immigration policies that were racially and ethnically selective and that repeatedly closed the nation's gates to newcomers. Although the United States proclaims itself an open society and declares that "all men are created equal," the nation aspired, for much of its history, to be white. The promise of democracy coexisted alongside slavery and deep and long-standing patterns of racial and ethnic exclusion (FitzGerald and Cook-Martín 2014; Gerstle 2015).

Historians have shown that early immigrants were essential to nation building in the United States. They were welcomed because of the need for labor for industrial growth and land settlement and development. Employers sought immigrants to fill labor shortages during periods of economic prosperity and industrial boom. However, when economic depression and tight labor markets reduced employment and suppressed wages, American-born whites began to see immigrants as competitors who were taking jobs from them. Anti-immigration sentiment began to take root in the form of *nativism*, which historian John Higham has defined as "intense opposition" to minority groups because of their "foreign (i.e., 'un-American') connection" (Higham 2008, 2). Nativism can be found in any society and is closely related to xenophobia (fear and resentment of foreigners). In the United States, nativism was initially religion based (expressed as anti-Catholicism and anti-Semitism), but as time passed, opposition to newcomers became racialized as well. Coupled with domestic economic conditions and shifts in foreign relations, nativism in the United States became a powerful force behind citizenship and anti-immigration legislation.

The Naturalization Act of 1790, the country's first citizenship law, gave every free European immigrant of "good moral character," regardless of nationality, language, religion, or gender, the opportunity to become a citizen of the United States after a residence of two years. These generous terms of civic membership made the United States a magnet for Europeans and established America's reputation as a nation of immigrants (Gerstle 2015). Nevertheless, the 1790 law reserved naturalization for whites alone; Native Americans, people of African descent, and Asians were barred from becoming U.S. citizens. Eighty years later, in the post–Civil War period, the Naturalization Act of 1870 allowed persons of African descent to become U.S. citizens, but citizenship remained out of reach for all other nonwhite persons. The racial restriction stipulated in the 1790 statute remained in force for more than 160 years, until the Immigration and Nationality Act of 1952 (also known as the McCarran-Walter Act) finally granted nonwhite immigrants—namely, Asians—eligibility for citizenship (FitzGerald and Cook-Martín 2014).

Historians trace the rise of America's first mass nativist movement to the Know-Nothing Party, which was originally a clandestine group that arose in the mid-nineteenth century. Growing to become one of the largest political parties of the time, the Know-Nothings were generally opposed to immigration, especially of Catholics. In the 1850s, the Know-Nothings and their one million members demanded legislative restrictions for incoming Irish and German Catholics, whom they portrayed as having an allegiance to the pope—a potential threat, they argued, to the nation. The Know-Nothings stirred up anti-Irish sentiment and sparked anti-Irish discrimination and vigilante attacks by Protestant gangs against Irish neighborhoods, Catholic schools, and Catholic churches. The group also organized politically to remove the children of Irish Catholic immigrants from parochial schools and to bar immigrants from holding public office and, in some cases, from voting (Gerstle 2015).

Southern and Eastern European Immigration

In the 1880s, immigrants from Southern and Eastern Europe, largely Italians and Jews, began to arrive in the United States. Between 1880 and 1920, more than 20 million immigrants arrived on American shores, making this new wave of immigration the largest the nation had ever experienced. The share of the foreign-born population peaked at an historic high, 14.8 percent, in 1890. Some American-born whites saw the influx as a "national crisis," and stereotypes of Eastern and Southern European newcomers as morally inferior, disease ridden, and crime-prone took hold in many parts of the country. Some native-born whites also typecast these immigrants as agents of anarchism, socialism, and violent radicalism, culminating in widespread discrimination and repression. For example, during the Haymarket Riot of 1886 in Chicago, eight people were killed in a labor protest that turned into a riot after a bomb was thrown at police. Because many of the rioters were immigrants (mostly Germans), the Haymarket Riot stimulated a national wave of xenophobia, and scores of foreign-born political activists and labor organizers were rounded up by the police in Chicago and elsewhere.

In the early twentieth century, the eugenics movement began to take root in the United States. Eugenic theory promoted the idea of racial superiority as hereditary and inspired the notion of ridding the nation of so-called "inferior" races—namely, anyone who was not Anglo-Saxon, French, or Scandinavian. Southern and Eastern Europeans were viewed as "inferior" and were characterized as possessing undesirable "genetic" traits—for example, low intelligence, mental disability, and an inclination to promiscuity, criminality, and pauperism. The view that racial mixing would be degenerative for Anglo-Saxon American people became predominant in the early twentieth century, lending support for legislation prohibiting intermarriage between Northwestern European whites and people of color.

Congress also sought to enact restrictions to reduce immigration from Southern and Eastern Europe from the end of the nineteenth century through the 1920s. In 1907, Congress authorized the establishment of a joint committee of inquiry called the Dillingham Commission. Chaired by Senator William Dillingham, the committee was composed of the country's foremost social scientists and political thinkers, most of whom advocated for immigration restriction. In 1911, the commission produced a 41-volume work, the Dillingham Commission Reports, based on an extensive quantitative and qualitative survey of the causes and consequences of immigration. Influenced by the eugenics movement, the commission sought to "scientifically" demonstrate that Eastern and Southern Europeans were not assimilating and were degrading the quality of American society. The analysis arrived at a definitive conclusion: immigration must be limited. Within a decade, almost all of their policy initiatives and recommendations were implemented into law, including literacy tests and a quota system based on nationality. The framing of immigration as a "problem," subject to federal solutions, stemmed directly from the commission's work (Benton-Cohen 2018; Zolberg 2006).

The Immigration Act of 1917 was, at the time, the most restrictive federal anti-immigration legislation ever enacted. Most notably, it created literacy requirements for the express purpose of excluding immigrants with little education from reaching American shores. The unstated intention of this provision was to reduce immigration from Eastern and Southern Europe, where the literacy rates were comparatively lower than for other parts of Europe. In 1924, the Immigration Act (Johnson-Reed Act) established numerical limits (quotas) on immigration based on the national and ethnic origins of those already in the United States (primarily Northwestern European) on the grounds that immigrants from those regions would better integrate into American culture. Together with the 1917 Act, the 1924 Act effectively ended mass immigration to the United States from most parts of the world, significantly reducing all immigration from Southern and Eastern Europe along with Asia. The 1924 law passed both houses of Congress with overwhelming margins, drawing votes from congressmen and senators from every region of the country. The legislation, which remained in effect until 1965, imposed a decidedly racial cast on American immigration policy (Gerstle 2015).

Asian Immigration

Congress instituted further measures to bar the entry of Asian immigrants. From the nation's earliest days, Asian immigrants faced intense nativism and hostility. These sentiments intensified when Chinese immigrants attracted by the gold rush began to arrive on the West Coast in the mid-nineteenth century. From that time, many white Americans viewed the Chinese, who were willing to work for lower wages than native-born workers, as economic competitors. As the public outcry against Chinese workers escalated, various discriminatory measures against Chinese immigrants were implemented; for example, they were often denied basic rights (such as the right to testify in court) and were forced to pay special taxes to work in mining.

White frustration with the post–Civil War economic recession, coupled with hostile views toward the Chinese, led to anti-Chinese aggression and violence, particularly in the West. Growing anti-Chinese sentiment eventually prompted Congress to pass the Chinese Exclusion Act of 1882—the first federal restriction imposed on the immigration of a particular racial group or nationality. The act prohibited the entry of Chinese immigrants over a period of 60 years, through 1943. Japanese immigrants, who followed the Chinese, met with similar resistance from native-born white Americans. In 1907, the federal government signed the Gentlemen's Agreement with the Japanese government to drastically limit immigration from Japan. A decade later, the previously mentioned Immigration Act of 1917 (also known as the Asiatic Barred Zone Act) banned entry from most of the Asia-Pacific region. An exception was made for Filipinos, who were classified as U.S. nationals under American colonial rule. Immigration from the Philippines, however, was restricted with the passage of the Tydings-McDuffie Act in 1934. As a result, the admission of Filipinos was limited to quotas of just 50 individuals per year.

The Johnson-Reed Act of 1924, as previously noted, was applied to Asian immigration as well, which meant a virtual halt of immigration from Asia. State and local laws complemented federal laws. For example, in the early part of the twentieth century, several western states passed alien land laws prohibiting any immigrant ineligible for citizenship from owning real estate. These land measures were mostly directed at Japanese immigrant farmers but also struck at East and South Asians generally, who, by the terms of the 1790 naturalization law, were ineligible for citizenship (Gerstle 2015). The policies and laws banning immigration from Asia, together with anti-Asian discriminatory laws, were tied to native views of Asians as the "Yellow Peril"—a race that was unassimilable, inferior to whites, and a threat to the living standards of the white American worker.

Mexican Immigration

Nationals of independent countries in the Western Hemisphere were exempt from quota restrictions due to U.S. foreign policy considerations. While some politicians supported quotas for Mexico and other Latin American countries, employers in railroads, mining, and agricultural and cattle interests in the Southwest opposed quotas on Mexican immigration. These employers needed immigrants to fill labor needs, especially in agriculture. Cheap manual labor was a boon to American employers, and Mexicans were welcome so long as they would provide labor and then return to their country of origin. As the Dillingham Commission reported in 1911, the Mexican was "less desirable as a citizen than as a laborer" (FitzGerald and Cook-Martín 2014, 13).

During economic downturns, however, Mexicans found themselves unwelcome, and they received hostile treatment from native-born Americans. For example, following the Great Depression, as joblessness among U.S. citizens soared, Mexican immigrants either voluntarily returned to Mexico or were pressured to leave by local residents in the Southwest.

Federal and local governments also used deportation and repatriation to forcibly remove an estimated 400,000 people of Mexican descent in the 1930s. Many were American citizens by virtue of birth on U.S. territory, and some had never set foot in Mexico. Regardless of their citizenship and legal status, these individuals were loaded on trains and buses and forced over the border. Some, like Ignacio Piña, recall the experience as hellish. In 2006, the then 81-year-old recalled that "plainclothes authorities came in with guns and told us to get out. . . . They didn't let us take anything," not even their birth certificates proving that they were U.S.-born citizens (Koch 2006). Piña and his family were jailed for 10 days and then sent by train to Mexico, where he spent 16 years before finally acquiring proof of his American birth and citizenship. According to *USA Today*, "If their tales seem incredible, a newspaper analysis of the history textbooks in most US middle and high schools may explain why: little has been written about the exodus, called 'The Repatriation'" (Koch 2006).

The mid-1950s saw another massive roundup of Mexican immigrants, mostly undocumented, called "Operation Wetback," which was launched by the Immigration and Naturalization Services (INS) in selected districts in California, Texas, and Arizona (Parrillo 2019; Zolberg 2006). In response to a widespread public outcry over growing undocumented immigration, the aim was to stem the flow of undocumented immigrant workers and to discourage the employers who hired such workers. The INS reported that the six-week operation netted 1.3 million departures (Zolberg 2006).

The Liberalization of Immigration Restrictions

During the 1960s, when the civil rights movement helped bring about momentous changes in American attitudes toward equal rights for people of all races and heritages, America's restrictive immigration policies finally underwent a significant shift. This shift, which was boosted by ethnic lobbying and changing geopolitics—including pressure from independent countries of Africa, Asia, and South America, along with Cold War security concerns—made the United States a more welcoming place for nonwhite immigrants than it had been for decades. Congress passed the Immigration and Nationality Act of 1965 (Hart-Celler Act), ending the race-based immigration restrictions that had been in place since 1924. The immigration bill, signed into law by President Lyndon B. Johnson, abolished the national origins quota system and made occupational skills and family ties with those already in the United States the criteria of admission. Johnson's speech at the signing of the bill acknowledged the 1924 national origins quota system as "un-American in the highest sense," a system that "violated the basic principle of American democracy" (LBJ Presidential Library n.d.).

The impact of the act was profound. Over the next 50 years, an immigration wave unprecedented in its global origins and racial diversity washed over the United States (figure 24.1). The numbers of immigrants increased substantially, from about 10 million in 1960 to nearly 45 million in 2018. Further, prior to the 1965 law, about three out of four immigrants to the United States were white; their share of the immigrating population dropped to about 11 percent in 2018. Those arriving from the Americas and Asia increased substantially post-1965 (as illustrated by data from 2018). By 2017, the foreign-born population constituted nearly 14 percent (43 million) of the American population (Pew Research Center 2015; Connor and Budiman 2019).

Hart-Celler, however, did not end immigration restrictions or make nativism a relic of the past. Public discourse remains filled with negative assertions regarding the effects of immigrants (both legal and undocumented) on the country. Some politicians, public intellectuals, and

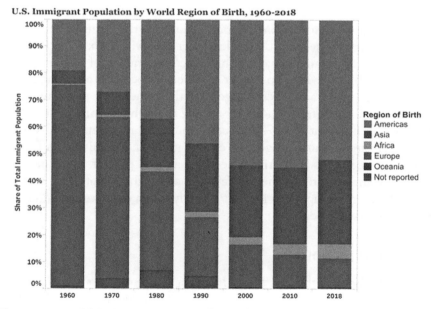

Figure 24.1. U.S. Immigrant Population by Region of Birth (in Percentages), 1960–2018.

(*Source*: Migration Policy Institute, https://www.migrationpolicy.org/programs /data-hub/charts/regions-immigrant-birth-1960-present)

opinion leaders, as well as many among the general public, express worries
about the impact that immigration and increased ethnoracial diversity
might pose to core beliefs and practices of the nation—worries that recall
those voiced in the late nineteenth and early twentieth centuries during
the influx of Southern and Eastern Europeans. Many expressions of public anxiety about America's increasing diversity reflect a long-standing
nationalist belief—namely that the United States is a white, Christian
nation (Gerstle 2015). Hence, nonwhite and non-Christian immigrants
are the primary targets of anti-immigrant sentiment today, including
Asians, Mexicans, and Muslims.

It should be noted, paradoxical though it may seem, that immigration restrictions have long coexisted with the popular narrative of the
United States as a "land of immigrants" and the home of liberal democracy. While many Americans take pride in their immigrant heritage, they
are starkly divided over new immigration to the United States. Donald
Trump, his administration, and his supporters increasingly embraced aus-
tere immigration measures during his presidency: for example, the travel
ban on seven Muslim countries (the first of its kind to ban a nationality since the 1882 Chinese Exclusion Act); various measures to restrict
legal immigration (e.g., granting of fewer visas and ending of temporary
legal immigrant status for Salvadorans residing in the United States); the
championing of a nearly 2,000-mile border wall with Mexico to shut out
undocumented immigrants; and the forced separation of children from
parents at the U.S.-Mexico border to deter undocumented immigration
from Latin America. Critics charge that these measures promote xenophobic, anti-immigration hostility among the public, while at the same
time being inherently "un-American" and contrary to national values.
Defenders argue that stronger law enforcement and immigration restrictions are necessary for national security and to protect the American
economy and culture. In the first few decades of the twenty-first century,
the debate on immigration has increasingly taken on a partisan and politically divisive tone.

FURTHER READING

Benton-Cohen, Katherine. 2018. *Inventing the Immigration Problem: The
  Dillingham Commission and Its Legacy.* Cambridge, MA, and London:
  Harvard University Press.
Connor, Phillip, and Abby Budiman. 2019. "Immigrant Share in U.S.
  Nears Record High but Remains below That of Many Other Coun-
  tries." FactTank: News in the Numbers. Pew Research Center, January
  30. Retrieved on October 30, 2020, at https://www.pewresearch.org

/fact-tank/2019/01/30/immigrant-share-in-u-s-nears-record-high-but
-remains-below-that-of-many-other-countries/.

FitzGerald, David Scott, and David Cook-Martín. 2014. *Culling the Masses: The Democratic Origins of Racist Immigration Policy in the Americas*. Cambridge, MA, and London: Harvard University Press.

Gerstle, Gary. 2015. "The Contradictory Character of American Nationality: A Historical Perspective." Pp. 33–58 in *Fear, Anxiety, and National Identity: Immigration and Belonging in North America and Western Europe*, edited by Nancy Foner and Patrick Simon. New York: Russell Sage.

Higham, John. 2008. *Strangers in the Land: Patterns of American Nativism 1860–1925*. Reprint, originally published in 1955. New Brunswick, NJ, and London: Rutgers University Press.

Koch, Wendy. 2006. "US Urged to Apologize for 1930s Deportations." *USA Today*, April 5.

LBJ Presidential Library. n.d. "LBJ on Immigration." Retrieved on October 30, 2020, at http://www.lbjlibrary.org/lyndon-baines-johnson /timeline/lbj-on-immigration.

Parrillo, Vincent N. 2019. *Strangers to These Shores: Race and Ethnic Relations in the United States*. 12th ed. New York: Pearson.

Pew Research Center. 2015. "Modern Immigration Wave Brings 59 Million to U.S., Driving Population Growth and Change through 2065." September 28. Retrieved on October 30, 2020, https://www.pewresearch.org/hispanic/2015/09/28/modern-immigration-wave-brings-59-million-to-u-s-driving-population-growth-and-change-through-2065/.

Quintero, Angelica. 2017. "America's Love-Hate Relationship with Immigrants." *Los Angeles Times*, August 2. Updated January 13, 2018. Retrieved on October 30, 2020, at https://www.latimes.com/projects/la -na-immigration-trends/.

Waters, Mary C., and Marisa Gerstein Pineau, eds. 2015. *The Integration of Immigrants into American Society*. Washington, DC: National Academies Press.

Zolberg, Aristide. 2006. *A Nation by Design: Immigration Policy in the Fashioning of America*. Cambridge, MA, and New York: Harvard University Press and Russell Sage.

Q25. DOES AFFIRMATIVE ACTION SYSTEMATICALLY DISADVANTAGE WHITES IN EMPLOYMENT AND EDUCATION?

Answer: No. The idea that affirmative action in employment and university admissions unfairly disadvantages qualified whites over unqualified minorities is false, though critics of race-conscious policies often use this argument to attack such programs. In fact, the use of quota systems and the hiring of unqualified candidates over more qualified ones are both prohibited by law. Research shows that affirmative action has increased the representation of Black and Hispanic Americans at universities and in workplaces that employ such policies, and it has reduced the representation of white males slightly. Nonetheless, present scholarship indicates that the United States remains racially stratified and unequal and that whites remain the most advantaged racial group when it comes to college admissions and the labor market.

The Facts: Affirmative action ranks among the most controversial social legislation from the latter half of the twentieth century in the United States. *Affirmative action* refers to policies designed to redress historical and present-day inequalities in American society. Its goal is to offer those who have been systematically disadvantaged increased opportunities in employment and education.

Both antidiscrimination laws and affirmative action aim to end discriminatory exclusion, but the logic and implementation of the two approaches differ. Antidiscrimination laws provide a mechanism for recompensing individuals victimized by discrimination and for changing the behavior of discriminatory organizations. Affirmative action policies, on the other hand, push organizations to act preemptively to identify and eliminate discriminatory barriers. In other words, whereas antidiscrimination laws offer redress to individuals after they have experienced discrimination, affirmative action aims to protect members of groups vulnerable to exclusion, thereby preventing systemic discrimination (Harper and Reskin 2005). Although affirmative action is often understood as a quota system in workplaces and schools, the use of explicit quotas (or "set asides") has been outlawed since 1978, when they were ruled unconstitutional by the U.S. Supreme Court.

Affirmative action policies were initiated to ensure nondiscrimination against African Americans in government employment. In 1941, President Franklin D. Roosevelt issued Executive Order 8802, which required defense contractors to pledge nondiscrimination in employment in government-funded projects, but it did not require them to implement affirmative action programs. Subsequent executive orders by virtually all presidents continued or expanded federal efforts to curb discrimination in employment and to increase minority employment opportunities among contractors and subcontractors that had business with the federal government.

The term "affirmative action" was first used in Executive Order 10925, which was issued by President John F. Kennedy in 1961. Kennedy's executive order mandated that federal contractors not only pledge nondiscrimination but take "affirmative action" to treat all qualified applicants and workers equally, without regard to race, creed, color, or national origin (Moore 2018; Katznelson 2005). In 1965, shortly after Congress passed the Civil Rights Act of 1964, President Lyndon B. Johnson issued Executive Order 11246 to ensure equal employment opportunities and nondiscrimination by federal contractors and subcontractors. Executive Order 11246 was amended in 1967 to include women.

Johnson's orders strengthened affirmative action obligations for federal contractors to act preemptively to identify and eliminate discriminatory barriers and to increase the employment of women and people of color. In the late 1970s, affirmative action requirements were extended to virtually all firms, educational institutions, and state and local governments receiving contracts or funds from the federal government. Today, Executive Order 11246, as amended and strengthened over the years, remains a key safeguard for workers employed by federal contractors, protecting them from discrimination on the basis of race, color, religion, sex, sexual orientation, gender identity, or national origin (Office of Federal Contract Compliance Programs n.d.).

While public policies of any scope and significance tend to attract avid supporters and opponents, affirmative action has been beset by controversy since its inception. Opponents of affirmative action contend that any deliberate recognition of race in decision-making is unfair and discriminatory and violates individual liberties protected by the U.S. Constitution. "Race preferences" are, in their view, reverse racism toward whites, particularly white males. On the other hand, proponents of affirmative action argue that race-conscious decision-making is necessary given the persistence of racial discrimination in American society and is essential for fostering racial integration. According to the latter perspective, affirmative action is essential to counteract the inequality entrenched in American society (Berry 2015; Katznelson 2005).

Defenders of affirmative action contend that the diversity achieved through race-sensitive policies has been shown to produce positive outcomes for both whites and nonwhites, thereby benefiting society at large. For example, some studies have found that diversity in schools results in positive learning outcomes, an increased ability to consider the perspectives of others, and the fostering of civic involvement for all students (Crosby, Iyer, and Sincharoen 2006). Other studies indicate that racial and gender diversity in the workplace is associated with better business performance by such tangible measures as increased sales revenue, greater market share, and greater relative profits in for-profit business organizations (Herring 2009).

Affirmative action in higher education has been subject to numerous legal challenges by white litigants. Plaintiffs typically argue that race-based preferences in public university admissions violate the equal protection clause of the Fourteenth Amendment and Title VI of the 1964 Civil Rights Act, which barred educational institutions receiving federal funding if they engaged in discriminatory practices. The U.S. Supreme Court first addressed this issue in a challenge to admissions at the University of California, Davis medical school brought by a white man (*Regents of the University of California v. Bakke*, 1978). The court ruled that a public school could not give categorical preference on the basis of race except to remedy past discrimination. The ruling also recognized that diversity was a "compelling state interest," signaling that states could consider race as a factor in university admissions. In other words, *Bakke* became the first case to uphold race-conscious admissions while outlawing racial quotas (Berry 2015; Harper and Reskin 2005).

Subsequently, the Supreme Court clarified its stance on affirmative action in cases brought against the University of Michigan in the late 1990s—the two most significant cases on affirmative admissions since 1978. In the case against Michigan's law school (*Grutter v. Bollinger*, 2003), the court reaffirmed *Bakke*, holding that diversity is a compelling state interest that warrants the explicit consideration of race by public educational institutions. In *Gratz v. Bollinger* (2003), however, the court struck down the University of Michigan's practice of automatically adding points to minority admission scores for those applying to the undergraduate college. However, the ruling indicated that universities could consider race to enhance diversity as part of the individualized assessments of each applicant (Berry 2015; Harper and Reskin 2005).

Since 2003, colleges and universities have continued to treat race as a "plus factor" when making selections among candidates for admission or scholarships; in other words, race is taken into consideration but is not the sole determining factor (Crosby, Iyer, and Sincharoen 2006). However, a handful of states—including California (1998), Florida (2001), and Michigan (2008)—have banned affirmative action in higher education. The majority of these bans were adopted by state constitutional amendments or by referenda (i.e., by popular vote). As a result, the percentage of Black and Hispanic students has dropped significantly in the top public universities in these states (Baker 2019; Harper and Reskin 2005; Menand 2020).

Has affirmative action worked? And has it diminished the opportunities of more qualified whites, as is often claimed by the opponents of affirmative action? Evaluation of the effects of affirmative action programs is as mixed as public debate on the subject. Research offers evidence that affirmative action does increase minority employment, college enrollments, and minority government contracts, with opportunities for white males decreasing slightly. A wide range of studies have demonstrated that affirmative action has shifted employment within the contractor sector from white males to minorities and women and that white applicants are replaced by minority candidates in college admissions. However, research findings also suggest that the magnitude of these shifts is not very large (Holzer and Neumark 2006). For example, studies of affirmative action in higher education generally show negligible effects on the admission prospects of white students (Charles et al. 2009). At elite universities, removing consideration of race would have a minimal effect on white applicants (Chung and Espenshade 2005). Historian Melvin Urofsky, author of *The Affirmative Action Puzzle* (2020), suggests it is difficult to have an accurate analysis of the impact of affirmative action on white men because there is little reliable data (Menand 2020).

In higher education, affirmative action has substantially increased the number of Black and Hispanic students at selective colleges and universities, while the share of white students—but not their numbers—has fallen (Crosby, Iyer, and Sincharoen 2006; Harper and Reskin 2005). In fact, an analysis of the racial and ethnic makeup of 100 highly selective schools by the *New York Times* (based on the data of the National Center for Educational Statistics) found that although Black and Hispanic students have gained ground at less selective colleges and universities, their representation at top institutions was lower in 2015 than in 1980. Between 1980 and 2015, white and Asian students continued to be overrepresented among freshmen at top colleges relative to the U.S. population, while Black and Hispanic students remained underrepresented (Ashkenas, Park, and Pearce 2017). White students are also more likely than Black, Hispanic, and Asian students to receive scholarships and still make up the overwhelming majority of scholarship recipients (Newkirk 2017).

Limited data regarding which employers practice affirmative action and what they specifically do to achieve this hampers accurate assessment of the impact of affirmative action on employment (Harper and Reskin 2005). In the private sector, only large companies with substantial government contracts are required by law to practice affirmative action. Yet many employers have voluntarily participated in affirmative action. Affirmative action has helped secure employment opportunities previously denied to white women and people of color and has improved their position in the labor market. It has also decreased levels of occupational segregation considerably; that is, uneven distribution of racial, ethnic, and gender groups across occupations has lessened, and workplaces have become more integrated. Further, despite criticism that affirmative action is detrimental to workplace efficiency, studies indicate that the increased presence of minority workers does not lower productivity or performance in organizations where affirmative action programs exist (Desmond and Emirbayer 2020; Harper and Reskin 2005; Holzer and Neumark 2006).

Affirmative action does not privilege unqualified minorities at the expense of qualified whites. It is illegal to hire an unqualified person over another who is more qualified or to hire a person who does not have the qualifications required for the job. As discussed above, the implementation of quotas in hiring and college admissions is also unlawful (Desmond and Emirbayer 2020). Although the Civil Rights Act prohibits hiring decisions based on a person's race or gender, covert discrimination against nonwhites continues to influence hiring and promotion decisions. Studies reveal that employers regularly pass over equally or better qualified candidates of color and hire whites (Sterba 2012). Whites are still more likely to be paid higher wages and evaluated more positively on the job compared to minority workers with the same qualifications. Accordingly, white Americans remain the most privileged racial group when it comes to employment, even when they are neither the most qualified candidate nor the most proficient employee. For specific examples of studies illustrating racial disparity in the American workplace, see Q15.

Evidence shows post-1965 affirmative action has done more to advance fair treatment across racial lines than any other public policy. Since the creation of equal opportunity and affirmative action programs, women and African Americans have seen greater employment opportunities in the economy as a whole, particularly in the public sector. The growth of the Black middle class in the second half of the twentieth century, for example, is attributed in part to increased opportunities afforded to Black students and workers through affirmative action programs. Without affirmative action, universities and workplaces in the United States would be far more segregated, and most white Americans would have far less contact with their fellow citizens of color.

Yet affirmative action continues to meet with challenges; its legality as policy is still being questioned, and the disputes surrounding it have grown more fractious. Since the 1980s, conservative politicians and the U.S. Supreme Court have shown growing reluctance toward the use of race-based remedies. In 2018, under the Trump administration, several guidance documents created by the Obama administration that encouraged affirmative action in school admissions were rescinded. Although this move does not have direct material impact (the decision regarding the legality of affirmative action resides in the courts rather than in administrative guidance), it nevertheless sent a clear signal of the Trump administration's negative stance toward affirmative action (Kamenetz 2018).

Anti–affirmative action sentiment has also gained traction among some Asian Americans. In 2014, Harvard University was sued for alleged discriminatory practices in the admissions process by Students for Fair Admissions, an anti–affirmative action group led by Edward Blum. Blum, a white conservative legal strategist, has been accused by his opponents of having strategized to obtain Asian American plaintiffs to dismantle affirmative action and civil rights protections benefiting people of color (Hinger 2018). The plaintiffs in this case argued that Harvard intentionally discriminates against Asian applicants by holding them to a higher standard than those for white, Black, and Hispanic American applicants. For instance, Asian American applicants are allegedly required to score 140 points higher on their SATs than their white counterparts to gain the same chance of admission (Lam 2017). Harvard rejected the statistical evidence presented by the plaintiffs; the University argued that it evaluates each applicant holistically, considering not only test scores but also nonnumerical factors (e.g., essays and recommendation letters), and that this means that those with the highest SAT scores are not necessarily admitted (Scott 2019). A federal judge ruled in 2019 that there was no evidence of explicit bias in Harvard's treatment of Asian applicants. In the decision, the federal judge stated that while Harvard's admissions program is "not perfect," it met the legal standard needed to ensure that it was not motivated by racial prejudice. It was also noted that "ensuring diversity at Harvard relies, in part, on race conscious admissions"(Hartocollis 2019, 2020; Kang 2019). Criticism toward affirmative action in the wake of the Harvard case typically centered on the "unfair benefits" given to students of color, in which Black and Latinx applicants were framed as "undeserving." Asian Americans, on the other hand, were seen as "victims" of race-conscious admissions. To be sure, data do show that Asian American applicants are held to a higher standard than their white counterparts (at least when it comes to standardized test scores), suggesting that some students of color, even those that outperform white students, remain comparatively and systemically disadvantaged in college admissions.

Supporters of affirmative action in higher education emphasize a number of structural factors that continue to systematically disadvantage applicants of color. Black, Latinx, and Native American students are more likely than white students to attend substandard schools that fail to prepare them for postsecondary education; many high-minority/high-poverty schools, due to inadequate funding, lack courses that are required by colleges and universities (e.g., fewer options for advanced placement [AP] courses) or extracurricular activities (see Q13 and Q14 on inequality in American schools). Studies reveal that standardized tests (such as the SAT or ACT) used for admissions decisions by most colleges and universities are biased toward middle-class white culture. Minority students from low-income families have limited access to high-priced preparatory courses and are disadvantaged by the high fees required for college applications. Impoverished students can apply for waivers, but not all will meet the criteria.

Though rarely discussed among critics of affirmative action, legacy programs give preference to children of alumni, who, at most colleges and universities, are white and have the most advantages to begin with. Data on legacy programs nationwide reveal that whites overwhelmingly benefit from such programs. Critics have termed such programs "affirmative action for whites." At Harvard, for example, one analysis found that between 2009 and 2015, legacy students were admitted at a rate of five times that of nonlegacy students (Larkin and Aina 2018). Proponents say that affirmative action policies remain necessary precisely because the admissions process in higher education continues to systematically advantage middle- and upper-class white applicants, while preventing low-income minority students from competing on an equal footing with white students.

FURTHER READING

Ashkenas, Jeremy, Haeyoun Park and Adam Pearce. 2017. "Even with Affirmative Action, Blacks and Hispanics Are More Underrepresented at Top Colleges Than 35 Years Ago." *New York Times*, August 24.
Baker, Dominique. 2019. "Why Might States Ban Affirmative Action?" Brown Center Chalkboard. Brookings, April 12. https://www.brookings.edu/blog/brown-center-chalkboard/2019/04/12/why-might-states-ban-affirmative-action/.
Berry, Ellen. 2015. *The Enigma of Diversity: The Language of Race and the Limits of Racial Justice*. Chicago and London: University of Chicago Press.
Charles, Camille Z., Mary J. Fischer, Margarita A. Mooney, and Douglas S. Massey. 2009. "Affirmative-Action Programs for Minority Students:

Right in Theory, Wrong in Practice." *Chronicle of Higher Education* 55(29): A29.

Chung, Chang Y., and Thomas J. Espenshade. 2005. "The Opportunity Cost of Admission Preferences at Elite Universities." *Social Science Quarterly* 86(2): 293–305. https://doi.org/10.1111/j.0038-4941.2005.00303.x.

Crosby, Faye J., Aarti Iyer, and Sirinda Sincharoen. 2006. "Understanding Affirmative Action." *Annual Review of Psychology* 57: 585–611. https://doi.org/10.1146/annurev.psych.57.102904.190029.

Desmond, Matthew, and Mustafa Emirbayer. 2020. *Race in America*. 2nd ed. New York and London: Norton.

Harper, Shannon, and Barbara Reskin. 2005. "Affirmative Action at School and on the Job." *Annual Review of Sociology* 31: 357–379. https://doi.org/10.1146/annurev.soc.31.041304.122155.

Hartocollis, Anemona. 2019. "Harvard Won a Key Affirmative Action Battle. But the War's Not Over." *New York Times*, October 2.

Hartocollis, Anemona. 2020. "The Affirmative Action Battle at Harvard Is Not Over." *New York Times*, February 2020.

Herring, Cedric. 2009. "Does Diversity Pay? Race, Gender, and the Business Case for Diversity." *American Sociological Review* 74(2): 208–224. https://doi.org/10.1177/000312240907400203.

Hinger, Sarah. 2018. "Meet Edward Blum, the Man Who Wants to Kill Affirmative Action in Higher Education." ACLU, October 18. Retrieved on June 25, 2020, at https://www.aclu.org/blog/racial-justice/affirmative-action/meet-edward-blum-man-who-wants-kill-affirmative-action-higher.

Holzer, Harry J., and David Neumark. 2006. "Affirmative Action: What Do We Know?" *Journal of Policy Analysis and Management* 25(2): 463–490. https://doi.org/10.1002/pam.20181.

Kamenetz, Anya. 2018. "Here's What's Going on with Affirmative Action and School Admissions." NPR, July 7. Retrieved on October 30, 2020, at https://www.npr.org/sections/ed/2018/07/07/626500660/everything-that-s-going-on-with-race-ethnicity-and-school-admissions-right-now.

Kang, Caspian. 2019. "Where Does Affirmative Action Leave Asian-Americans?" *New York Times Magazine*, August 28.

Katznelson, Ira. 2005. *When Affirmative Action Was White: An Untold History of Racial Inequality in Twentieth-Century America*. New York and London: Norton.

Lam, Andrew. 2017. "White Students' Unfair Advantage in Admissions." *New York Times*, January 30.

Larkin, Max, and Mayowa Aina. 2018. "Legacy Admissions Offer an Advantage—And Not Just at Schools Like Harvard." NPR, November 4.

Menand, Louis. 2020. "The Changing Meaning of Affirmative Action." *The New Yorker*, January 13.

Moore, Wendy Leo. 2018. "Maintaining Supremacy by Blocking Affirmative Action." *Contexts* 17(1): 54–59. https://doi.org/10.1177/1536504218766552.

Newkirk, Vann R. 2017. "The Myth of Reverse Racism." *The Atlantic*, August 5. https://www.theatlantic.com/education/archive/2017/08/myth-of-reverse-racism/535689/.

Office of Federal Contract Compliance Programs. n.d. "History of Executive Order 11246." U.S. Department of Labor. Retrieved on October 30, 2020, at https://www.dol.gov/agencies/ofccp/about/executive-order-11246-history.

Reskin, Barbara. 1998. *The Realities of Affirmative Action in Employment.* Washington, DC: American Sociological Association.

Scott, Jaschik. 2019. "Judge Upholds Harvard's Admission Policies." Inside Higher Ed, October 7. Retrieved on October 30, 2020, at https://www.insidehighered.com/admissions/article/2019/10/07/federal-judge-finds-harvards-policies-do-not-discriminate-against.

Sterba, James. 2012. "Race and Gender Discrimination: Contemporary Trends." Pp. 122–127 in *Rethinking the Color Line: Readings in Race and Ethnicity*, 5th ed., edited by Charles A. Gallagher. New York: McGraw Hill.

Q26. ARE MOST WELFARE RECIPIENTS IN AMERICA BLACK?

Answer: No. In fact, the majority of people who benefit from social welfare programs in the United States are white. White Americans participate in the highest numbers in most welfare programs as compared to all other racial groups—which is to be expected given that they currently make up the largest share of the American population of any single racial or ethnic group.

The Facts: The American welfare system consists of a broad range of "safety net" programs that offer food, education, job training, unemployment benefits, health care, workers' compensation, and housing assistance for low-income Americans at the federal, state, and local levels. Because these programs are funded by taxpayer money, welfare assistance is often front and center in political and public debates over government spending. Racial stereotypes often cloud these discussions, and a commonly held myth is that the majority of welfare recipients in the United States are Black.

Former president Ronald Reagan, for example, was able to politically capitalize on this racial myth in the late 1970s and early 1980s when speaking of welfare reform on the campaign trail and during his presidency. He spoke of Cadillac-driving "welfare queens" who brazenly defrauded the welfare system, drawing on the real-life story of Linda Taylor, who was convicted of welfare fraud in 1977. Taylor had Black and white ancestry, though for many Americans, she would come to symbolize Black people who defrauded the system. Journalist Bryce Covert wrote that because "the face of poverty in popular media had become black," Taylor came "to represent a group toward which white Americans were growing resentful. Without articulating explicit racial animus, Reagan conveyed a story that spoke to people's racist ideas about public benefits and lazy black people" (Covert 2019).

When criticizing the federal food stamp program, Reagan also repeatedly told the story of a "strapping young buck" brazenly buying T-bone steaks with food stamps while other hard-working Americans were patiently "waiting in line to buy hamburger." Through his choice of words, Reagan explicitly linked food stamps with Blackness—the term "buck" was widely understood to be an epithet historically used in the United States to specifically refer to physically imposing young Black men. He later toned down the racial language by changing "strapping young buck" to "some young fellow," though by then his description of African Americans bilking the welfare system was arguably already cemented in the minds of many Americans.

Welfare's association with Blackness in the public imagination persists today. A 2018 YouGov poll, for example, found that most Americans overestimated the numbers of Black Americans utilizing welfare programs (Delaney and Edwards-Levy 2018). And in 2017, a meeting with then President Donald Trump and the Congressional Black Caucus included an exchange in which one Caucus member reportedly told Trump that welfare reform would be detrimental to her constituents, adding that "not all of whom are Black." A seemingly surprised Trump responded, "Really? Then what are they?" (Sit 2018). Perhaps his question merely reflected his surprise that she had non-Black residents in her district, but his words may also reflect his assumption, and that of other Americans, that welfare recipients are, for the most part, Black.

In reality, white Americans participate in the highest numbers as compared to all other racial groups in both Medicaid (a health-care program for those with limited financial resources) and SNAP (Supplemental Nutrition Assistance Program, which provides assistance to buy food—previously called "food stamps"). In TANF (Temporary Assistance for Needy Families), which provides short-term cash to help families achieve self-sufficiency, Hispanic Americans show the highest participation, followed by Black and white Americans who participate in the program in near equal numbers. See figure 26.1 (a, b, and c) for a racial breakdown of recipients enrolled in each program.

Importantly, however, while whites benefit the most from the majority of social welfare programs (in raw numbers), African Americans benefit more so per capita. In other words, enrollment in welfare programs is overwhelmingly white because whites also constitute the largest share of the U.S. population (63.7 percent, according to the 2010 census). Conversely, African Americans made up approximately 13 percent of the U.S. population in 2010, but a considerably higher percentage of African Americans were enrolled in Medicaid (20 percent), SNAP (25 percent), and TANF (almost 29 percent) in 2018.

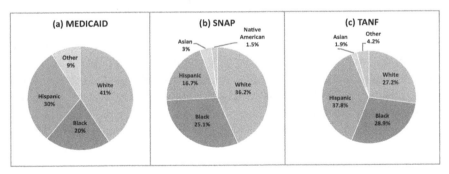

Figure 26.1 (a, b, c). Racial Breakdown of Recipients in Three Commonly Used American Welfare Programs in 2018.

(*Sources:* Medicaid (Henry J. Kaiser Family Foundation-KFF) https://www.kff.org /medicaid/state-indicator/distribution-by-raceethnicity-4/?currentTimeframe=0 &selectedDistributions=white--black--hispanic--other--total&sortModel=%7B %22colId%22:%22Location%22,%22sort%22:%22asc%22%7D; SNAP (United States Department of Agriculture-USDA) https://fns-prod.azureedge.net /sites/default/files/resource-files/Characteristics2018.pdf ; TANF (Department of Health and Human Services-HHS) https://www.acf.hhs.gov/sites/default/files/ofa /fy18_characteristics_web_508_2.pdf)

To explain this overrepresentation, it is important to recognize the relatively higher poverty rate of African Americans (as compared to whites) and the contributing factors to poverty: African Americans experience unequal educational opportunities nationwide relative to white Americans (see Q13 and Q14), persistent discrimination in employment (see Q15), and a wide wealth gap with white Americans. For instance, for every $100 in white family wealth, Black families hold a mere $5.04 (Badger 2017). For more on contributors to the significant disparity in wealth between Blacks and whites, see Q12 and Q17.

Beyond Black and white, *all* racial groups benefit from America's welfare programs. Native Americans, for example, are overrepresented in SNAP, which is not surprising given that they, too, experience high rates of poverty; their poverty rate is approximately twice that of the national average (in 2017, 28.3 percent of Native Americans lived in poverty as compared to 14.6 percent for the nation as a whole) (National Congress of American Indians n.d.). Hispanic Americans participate in SNAP on par with their representation in the U.S. population, though they are overrepresented in Medicaid and TANF (undocumented Hispanic immigrants are ineligible for these programs). Some Asian American groups also participate in social welfare programs in high numbers. Approximately 12 percent of Asian Americans live below the poverty level, and SNAP participation is particularly high among the Bhutanese (approximately 67 percent use SNAP), Burmese (44 percent), Hmong (32 percent), Cambodians (23 percent), Laotians (21 percent), Bangladeshis (15 percent), and Pakistanis (11 percent) (Tran 2018). Some of these Asian ethnic groups participate in SNAP at much higher rates than Black and Hispanic Americans.

Finally, studies show that insidious racial stereotypes regarding welfare (such as "welfare is for Black people") lessen white support for social welfare programs. Research by Stanford sociologist Robb Willer and Berkeley sociologist Rachel Wetts found that white Americans support welfare programs when they perceive themselves as beneficiaries, but they are willing to cut programs if they believe that Black Americans and other people of color primarily benefit (Wetts and Willer 2018). This is particularly important because the white majority has significant power to cut welfare programs given that they (1) make up the largest voting bloc and (2) are often in positions of power to make decisions about public policy, including policies regarding social welfare programs.

Wetts, in an interview with NPR in 2018, noted that "even though members of all racial groups are using [welfare] programs, white Americans tend to perceive them as mostly benefiting African-Americans.

So, there's a misconception of who the primary beneficiaries are of these programs" (Chow 2018). Ironically, however, as white support wanes for programs intended to aid the most vulnerable Americans, poor whites are the most likely to be affected when these programs are cut. For example, in 2018 and 2019, the Trump administration proposed new cuts to SNAP that would affect more than five million American families (Picchi 2019). Critics charged that the cuts would increase food insecurity for many Americans and, according to multiple analyses, would most likely hit poor white Americans the hardest (Rohrlich 2018; Van Dam 2018).

FURTHER READING

Badger, Emily. 2017. "Whites Have Huge Wealth Edge over Blacks (But Don't Know It.)" *New York Times*, September 18.

Chow, Kat. 2018. "Why More White Americans Are Opposing Government Welfare Programs." Code Switch. NPR, June 8.

Covert, Bryce. 2019. "The Myth of the Welfare Queen." *The New Republic*, July 2.

Delaney, Arthur, and Ariel Edwards-Levy. 2018. "Americans Are Mistaken about Who Gets Welfare." HuffPost, February 5.

Haney Lopez, Ian. 2014. *Dog Whistle Politics: How Coded Racial Appeals Have Reinvented Racism & Wrecked the Middle Class.* Oxford, UK: Oxford University Press.

National Congress of American Indians. n.d. "Demographics." Retrieved on November 30, 2020, at https://www.ncai.org/about-tribes /demographics.

Picchi, Aimee. 2019. "Food Stamps Could Hit Up to 5.3 Million Households." CBS News, December 10.

Rohrlich, Justin. 2018. "Trump's Food Stamp Cut Will Hit His Single, White, Male Base the Hardest." Quartz, December 21.

Sit, Ryan. 2018. "Trump Thinks Only Black People Are on Welfare, but Really, White Americans Receive the Most Benefits." *Newsweek*, January 12.

Tran, Victoria. 2018. "Asian Americans Are Falling through the Cracks in Data Representation and Social Services." Urban Institute, June 19. Retrieved on January 31, 2020, at https://www.urban.org/urban-wire /asian-americans-are-falling-through-cracks-data-representation-and -social-services.

Van Dam, Andrew. 2018. "Trump's GOP Is Looking to Deeply Cut Food Stamps—Hitting His Voters Hard." *Washington Post*, June 25.

Wetts, Rachel, and Rob Willer. 2018. "Privilege on the Precipice: Perceived Racial Status Threats Lead White Americans to Oppose Welfare Programs." *Social Forces* 97(2): 793–822.

Q27. DO AMERICAN INDIANS AND ALASKA NATIVES GET COLLEGE, HEALTH CARE, AND HOUSING FOR FREE?

Answer: Yes and no. A commonly held misconception of American Indians and Alaska Natives by non-Native people is that they receive free college tuition, health care, housing, and other "freebies" from the U.S. government. In reality, although they receive some benefits as agreed upon through prior treaties with the U.S. government, most treaty obligations are "unmet and almost always underfunded" (Partnership with Native Americans n.d.). Consequently, the image that some non-Native Americans have of Native peoples awash in "free stuff" does not match with their lived reality.

The Facts: This section examines common stereotypes and misconceptions surrounding so-called freebies, such as free college, health care, and housing for Native Americans.

College Tuition Is Not Automatically Free

The Bureau of Indian Education (BIE), a branch of the U.S. Department of Interior, oversees more than 180 primary and secondary schools across the nation, in addition to two postsecondary schools (Haskell Indian Nations University in Kansas and Southwestern Indian Polytechnic Institute in New Mexico). The BIE also provides support to 24 tribal colleges and universities across the nation, which collectively serve over 25,000 students. Though these colleges and universities are intended for Indigenous students, tuition is not free.

The BIE does provide some financial assistance to American Indian and Alaska Native college students to attend these and other schools via scholarships, though Native students must compete for them, and in many cases, scholarships are based on financial need. In other cases, students may receive some aid from their affiliated tribes (i.e., tribal scholarships)—though aid varies widely from tribe to tribe. A handful of states also provide tuition waivers or tuition reductions (usually in the form of in-state tuition) for Native American students. However, many of these state programs have firm stipulations for eligibility; for example, students must be enrolled in a federally recognized tribe, possess one-fourth or more proven Native American or Alaska Native ancestry, live in a specific state, or belong to a particular tribe. More specifically, some colleges and universities have tuition-free or reduced tuition programs for Native American students, though these schools are the exception rather than the rule, and students must still compete for admission. As such, there are available scholarships and programs that American Indian and Alaskan Native students can apply to and compete for, though the vast majority do not receive a "free ride" to college (for more information, see Meier 2018).

Health Care Is "Free" but Limited

The Indian Health Service (IHS), an agency within the U.S. Department of Health and Human Services, does provide health care for "federally recognized American Indian and Alaska Natives in the United States" (see https://www.ihs.gov/). According to the IHS website, "The provision of health services to members of federally-recognized tribes grew out of the special government-to-government relationship between the federal government and Indian tribes. This relationship, established in 1787, is based on Article I, Section 8 of the Constitution, and has been given form and substance by numerous treaties, laws, Supreme Court decisions, and Executive Orders. The IHS is the principal federal health care provider and health advocate for Indian people" (see https://www.ihs.gov /aboutihs/).

In a nutshell, Native Americans ceded most of their land to the U.S. government in previous treaties, and in return, the federal government promised health care to Native Americans. However, the IHS is not free insurance. Rather, the IHS is a collection of hospitals and clinics where Native Americans can receive care—much like the U.S. Department of Veterans Affairs (VA) provides for military veterans, though the IHS is much smaller. Funding is uneven, and, as a consequence, access to services can vary widely from one location to another (Artiga, Arguello, and Duckett 2013). Moreover, obtaining health care outside the IHS is difficult because of the high rates of poverty and low rates of insurance among Native Americans. Though the IHS is supposed to pay for care in the private sector when services are unavailable at IHS facilities, many Native Americans find their efforts to secure needed medical care denied because of lack of funding (Whitney 2017).

In addition, accessing IHS care is difficult for many. IHS services are limited to "members of and descendants of members of federally recognized tribes that live on or near federal reservations" (Artiga, Arguello, and Duckett 2013). Consequently, a significant portion of those who identify as Native Americans are excluded, including those who belong to state-recognized tribes (but not federally-recognized tribes), those currently without official tribal membership, and those who live far from reservations (only about 22 percent of Native Americans live on reservations or land trusts, and more than half of all Native Americans live in urban areas) (Artiga, Arguello, and Duckett 2013; Friedman 2016). As such, less than half of all American Indians and Alaska Natives actually have IHS health care—approximately 2.56 million of the nation's 5.2 million American Indians and Alaska Natives (Indian Health Service 2019).

Even those that live on or near reservations who are eligible for IHS health-care benefits can struggle to access care because facilities can be difficult to reach. A 2016 NPR story chronicled one family living on the Cheyenne River Indian Reservation in South Dakota. Because there are no facilities near their home or even in their town, family members had to wait two hours for the arrival of an ambulance. For others, distance even prevents them from accessing routine medical checkups, which are essential for preventative care. In Alaska, many reservations are located in remote areas and are only accessible by plane or boat (Dovey 2016). For Native peoples living in isolated, rural areas (in Alaska, but also in the continental United States), seeing a doctor can be challenging, costly, and time consuming.

Finally, Congress chronically underfunds the IHS. This is particularly problematic because Native Americans often live in poverty and, as a consequence, have "more serious health problems than the general public, including higher rates of diabetes, liver disease and unintentional injuries" (Friedman 2016). In 2016, for example, the entire IHS budget was $4.8 million—about $1,297 per person. Compare that to nearly $7,000 per inmate in the federal prison system (Whitney 2017). Poor funding has resulted in problems in such areas as understaffing, reliance on health-care providers without proper credentials, long wait times, and a shortage of medical equipment and facilities. These issues have contributed to what some eyewitnesses have described as "horrifying" and "unacceptable" conditions in IHS facilities (Dovey 2016). For example, services that most Americans expect to see in hospitals, such as emergency rooms and MRI machines, are entirely absent in some IHS facilities (Friedman 2016).

The effects of a grossly underfunded IHS can be observed in the high rates of COVID-19 among Native Americans in 2020. The virus ravaged Native communities and spread like wildfire across many reservations; in May 2020, the Navajo Nation had infection rates higher than any U.S. state (Warren and Haaland 2020). According to the Centers for Disease Control and Prevention (CDC), Native communities are especially vulnerable to epidemics due to high rates of poverty and related problems, such as overcrowded housing, lack of access to running water (handwashing is essential to slow the spread of the virus), and chronic health conditions. Importantly, limited medical resources have further exacerbated the problem. According to the National Indian Health Board, only about half of tribes reported they received COVID-19 information from federal or state governments or desperately needed supplies, such as testing kits necessary to identify, trace, and ultimately contain the virus (Bawden and Civic Nation 2020).

Collectively, critics say that these problems further exacerbate Native American disparities in health compared to the general American population, including comparatively high mortality and low life expectancy. On average, the life expectancy of Native Americans is 5.5 years lower than the national average (Indian Health Service 2019), and in some states, their life expectancy is a stunning 20 years shorter (Whitney 2017). Limited access to and availability of adequate medical care partially explain these staggering statistics.

Housing Is Not Free

Finally, though many non-Native Americans believe that Native Americans receive free housing on reservations, this is also a myth. First, the federal government, not Native Americans, own most reservation land in the United States, holding it "in trust" for Native Americans. For this reason, Native families rarely own their land or even their homes on reservations, which means that they cannot build equity or mortgage their assets for loans as do other Americans—which keeps them impoverished. Second, the Bureau of Indian Affairs (BIA) and the U.S. Department of Housing and Urban Development (HUD) sometimes assist Native Americans with housing, but the homes are not free. In fact, many Native American families on reservations live in government-built housing and make rental payments to the U.S. government. Others live in trailers or makeshift homes in what is often described as "third world" conditions. For example, 40 percent of housing on reservations is considered "substandard" as compared to 6 percent nationwide (National Congress of

American Indians n.d.), meaning they are in need of substantial repair or without basic indoor plumbing, electricity, or phone service. The rate of homelessness on Native American reservations is also higher than the national average, though the numbers are difficult to gauge because those without housing more often "go from one family member's home to another" rather than live on the streets (Biess 2017). This practice has the ripple effect of worsening the problem of crowding in Native American households. In fact, it has been estimated that nearly one-third of homes on reservations are overcrowded (National Congress of American Indians n.d.).

In sum, college tuition is not free, health care is limited, and housing assistance is deeply flawed. Further, Native Americans are often stereotyped as rich due to the profits that tribes make from casinos. A 1988 law allowed federally recognized tribes to legally operate casinos, though eligible tribes constitute only 573 of the more than 1,000 tribes in the United States. Of the 573 tribes, only 242 operated casinos as of 2014, and fewer than 15 percent of those ran thriving casinos (Partnership with Native Americans. n.d.). In fact, the vast majority of Native Americans do not benefit from casino revenues but live in poverty. One in four Native Americans live below the federal poverty line, and Native Americans

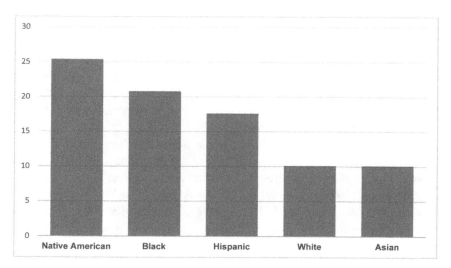

Figure 27.1. United States Poverty Rate by Race in 2018 (in Percentages).

(*Source*: https://www.povertyusa.org/facts)

have the highest poverty rate of any racial group in the nation (see figure 27.1 for a comparison of poverty rates by race in 2018).

Many Native Americans live in desperate conditions, and in some parts of the country, the situation for Indigenous people is especially dire. The Pine Ridge Indian Reservation in South Dakota, for example, is home to nearly 20,000 people and is the poorest county in the country. Ninety-seven percent of the population in Pine Ridge lives below the poverty line. The high poverty rate is related to the lack of commercial infrastructure on or near the reservation and the subsequent high unemployment rate (about 90 percent). Approximately 17 people live in each family home (in homes that generally only have two to three bedrooms). About a third of the homes on the reservation have no electricity, water, or a sewage system (Friends of Pine Ridge Reservation n.d.). In stark contrast to the myth that Native Americans profit from endless "free stuff" and "special benefits" from the federal government, their lived reality is much different.

FURTHER READING

Artiga, Samantha, Rachel Arguello, and Philethea Duckett. 2013. "Health Coverage and Care for American Indians and Alaska Natives." KFF, October 7. Retrieved on February 18, 2020, at https://www.kff.org/disparities-policy/issue-brief/health-coverage-and-care-for-american-indians-and-alaska-natives/.

Bawden, Mercedes, and Civic Nation. 2020. "COVID-19's Threat to Native Communities." *Forbes*, May 19.

Biess, Jennifer. 2017. "Homelessness in Indian Country Is a Hidden, but Critical, Problem." Urban Institute, April 10. Retrieved on February 18, 2020, at https://www.urban.org/urban-wire/homelessness-indian-country-hidden-critical-problem.

Dake, Lauren. 2017. "The Quiet Crisis: Mass Eviction Shows Toll of Homelessness on Native Americans." *The Guardian*, June 12.

Dovey, Dana. 2016. "Healthcare on Native American Reservations Is 'Horrifying': In the U.S., Who You Are Affects How You Are Treated." Medical Daily, February 5. Retrieved on February 18, 2020, at https://www.medicaldaily.com/native-american-reservations-healthcare-terrible-372442.

Friedman, Misha. 2016. "For Native Americans, Health Care Is a Long, Hard Road Away." NPR, April 13.

Friends of Pine Ridge Reservation. n.d. "Statistics about Pine Ridge Reservation." Retrieved on February 18, 2020, at https://friendsof

pineridgereservation.org/about-pine-ridge-reservation-and-foprr /statistics-about-pine-ridge-reservation/.

Indian Health Service. 2019. "Disparities." Retrieved on February 18, 2020, at https://www.ihs.gov/newsroom/factsheets/disparities/.

Meier, Kelly S. 2018. "Tuition-Free College for Native Americans." The Classroom. Retrieved on February 18, 2020, at https://www.theclass room.com/tuition-free-college-for-native-americans-13609768.html.

National Congress of American Indians. n.d. "Housing & Infrastructure." http://www.ncai.org/policy-issues/economic-development-commerce /housing-infrastructure.

Partnership with Native Americans. n.d. "5 Native American Funding Facts." Retrieved on February 18, 2020, at http://www.nativepartner ship.org/site/DocServer/PWNA_Reservation_Funding_Facts.pdf?doc ID=5861.

Warren, Elizabeth, and Deb Haaland. 2020. "The Federal Government Fiddles as Covid-19 Ravages Native Americans." *Washington Post*, May 26.

Whitney, Eric. 2017. "Native Americans Feel Invisible in the U.S. Health Care System." NPR, December 12.

6

❖❖❖

Immigration

In February 2017, a 52-year-old white navy veteran fired multiple shots in a Kansas bar, killing one patron and wounding two others. Two of the victims, Srinivas Kuchibhotla and Alok Madasani, were Indian-born immigrants who worked as engineers at the same technology company. The assailant had approached the men and aggressively interrogated them about their immigration status: "Where are you from?" "How did you get into this country?" "Are you here legally?" When patrons complained about the harassment, he was escorted out of the establishment. He later returned to the bar with a handgun, however, and fired at the two Indian friends at least eight times at close range. Kuchibhotla was fatally shot, and Madasani and another bar patron, Ian Grillot, who tried to stop the shooter, were wounded. Witnesses recalled the gunman yelling, "Get out of my country!" before opening fire.

Two and a half years later, in August 2019, a 21-year-old white man walked into a crowded Walmart Superstore in El Paso, Texas, with a semiautomatic rifle and attempted to shoot as many Latinx people as possible. Before surrendering to police, he killed 23 people and injured 23 more. The gunman admitted that he purposely targeted Mexicans, and police discovered that, just prior to the killing, he had posted an online anti-immigrant manifesto declaring, "This attack is a response to the Hispanic invasion of Texas." The mass shooting has been described in the media as the deadliest anti-Latinx attack in modern U.S. history.

Such terrorizing explosions of violence are rare, but every such incident is devastating to the victims, their families, and their communities. They are chilling reminders to Americans of the resentment, suspicion, and anger that some people feel toward those who look "different" or "un-American." This hostility, particularly toward people of color, has been cited as an important factor in the increasingly staunch opposition to immigration—whether legal or undocumented—in twenty-first-century America. While some of the opposition is specifically related to broader prejudices against nonwhite immigrants and a perceived threat to "white America," other calls to curb undocumented immigration have focused on more general concerns regarding the impact of undocumented immigrants (e.g., they may drain social services, bring in crime) and the fact that undocumented entry into the United States is a violation of federal law. Immigration advocates, on the other hand, often express support for legal and undocumented immigrants on humanitarian grounds, emphasizing their belief that immigrants are and have always been a net benefit to American society.

The impassioned public debate regarding immigration in the United States suggests deeper concerns about the ways in which mass migration is reshaping society and culture. Many wonder what sort of Americans recent immigrants will become. Large numbers of Americans regard immigrants as a source of strength and vitality for the country. But even some of those who believe that immigration has a generally positive or benign impact on American society express concern that today's largely nonwhite immigrants may not assimilate to American society or that they may disadvantage native-born Americans in terms of employment. As the influx of immigrants continues to rapidly transform American society, immigration has become a crucial sociopolitical issue and will likely remain so throughout the twenty-first century.

This chapter addresses several salient themes regarding immigration to the United States. Question 28, "Are immigrants more likely to commit crime than native-born Americans?," reviews the large body of research in criminology and sociology on the issue. Question 29, "Are most undocumented immigrants from Mexico?," examines available data on the trends of undocumented immigration and discusses the dramatic change in the composition of this population from the last few decades of the twentieth century to the present. Question 30, "Are immigrants today assimilating into American society as did earlier waves?," considers whether the claim that today's immigrants from non-European countries resist assimilation is valid in light of current research. Some Americans also believe that immigrants unfairly benefit from welfare programs, take jobs from native-born

Americans, and lower wages for everyone. The last two questions in the chapter address these beliefs: "Do undocumented immigrants drain America's welfare system?" (Question 31), and "Do immigrants take jobs away from or lower the wages of native-born Americans?" (Question 32).

Q28. ARE IMMIGRANTS MORE LIKELY TO COMMIT CRIME THAN NATIVE-BORN AMERICANS?

Answer: No. Research and empirical evidence, both past and present, offer little support for the claim that immigrants are more likely to commit crime than native-born Americans. On the contrary, a growing body of evidence reveals that immigrants are less likely to commit crime than native-born Americans and that high rates of immigration are generally associated with lower rates of crime.

The Facts: In 2015, in a speech announcing his presidential candidacy, Donald Trump promised to seal the U.S. southern border with "a great wall," claiming, "When Mexico sends its people, they're not sending their best. . . . They're sending people that have lots of problems. . . . They're bringing drugs. They're bringing crime. They're rapists." He attempted to temper his remarks with, "And some, I assume, are good people," though his preceding words explicitly linked Mexican immigrants, particularly those who cross the border without papers, with crime (see Trump 2015 for a full transcript).

The perception that the foreign-born and *illegal aliens* in particular (the latter is a term used for immigrants without legal status—also called *undocumented* or *unauthorized* immigrants) are more prone to criminality is deeply rooted in American public opinion. Such beliefs have been used to justify support from conservative media and lawmakers for measures to reduce immigration—both undocumented and legal. Prejudice against immigrants is long-standing and dates to the late nineteenth and early twentieth centuries, when the criminal stereotype was attached to immigrants from Ireland and from Southern and Eastern Europe (see Q24). Generally poor, their neighborhoods were stigmatized as disorganized and disorderly, which, many theorized, led to higher crime rates. Studies have challenged these stereotypes and have shown that, in fact, early immigrants were less likely to be arrested or convicted of crimes than their native-born counterparts (Wadsworth 2010; Waters and Pineau 2015).

Although purported links between immigration and crime have been at the forefront of criminological inquiry since the early twentieth century, the issue has taken on added significance since the 1990s, when the United States began to experience the largest wave of immigration in its history—in both absolute and relative terms (Light and Miller 2018). Today, immigrant crime stereotypes raised by politicians and the media are frequently used by opponents of immigration to characterize many immigrants of color, particularly those from Mexico and Central and South America, as prone to criminality.

As with earlier waves of immigration, accusations that recent immigrants are more likely to engage in criminal behavior have been largely contradicted by empirical evidence. Contemporary scholars have attempted to answer two key questions: (1) are immigrants more likely to commit crime than the native born, and (2) do immigrants affect the overall crime rate in the United States? Although findings have been mixed, the bulk of research to date reveals that immigrants are less likely to engage in criminal behavior than native-born Americans and that higher immigration is associated with lower crime rates (Rumbaut 2009; Rumbaut and Ewing 2007; Waters and Pineau 2015). Studies also show that immigrants are less likely than the native born to be repeat offenders among high-risk adolescents. Immigrant youth who were students in U.S. middle and high schools in the mid-1990s have among the lowest delinquency rates of all young Americans (Ewing, Martínez, and Rumbaut 2015). However, evidence also suggests that the lower propensity of immigrants to commit crime does not carry over to their offspring. The U.S.-born children of immigrants, called the *second generation*, appear to engage in criminal behavior at rates similar to those of other native-born Americans—a trend scholars have termed the *assimilation paradox* (Orrenius and Zavodny 2019; Ousey and Kubrin 2018; Rumbaut and Ewing 2007).

Criminal justice statistics (typically drawing on the FBI's Uniform Crime Reports [UCR] and the Bureau of Justice's National Crime Victimization Survey [NCVS]) reveal a general decline in reported violent and property crime in the United States since the 1980s. This drop coincided with a period when both legal and illegal immigration were surpassing historic highs. In the final decades of the twentieth century, crime rates declined nationally as well as in cities and regions of high immigrant concentration, for example, in major metropolitan areas such as Los Angeles, New York, Chicago, and Miami, and in border cities such as San Diego and El Paso (Rumbaut and Ewing 2007).

In fact, an increase in immigration appears to reduce crime (Adelman et al. 2017; Ewing, Martínez, and Rumbaut 2015; Sampson 2008). A study of 180 Chicago neighborhoods from 1995 to 2004 revealed that areas with high immigration tended to experience reductions in crime rates (Sampson 2008). Another study—examining longitudinal trends for 200 metropolitan areas that experienced rapid increases in immigrants (1970–2010)—found reduced violent and property crimes (Adelman et al. 2017). Immigrant presence also appears to benefit native-born Americans through a decline in overall crime rates. To some extent, this may be because immigrants contribute to local labor markets by creating jobs and revitalizing inner-city neighborhoods in ways that improve conditions for immigrants and native-born workers alike (Adelman et al. 2017).

Some critics argue that it is *undocumented* immigrants that are responsible for increases in crime—not immigrants overall. According to this view, immigrants in the United States illegally are more likely than legal immigrants to engage in crime due to economic deprivation and social isolation associated with their legal vulnerabilities (Light and Miller 2018). Although there are comparatively fewer studies of criminal behavior among undocumented immigrants, the available research generally suggests that they also have a lower propensity to commit crime than the native born (Flagg 2019; Orrenius and Zavodny 2019). While studies show that criminal activity among undocumented immigrants is higher than for legal immigrants, this rate is still lower by comparison with that of native-born Americans, regardless of country of origin or level of education (Wadsworth 2010). And on closer examination, state-level analyses reveal that undocumented immigrants do not generally increase crime. Between 1990 and 2014, undocumented immigration did not increase violent crime; in fact, it was associated with a slight decrease (Light and Miller 2018). Between 1990 and 2013, when the number of undocumented immigrants in the United States more than tripled, from 3.5 million to 11.2 million, the UCR data indicated that both violent and property crime rates fell nationally.

Immigrants, both authorized and unauthorized, are also less likely than native-born Americans to be incarcerated (Adelman et al. 2017; Ewing, Martínez, and Rumbaut 2015; Waters and Pineau 2015). According to the American Community Survey (ACS) of 2010, roughly 1.6 percent of immigrant males (aged 18–39) are serving time in prison, compared to 3.3 percent of native-born males. This disparity in incarceration rates has existed for decades. Between 1980 and 2000, the incarceration rates of the native born were anywhere from two to five times higher than those of immigrants. The 2010 census data further revealed that young, undereducated Mexican, Salvadoran, and Guatemalan men (who make up the bulk of the undocumented population) had significantly lower incarceration rates than similarly positioned native-born men (i.e., those who are young and undereducated—without a high school diploma).

In 2010, native-born men (those without a diploma and aged 18–30) had an incarceration rate of 10.7 percent—more than triple that of foreign-born Mexican men and five times greater than that of foreign-born Salvadoran and Guatemalan males (Ewing, Martínez, and Rumbaut 2015).

Scholars have proposed several explanations for these results and findings. First, many immigrants seek to avoid police scrutiny—especially if they are undocumented—for fear of deportation. Second, those who choose to leave their countries of origin for the United States tend to be motivated to improve their lives (a phenomenon termed *positive selection bias*), which may lead to a low propensity to commit crime. Third, immigrants may be more likely to have close family and community ties, which tend to reduce the propensity to commit crime, despite personal circumstances marked by economic disadvantage (Orrenius and Zavodny 2019; Sampson 2008). Furthermore, a decrease in crime in areas with high immigrant concentrations has been attributed to the phenomenon of *immigration revitalization*, whereby immigration is seen as having revitalized urban areas that had previously experienced population decline. According to this model, immigrant influx leads to population growth and to a lower vacancy rate, which helps strengthen the social order in their communities (Sampson 2008).

FURTHER READING

Adelman, Robert, Lesley Williams Reid, Gail Markle, Saskia Weiss, and Charles Jaret. 2017. "Urban Crime Rates and the Changing Face of Immigration: Evidence across Four Decades." *Journal of Ethnicity in Criminal Justice* 15(1): 52–77. https://doi.org/10.1080/15377938.2016.1261057.

Ewing, Walter A., Daniel E. Martínez, and Rubén G. Rumbaut. 2015. *The Criminalization of Immigration in the United States.* Special Report. Washington, DC: American Immigration Council. Retrieved on October 30, 2020, at https://www.americanimmigrationcouncil.org/sites/default/files/research/the_criminalization_of_immigration_in_the_united_states.pdf.

Flagg, Anna. 2019. "Is There a Connection between Undocumented Immigrants and Crime?" *New York Times*, May 13. Retrieved on October 30, 2020, at https://www.nytimes.com/2019/05/13/upshot/illegal-immigration-crime-rates-research.html.

Light, Michael T., and Ty Miller. 2018. "Does Undocumented Immigration Increase Violent Crime?" *Criminology* 56(2): 370–401. https://doi.org/10.1111/1745-9125.1217.

Orrenius, Pia, and Madeline Zavodny. 2019. "Do Immigrants Threaten US Public Safety?" *Journal on Migration and Human Security* 7(3): 52–61. https://doi.org/10.1177/2331502419857083.

Ousey, Graham C., and Charis E. Kubrin. 2018. "Immigration and Crime: Assessing a Contentious Issue." *Annual Review of Criminology* 1: 63–84. https://doi.org/10.1146/annurev-criminol-032317-092026.

Rumbaut, Rubén. 2009. "Undocumented Immigration and Rates of Crime and Imprisonment: Popular Myths and Empirical Realities." Appendix D, pp. 119–139, in *The Role of Local Police: Striking a Balance between Immigration Enforcement and Civil Liberties*, edited by Anita Khashu. Washington, DC: Police Foundation. Retrieved on October 30, 2020, at https://www.policefoundation.org/wp-content/uploads/2015/06/Appendix-D_0.pdf.

Rumbaut, Rubén G., and Walter A. Ewing. 2007. *The Myth of Immigrant Criminality and the Paradox of Assimilation: Incarceration Rates among Native and Foreign-Born Men*. Special Report. Washington, DC: American Immigration Law Foundation, Immigration Policy Center. Retrieved on October 30, 2020, at https://www.americanimmigrationcouncil.org/sites/default/files/research/Imm%20Criminality%20%28IPC%29.pdf.

Sampson, Robert J. 2008. "Rethinking Crime and Immigration." *Contexts* 7(1): 28–33. https://doi.org/10.1525/ctx.2008.7.1.28.

Trump, Donald. 2015. "Here's Donald Trump's Presidential Announcement Speech." *TIME*, June 16. Retrieved on July 22, 2020, at https://time.com/3923128/donald-trump-announcement-speech/.

Wadsworth, Tim. 2010. "Is Immigration Responsible for the Crime Drop? An Assessment of the Influence of Immigration on Changes in Violent Crime between 1990 and 2000." *Social Science Quarterly* 91(2): 531–553. https://doi.org/10.1111/j.1540-6237.2010.00706.x.

Waters, Mary C., and Marisa Gerstein Pineau, eds. 2015. *The Integration of Immigrants into American Society*. Washington, DC: National Academies Press.

Q29. ARE MOST UNDOCUMENTED IMMIGRANTS FROM MEXICO?

Answer: No. Mexicans constitute the single largest group of undocumented immigrants in the United States, though notably, they make up less than half of the total undocumented immigration population. Further, although they currently represent the largest bloc of undocumented immigrants, this is rapidly changing due to the declining numbers of illegal Mexican entrants since 2009 and the rapid rise of undocumented immigrants from countries in Central America and Asia.

The Facts: According to the most recent available estimates (based on data from 2017), there are 10.5 million undocumented immigrants in the United States, representing 3.2 percent of the total U.S. population (Krogstad, Passel, and Cohn 2019). This number represents a drop from 4 percent in 2007, when the undocumented population peaked (Warren 2019). Since 1980, demographers have developed an indirect methodology to gauge the size of the undocumented population, and annual estimates are regularly published by the Pew Research Center as well as by the Department of Homeland Security's Office of Immigration Statistics. For example, estimation procedures for undocumented Mexicans begin with the number of Mexican immigrants included in the U.S. Census or Current Population Survey. This is then adjusted for undercounting and other reporting errors, from which estimated migrant deaths and return migrations are subtracted. The estimation procedures are similar but not identical among researchers, resulting in different estimates for the absolute numbers of undocumented immigrants. Nevertheless, the trends remain basically the same (Massey and Gentsch 2014).

With an extensive shared border between the two nations, Mexico has long supplied the largest flow of undocumented migrants to the United States. By 2007, Mexicans made up the majority (57 percent) of the total undocumented population. However, the number of undocumented Mexican immigrants in the United States has declined over the past decade. According to Pew Research Center estimates (based on government data), there were 4.9 million undocumented Mexican immigrants living in the United States in 2017, down from the peak of 6.9 million in 2007. Though Mexicans no longer form the majority of those living in the United States illegally, the group still constitutes just under half (47 percent) of the total undocumented immigrant population (Gonzalez-Barrera 2015; Krogstad, Passel, and Cohn 2019; Passel and Cohn 2019). The decrease in undocumented Mexican immigrants was the major factor driving down the overall undocumented population in the United States by 1.7 million between 2007 and 2017 (Passel and Cohn 2019).

The most likely reasons for the decline of undocumented immigrants from Mexico include stricter enforcement of U.S. immigration laws, particularly at the U.S.-Mexico border during the Bush and Obama administrations; the slow recovery of the U.S. economy after the Great Recession (2008); and improved economic conditions in Mexico (Gonzalez-Barrera 2015; Warren 2019). The Obama administration deported roughly three million immigrants between 2009 and 2016, a significant increase on the two million immigrants deported by the Bush administration between 2001 and 2008. In 2017, the Trump administration deported 295,000 immigrants, the lowest annual total since 2006 (Radford 2019); however, harsh anti-immigration rhetoric and increasingly punitive changes to immigration policy under President Trump (e.g., separating children from parents at the border) have likely contributed to already reduced flows of undocumented immigrants from Mexico (Pierce, Bolter, and Selee 2018).

The drop in Department of Homeland Security apprehensions at the U.S.-Mexico border mirrored the decline in undocumented population growth, falling from 1.6 million in 2000 to about 300,000 in 2017. Undocumented population growth stopped, as undocumented arrivals fell from 1.4 million in 2000 to about 550,000 in 2007, and continuing thereafter at about that level. In the meantime, the number of undocumented immigrants leaving the United States increased steadily, from 370,000 in 2000 to 770,000 in 2016—the majority being Mexicans (Warren 2019). The increased departures among undocumented Mexicans are likely the result of a weak U.S. labor market, improved economic opportunities in Mexico, and deportation by the Department of Homeland Security (Gonzalez-Barrera 2015; Rosenblum and Ruiz Soto 2015; Warren 2019).

While the number of undocumented Mexicans in the United States has decreased in the last decade, undocumented immigrants from other parts of the world have increased. Available data show that there were approximately 5.5 million non-Mexican undocumented immigrants in 2017, up from 5.3 million in 2007. Undocumented immigrants from Central America, Asia, and Africa grew rapidly after 2000—with numbers from Central America and Asia tripling and those from Africa doubling (Rosenblum and Ruiz Soto 2015). The number of Central American undocumented immigrants rose from 1.5 million in 2007 to 1.9 million in 2017. This growth was mainly fueled by immigrants from El Salvador, Guatemala, and Honduras. The number of undocumented immigrants from Asia rose from 1.3 million in 2007 to 1.5 million in 2017, with the largest groups coming from China, India, Korea, and the Philippines. Between 2007 and 2017, for example, the number of undocumented Indian immigrants grew by over 60 percent, from 325,000 to 525,000 persons—about 5 percent of the total undocumented immigrant population (Passel and Cohn 2019). In 2017, of the total population of people living in the United States without legal authorization, Central Americans and Asians represented 18 percent and 14 percent, respectively. See figure 29.1 for a breakdown of undocumented immigrants in 2017.

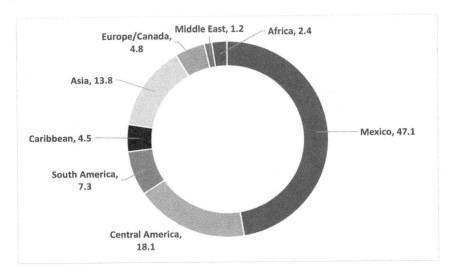

Figure 29.1. Estimated Percentages of Undocumented Immigrants in the United States, 2017.
(*Source:* Passel and Cohn [2019])

Possible explanations for the recent rise in immigration from the Northern Triangle (El Salvador, Guatemala, and Honduras) are drug wars, high rates of homicide and other violent crimes, crushing poverty, and political upheaval. Moreover, Northern Triangle migrants are generally attracted to the United States for the same reasons as other migrants, both legal and illegal: to gain economic opportunity and to join relatives already living in the country (Cohn, Passel, and Gonzalez-Barrera 2017). On the other hand, experts argue that the primary reason underlying increased undocumented immigrants from Asia is directly related to rising incomes in some Asian countries. With thriving economies in places such as China, India, and South Korea, people there can afford to migrate to the United States—legally or illegally (Phippen 2015). The growth of undocumented African immigrants—though they still constitute a small fraction of the undocumented population in the United States (less than 3 percent)—is owed to increasing violence and insecurity in countries such as Nigeria and Ghana, the two major source countries of undocumented Africans (Rosenblum and Ruiz Soto 2015). Other than Central America, Asia, and Africa, undocumented immigrants come from all corners of the globe, including South America, Europe, Canada, Oceania, and the Caribbean. Yet, the numbers of the latter remain relatively small (Rosenblum and Ruiz Soto 2015).

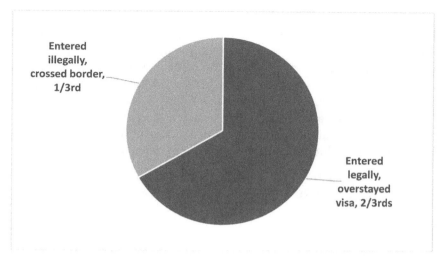

Figure 29.2. Estimated Arrival of Undocumented Immigrants to the United States, 2010–2016.
(*Source*: Warren [2019], Center for Migration Studies)

The decline in undocumented immigrants from Mexico and the increase in flow from other countries represent a marked change in how recent arrivals enter the country. A growing share of undocumented immigrants do not cross the border illegally (as many Americans might imagine); they often originally arrive in the United States legally with visas (for tourism, study, or business) and subsequently overstay their mandated departure date. According to the Pew Research Center, "overstays" have made up a large majority of undocumented immigrant arrivals since 2010 (Passel and Cohn 2019). Put differently, from 2010 to 2016, about two-thirds of undocumented arrivals overstayed temporary visas; only one-third entered the country by crossing the southern border. The largest share of overstayers are from Mexico (one million). Other large groups of overstayers are from China, India, Venezuela, the Philippines, Brazil, and Colombia (Jordan 2019; Warren 2019). For a breakdown of the two methods of arrival of undocumented immigrants to the United States from 2010 to 2016—and for consideration within the context of the building of a wall along the southern border—see figure 29.2. While an imposing wall may curb some undocumented entry, particularly those who cross illegally into the United States over the border, most undocumented immigrants enter by other means.

Undocumented populations in the United States today are not composed solely of Mexicans. Despite the stereotypes about illegal immigration that permeate media narratives, political speeches, and the public
imagination, there are three salient realities: (1) just under half of all
undocumented immigration is from Mexico, with that percentage in
decline; (2) undocumented immigration has increased from Central
America and Asia; and (3) in recent years, most of those who are in the
United States illegally did not surreptitiously cross the U.S.-Mexico border but first arrived legally and then overstayed their visas.

FURTHER READING

Baker, Bryan. 2018. *Estimates of the Illegal Alien Population Residing in the
United States: January 2015.* Office of Immigration Statistics, Department of Homeland Security. Retrieved on November 9, 2020, at
https://www.dhs.gov/sites/default/files/publications/18_1214_PLCY
_pops-est-report.pdf.
Cohn, D'Vera, Jeffrey S. Passel, and Ana Gonzalez-Barrera. 2017. "Rise in
U.S. Immigrants from El Salvador, Guatemala and Honduras Outpaces
Growth from Elsewhere." Pew Research Center, December 7. Retrieved
on November 9, 2020, at https://www.pewresearch.org/hispanic
/2017/12/07/rise-in-u-s-immigrants-from-el-salvador-guatemala-and
-honduras-outpaces-growth-from-elsewhere/.
Gonzalez-Barrera, Ana. 2015. "More Mexicans Leaving Than Coming to
the U.S." Pew Research Center, November 19. Retrieved on November 9, 2020, athttps://www.pewresearch.org/hispanic/2015/11/19
/more-mexicans-leaving-than-coming-to-the-u-s/.
Jordan, Miriam. 2019. "The Overlooked Undocumented Immigrants:
From India, China, Brazil." *New York Times*, December 1.
Krogstad, Jens Manuel, Jeffrey S. Passel, and D'Vera Cohn. 2019. "5 Facts
about Illegal Immigration in the U.S." Fact Tank: News in the Numbers, June 12. Pew Research Center. Retrieved on November 9, 2020,
at   https://www.pewresearch.org/fact-tank/2019/06/12/5-facts-about
-illegal-immigration-in-the-u-s/.
Massey, Douglas S., and Kerstin Gentsch. 2014. "Undocumented Migra-
tion to the United States and the Wages of Mexican Immigrants."
International Migration Review 48(2): 482–499.
Passel, Jeffrey S., and D'Vera Cohn. 2019. "Mexicans Decline to Less Than
Half the U.S. Unauthorized Immigrant Population for the First Time."
Fact Tank: News in the Numbers, June 12. Pew Research Center.

Retrieved on November 9, 2020, at https://www.pewresearch.org/fact
-tank/2019/06/12/us-unauthorized-immigrant-population-2017/.

Phippen, J. Weston. 2015. "Asians Now Outpace Mexicans in Terms
of Undocumented Growth." *The Atlantic*, August 20. Retrieved on
November 9, 2020, at https://www.theatlantic.com/politics/archive
/2015/08/asians-now-outpace-mexicans-in-terms-of-undocumented
-growth/432603/.

Pierce, Sarah, Jessica Bolter, and Andrew Selee. 2018. *U.S. Immigration
Policy under Trump: Deep Changes and Lasting Impacts.* Washington, DC:
Migration Policy Institute. Retrieved on November 9, 2020, at https://
observatoriocolef.org/wp-content/uploads/2018/07/TCMTrumpSpring
2018-FINAL.pdf.

Radford, Jynnah. 2019. "Key Findings about U.S. Immigrants." Fact
Tank: News in the Numbers, June 17. Pew Research Center. Retrieved
on November 9, 2020, at https://www.pewresearch.org/fact-tank/2019
/06/17/key-findings-about-u-s-immigrants/.

Rosenblum, Marc R., and Ariel G. Ruiz Soto. 2015. *An Analysis of Unauthorized Immigrants in the United States by Country and Region of Birth.*
Washington, DC: Migration Policy Institute. Retrieved on November 9, 2020, at https://www.migrationpolicy.org/research/analysis-un
authorized-immigrants-united-states-country-and-region-birth.

Warren, Robert. 2019. "Sharp Multiyear Decline in Undocumented
Immigration Suggests Progress at US-Mexico Border, Not a National
Emergency." Center for Migration Studies. Retrieved on November 9,
2020, at https://cmsny.org/publications/essay-warren-022719/.

Q30. ARE IMMIGRANTS TODAY ASSIMILATING INTO AMERICAN SOCIETY AS DID EARLIER WAVES?

Answer: Yes. Based on several leading indicators of assimilation, today's immigrants and their offspring (who are mostly nonwhite) are assimilating into U.S. society at a similar or even faster rate than past waves of immigrants (who were primarily from Europe).

The Facts: Throughout American history, each new wave of immigrants has been accused by some native-born Americans of failing to assimilate. Italian, Polish, and other European immigrants who came to the United States at the end of the nineteenth century faced this criticism: but they proved such notions wrong, as they and their children learned English, left the immigrant enclaves of the cities, bought homes in suburbia, attained jobs in the mainstream labor market, and became American citizens, all while integrating into their communities in a myriad of other ways. The process of assimilation among past European immigrants, however, required much effort over several generations (Jiménez 2011; U.S. Chamber of Commerce 2016).

The passage of the Hart-Celler Act of 1965—the landmark immigration law that liberalized restrictive immigration policies that had been in place in the United States since the 1920s—resulted in a surge of immigration from Asia and Latin America. Today, these new immigrants constitute the majority of all immigrants to the United States. Asian and Hispanic immigrants now face the same charge of nonassimilation as their European predecessors. They are often seen as unwilling to integrate into American society and are perceived as a threat to American identity and culture.

However, the claim that recent nonwhite immigrants are not assimilating into American society has little empirical support. Evidence suggests that despite their racial difference from the white majority (a factor often seen as a barrier to assimilation), new immigrants are not only assimilating, but they are doing so at an even faster rate than earlier European immigrants. Evidence further shows that they are ascending the socioeconomic ladder—just as did earlier waves of immigrants (Alba 2009; Smith 2003; Steinberg 2004; U.S. Chamber of Commerce 2016; Waters and Pineau 2015).

Assimilation is complex but has been defined as the decline of "ethnic distinction" and of "cultural and social differences" (Alba and Nee 2003, 11). Scholars have identified a number of social indicators to gauge assimilation, such as English fluency, educational and economic attainment, rates of intermarriage, and residential integration (residential proximity with the dominant group). Based on these measures, a report by the National Academies of Sciences, Engineering, and Medicine (Waters and Pineau 2015) concluded that current immigrants and their descendants are integrating into U.S. society. Moreover, data show that integration is reinforced over time and that subsequent generations (children and grandchildren of immigrants) are closer to native-born Americans than to their parents culturally. The following are some key findings regarding the major indicators of assimilation.

English Fluency

Numerous studies find that today's immigrants and their offspring learn English at the same or faster rate than earlier waves of immigrants

(Steinberg 2004; Waters and Pineau 2015). Moreover, with each new generation, the move toward English occurs rapidly. For instance, one 2012 study revealed that although only 38 percent of foreign-born Latinx immigrants speak English very well, 92 percent of their U.S.-born adult children do, and this figure increases to 96 percent by the third generation (Taylor et al. 2012). Conversely, the usage of ancestral languages drops significantly with each new generation (Rumbaut, Massey, and Bean 2006). Although today's society may be more conducive to retention of the immigrant mother tongue (given the continued inflow of new immigrants), the research findings are clear that today's immigrants move rapidly toward monolingualism (i.e., speaking English only).

Educational and Economic Attainment

Research shows significant improvement in educational attainment among today's immigrants and their offspring. Due in part to the preference given to highly skilled immigrants by the Hart-Celler Act of 1965, today's immigrant population already includes a significant proportion of highly educated professionals. More than one-quarter of today's foreign-born immigrants have a college education or more, and their children generally do exceptionally well in school (Waters and Pineau 2015). Further, among those who arrive with little education, there is substantial educational improvement by the second generation. For example, one 2013 survey found that second generation adults are more likely than the first generation to finish high school (90 percent vs. 72 percent, respectively) and to attain a college degree (36 percent vs. 29 percent, respectively) (Pew Research Center 2013).

As for economic attainment, immigrant workers make dramatic progress the longer they live in the United States, but their children do even better (see Myers and Pitkin 2010). The children of Mexican and Central American immigrants, in particular, make a large leap, with 22 percent of second-generation Mexican men and 31 percent of second-generation Central American men in professional or managerial positions (in comparison with 6.8 percent among first-generation Mexican men and 9.3 percent among first-generation Central American men). Second-generation Hispanic women make even greater progress: 37.2 percent of them hold professional and managerial occupations as compared to 16.7 percent for first-generation Hispanic women (Waters and Pineau 2015). Additional measures of economic attainment similarly show generational improvement: adults of the second generation do even better than those in the first generation in terms of median household income

($58,000 vs. $46,000, respectively) and home ownership (64 percent vs. 51 percent, respectively) (Pew Research Center 2013). The overall poverty rate also declines with each new generation, from more than 18 percent (first-generation immigrants) to 13.6 percent (second generation) to 11.5 percent (third generation) (Waters and Pineau 2015).

Intermarriage

Historically, intermarriage between ethnic/racial minority immigrants and native-born whites has been considered a sign of assimilation (Waters and Pineau 2015). Steadily rising rates of intermarriage of individuals from different ethnic and racial groups demonstrate the extent to which cultural and racial differences have diminished as obstacles to such relationships. Data show frequent intermarriage of whites with either Asians or Hispanics, especially among the U.S. born (Alba 2009). A study based on the 1990 census, for example, found that 40 percent of second-generation Asians married non-Asians and most Asians who outmarried did so with whites. Rates of intermarriage for Hispanics were lower than for Asians, but were high nevertheless: almost one-third of U.S.-born Hispanics between the ages of 25 and 34 were married to non-Hispanic whites (Steinberg 2004). According to census data from 2015, the most common intermarriage among newlywed couples is Hispanic and white (42 percent), followed by Asian and white (15 percent) (Livingston and Brown 2017).

Residential Integration

Assimilation is also measured by location of residence. Assimilation is considered to be taking place if, over time, immigrants and their descendants live in neighborhoods that are less defined by members of their ethnoracial or national origin. Residential patterns among immigrant groups indicate that with each new generation, immigrants become more dispersed across regions, cities, and neighborhoods, gradually becoming less segregated from native-born whites. Both Hispanics and Asians show some level of segregation from the white majority (see Q11), though data reveal that their rates of segregation decline as they spend more time living in the United States. With time and successive generations, immigrants are more likely to move from urban ethnic enclaves into suburbs—areas that are often predominantly white. Furthermore, while many new immigrants continue to settle and concentrate in traditional immigrant "gateway" states (e.g., California, New York, Texas, and Florida), studies in the 2010s have documented a heightened trend of immigrant dispersal across the country, including the South and Midwest—regions that have historically had low levels of immigration (Jiménez 2011; Waters and Pineau 2015). Suburbanization and the geographic dispersal of new immigrants indicates the greater possibility for contact and the formation of social relationships with whites.

Taken together, all of these indicators suggest that today's nonwhite immigrants and their U.S.-born offspring are assimilating into American society just as did past immigrants and their descendants from Europe. Perhaps native-born Americans perceive that new immigrants resist assimilation or assimilate more slowly than earlier waves of European immigrants because collective memory can be deceptive. Early European immigrants are remembered as assimilating faster than they actually did because they immigrated more than a century ago (in the late nineteenth and early twentieth centuries). The trials associated with their integration into American society have been obscured or minimized in the telling and retelling of family immigration stories over time, and their multigenerational struggles to assimilate are downplayed.

Furthermore, the stereotype that new immigrants fail to assimilate or assimilate at a slow rate may exist because the majority of immigrants since 1965, many of whom are from Asia and Latin America, are racially (and physically) distinct from the majority white population. Hence, they are more visible than earlier waves of European immigrants, who, despite cultural differences, more easily blended into American society because of their physical similarities to native-born whites (e.g., similar skin color and features). Asian and Hispanic immigrants, on the other hand, stand out; thus, when they settle in ethnic enclaves in large numbers or speak their native tongues in public spaces, they are more noticeable to the native-born population, which, as a consequence, is perceived as resisting assimilation. However, despite the stereotype, research suggests that today's nonwhite immigrants and, in particular, their U.S.-born offspring are assimilating into American society as did past immigrants and their descendants from Europe. According to some measures, data show that these newer immigrants are assimilating at an even faster rate than their predecessors.

FURTHER READING

Alba, Richard. 2009. *Blurring the Color Line: The New Chance for a More Integrated America.* Cambridge, MA: Harvard University Press.

Alba, Richard, and Victor Nee. 2003. *Remaking the American Mainstream: Assimilation and Contemporary Immigration.* Cambridge, MA: Harvard University Press.

Jiménez, Thomás R. 2011. *Immigrants in the United States: How Well Are They Integrating into Society?* Washington, DC: Migration Policy Institute.

Livingston, Gretchen, and Anna Brown. 2017. "Intermarriage in the U.S.: 50 Years after Loving v. Virginia." Pew Research Center, May 17. Retrieved on November 9, 2020, at https://www.pewsocialtrends.org /2017/05/18/intermarriage-in-the-u-s-50-years-after-loving-v-virginia/.

Myers, Dowell, and John Pitkin. 2010. *Assimilation Today: New Evidence Shows the Latest Immigrants to America Are Following in Our History's Footsteps.* Washington, D.C.: Center for American Progress. Retrieved on November 9, 2020, at https://cdn.americanprogress.org/wp-content /uploads/issues/2010/09/pdf/immigrant_assimilation.pdf.

Pew Research Center. 2013. "Second-Generation Americans: A Portrait of the Adult Children of Immigrants." Pew Research Center, February 7. Retrieved on November 9, 2020, at https://www.pewsocialtrends.org /2013/02/07/second-generation-americans/.

Rumbaut, Rubén G., Douglas Massey, and Frank D. Bean. 2006. "Linguistic Life Expectancies: Immigrant Language Retention in Southern California." *Population and Development Review* 32(3): 447–460.

Smith, James P. 2003. "Assimilation across the Latino Generations." *AEA Papers and Proceedings* 93(2): 315–319.

Steinberg, Stephen. 2004. "The Melting Pot and the Color Line." Pp. 235–247 in *Reinventing the Melting Pot: The New Immigrants and What It Means to Be an American,* edited by Tamar Jacoby. New York: Basic Books.

Taylor, Paul, Mark Hugo Lopez, Jessica Hamar Martínez, and Gabriel Velasco. 2012. "When Labels Don't Fit: Hispanics and Their Views of Identity." Pew Research Center, April 4. Retrieved on November 9, 2020, at https://www.pewresearch.org/hispanic/2012/04/04 /when-labels-dont-fit-hispanics-and-their-views-of-identity/.

U.S. Chamber of Commerce. 2016. *Immigration: Myths and Facts.* Washington, DC: U.S. Chamber of Commerce. Retrieved on November 9, 2020, athttps://www.uschamber.com/sites/default/files/documents /files/022851_mythsfacts_2016_report_final.pdf.

Waters, Mary C., and Marisa Gerstein Pineau, eds. 2015. *The Integration of Immigrants into American Society.* Washington, DC: National Academies Press.

Q31. DO UNDOCUMENTED IMMIGRANTS DRAIN AMERICA'S WELFARE SYSTEM?

Answer: No. Data show that undocumented immigrants do not constitute a net drain on the welfare system in the United States. This is because (1) they are ineligible for most federal public benefit programs; (2) many do not utilize welfare, even in cases when they might be eligible by law, due to fear of deportation; and (3) they often pay, through taxes, into welfare programs. Experts argue that undocumented immigrants in fact make a net positive contribution to public coffers, as they pay more in taxes than they receive in welfare benefits.

The Facts: Undocumented immigration has long been a contentious issue in the United States, though perhaps even more so in recent decades. Opponents of undocumented immigration argue, among other things, that they are a financial burden to the country—in particular, that they drain the U.S. welfare system.

The belief that undocumented immigrants enter the United States for the purpose of accessing welfare benefits is widespread, but in reality, undocumented immigrants are excluded by law from most benefits. In 1996, Congress passed the Welfare Reform Act and the Illegal Immigration Reform and Immigrant Responsibility Act, partly to curtail unauthorized migration by limiting the public benefits available to noncitizen immigrants (Bean and Stevens 2003). Undocumented immigrants are ineligible for most federal public benefit programs, except under rare circumstances, such as Emergency Medicaid (e.g., labor and delivery costs for low-income pregnant undocumented immigrants). Immigrants without legal status are also ineligible for Social Security, Supplemental Security Income, Temporary Assistance for Needy Families (TANF), Medicaid, Medicare, the Supplemental Nutrition Assistance Program (SNAP, formerly known as "food stamps"), and Nonemergency Medicaid (Fox 2016). Even most legal immigrants cannot access these benefits until they have been in the United States for at least five years (U.S. Chamber of Commerce 2016). Undocumented immigrants are similarly ineligible under the Affordable Care Act ("Obamacare"), and they are unable to purchase subsidized private health insurance through federal and state exchanges (Marrow and Joseph 2015).

Following the Supreme Court decision *Plyler v. Doe* (1982), all children residing in the United States are required by federal law to be provided with a K-12 education, regardless of their immigrant status, including the undocumented. In many states, however, undocumented immigrants are prevented from accessing in-state tuition for higher education, including many who have completed their entire K-12 education in that particular state. Given these restrictions against undocumented (and in some cases, legal) immigrants, it is not surprising that U.S. citizens are more likely to receive public benefits than noncitizens (both legal and undocumented) (U.S. Chamber of Commerce 2016).

In addition, research has found that undocumented immigrants typically underutilize the few public services and benefits available to them, such as emergency medical treatment under Medicaid—likely due to fears that if they do so, their undocumented status will be revealed, and they will be subject to deportation. Even legal immigrant families are less likely to use SNAP than native-born families. An analysis of the 2008 and 2009 American Community Survey of the Census Bureau revealed that while more than two-thirds of children in poor families with U.S.-born parents received SNAP in 2008 and 2009, less than half of children in poor families with foreign-born parents received SNAP in the same years. Similarly, 18 percent of children with native-born parents used TANF, compared to 12 percent of children with immigrant parents (Gellat and Koball 2014). Another analysis, based on the 1995–2010 Current Population Survey of the Census Bureau, similarly showed that among lower-income households with children, those led by immigrants participated in SNAP and TANF at lower rates than native-led households. However, depending on how the household is defined, the statistical results vary. Using the same Current Population Survey for the period 2011–2013, another study found that the immigrant households use certain programs—including TANF and SNAP—at higher rates than households led by the native born (National Academies of Sciences, Engineering, and Medicine 2017). Children in poor families with U.S.-born parents are more likely to have public health insurance coverage than those with immigrant parents, and data suggest that undocumented immigrants utilize health care less than U.S.-born Americans. Only 7.9 percent of undocumented immigrants incur publicly financed health expenditures (averaging $140 per person annually), compared to 30.1 percent of U.S. citizens (receiving $1,385 per person annually) (U.S. Chamber of Commerce 2016).

It should be noted that the fiscal impact of undocumented immigration depends on (1) the level on which the data are interpreted (whether national, state, or local) and (2) the immigrant generation considered. For example, one 2018 study found that undocumented immigration appears to have a negative impact on taxes and public spending, if considering state and local levels and excluding federal spending. Analysis at the federal level, on the other hand, shows positive gains contributed by undocumented immigrants. In addition, while foreign-born immigrants and their dependents—both documented and undocumented—may place a burden on state and local budgets, the second and third generations of immigrants add to both (Marrow et al. 2018). Careful consideration is required to fully understand the impact of undocumented immigration on the welfare system.

Moreover, public discussion has typically focused on the economic costs as opposed to the benefits of the influx of young immigrants in terms of tax contributions, including those that arrive illegally. Few studies assess the contributions of undocumented foreign-born individuals, but those that have done so have found that undocumented immigrants contribute more than they take from the public treasury. For example, one study based on the Current Population Survey and Medical Expenditure Panel Surveys examined Medicare Trust Fund contributions and withdrawals by undocumented immigrants. The study found that between 2000 and 2011, undocumented immigrants contributed $2.2 billion to $3.8 billion more than they withdrew annually (a total surplus of $35.1 billion) (Zallman et al. 2016). In effect, undocumented immigrants have prolonged the life of the Medicare Trust Fund.

Undocumented immigrants also pay a variety of local, state, and federal taxes, including income tax and Medicare, through payroll taxes (i.e., taxes withheld from wages). Although it is impossible to know the exact number of undocumented immigrant workers who pay payroll taxes, analysts estimate that approximately three-quarters of them do contribute taxes (Porter 2005). The extent of their contribution to Social Security is particularly significant. Recent immigrants benefit Social Security because they tend to be of working age and contribute more than they take from the system. Undocumented immigrants help even more because they are unlikely to collect benefits (Porter 2005). Unlike most U.S. citizens, who will receive some form of public pension in retirement and are eligible for Medicare when they turn 65, undocumented immigrants are not entitled to these benefits—even if they have paid annually into these programs through taxes.

Given the widespread belief that undocumented immigrants are paid "off the books," it might seem counterintuitive that they contribute to the nation's retirement system. How is this possible? The Immigration Reform and Control Act (IRCA) of 1986, in an effort to reduce undocumented migration, set penalties for employers who knowingly hire undocumented immigrants. Consequently, most undocumented immigrant workers buy fraudulent identifications or IDs (typically consisting of a green card and a Social Security card) to gain jobs. These fake IDs provide cover for employers who, if asked, can plausibly assert that they believed their workers were legal. This also means that workers must be paid "by the book," with payroll tax deductions. In 2007, an estimated 5.6 million undocumented workers paid $12 billion into the Social Security system (Becerra et al. 2012; Porter 2005). As incorrect or fictitious Social Security numbers are not linked to individuals who can potentially receive Social Security benefits one day, the majority of contributions to Social Security from undocumented immigrants go into the "earnings suspense file" (a surplus account), which has grown with the increase of undocumented immigration. During the 1990s, $189 billion in wages were added to the suspense file (Porter 2005). In 2010, the Social Security Administration estimated that undocumented immigrants paid $13 billion into the Social Security trust funds that year and only received about $1 billion in benefits. This means that undocumented immigrants contributed roughly $12 billion to the Social Security program in 2010 alone (Goss et al. 2013).

In addition to the financial benefits for Social Security and Medicare, undocumented immigrants also provide revenue to state and local governments as a result of their purchases, taxes, and employment. Becerra et al. (2012) suggest that while some studies have reported that the cost to states with high numbers of undocumented immigrants outweighs their economic contributions, several states (e.g., Arizona and Florida) reported that undocumented immigrants contribute more in state and local taxes than they receive in government services and benefits. Texas and Arizona, states with particularly high undocumented immigrant populations, have estimated that the state would lose considerable gross state product and jobs if all undocumented immigrants were to leave or be deported. Even studies that report an overall economic loss as a result of providing services to undocumented immigrants indicate that the losses are negligible once the economic benefits of undocumented immigrants are taken into consideration (Becerra et al. 2012; Marrow et al. 2018)

In sum, although there are some costs associated with undocumented immigrants in the United States, their *overall* economic contribution, including employment, purchases, and tax revenue generated and contributions to the gross national product via employment, results in financial benefit to the United States at the federal level and also for some local and state governments.

FURTHER READING

Bean, Frank D., and Gillian Stevens. 2003. *America's Newcomers and the Dynamics of Diversity*. New York: Russell Sage.

Becerra, David, David K. Androff, Cecilia Ayón, and Jason T. Castillo. 2012. "Fear vs. Facts: Examining the Economic Impact of Undocumented Immigrants in the U.S." *Journal of Sociology & Social Welfare* 39(4): 111–135.

Fox, Cybelle. 2016. "Unauthorized Welfare: The Origins of Immigrant Status Restrictions in American Social Policy." *Journal of American History* 102(4): 1051–1074.

Gellat, Julia, and Heather Koball, eds. 2014. *Immigrant Access to Health and Human Services: Final Report.* October. Washington, DC: Urban Institute. Retrieved on November 9, 2020, at https://www.urban.org /sites/default/files/publication/33551/2000012-Immigrant-Access-to -Health-and-Human-Services.pdf.

Goss, Stephen, Alice Wade, J. Patrick Skirvin, Michael Morris, K. Mark Bye, and Danielle Huston. 2013. *Effects of Unauthorized Immigration on the Actuarial Status of the Social Security Trust Funds.* Actuarial Note, no. 151, April. Baltimore, MD: Office of the Chief Actuary, Social Security Administration. Retrieved on November 9, 2020, at https:// www.ssa.gov/oact/NOTES/pdf_notes/note151.pdf.

Lipman, Francine J. 2006. "The Taxation of Undocumented Immigrants: Separate, Unequal, and without Representation." *Harvard Latino Law Review* 9: 1–58.

Lowrey, Annie. 2018. "Are Immigrants a Drain on Government Resources?" *The Atlantic*, September 29. Retrieved on November 9, 2020, at https://www.theatlantic.com/ideas/archive/2018/09/are -immigrants-drain-government-resources/571582/.

Marrow, Helen B., and Tiffany D. Joseph. 2015. "Excluded and Frozen Out: Unauthorised Immigrants' (Non)Access to Care after US Health Care Reform." *Journal of Ethnic and Migration Studies* 41(14): 2253–2273.

Marrow, Helen B., Will Tyson, Susan C. Pearce, Martha Crowley, and Kim Ebert. 2018. "Is Unauthorized Immigration and Economic Drain on American Communities? Research Says No." *Contexts: Sociology for the Public: Guest Posts*, May 21. Retrieved on November 9, 2020, at https://contexts.org/blog/unauthorized-immigration-local-economies/.

National Academies of Sciences, Engineering, and Medicine. 2017. *The Economic and Fiscal Consequences of Immigration.* Washington, DC: National Academies Press. https://doi.org/10.17226/23550.

Porter, Eduardo. 2005. "Illegal Immigrants Are Bolstering Social Security with Billions." *New York Times*, April 5.

U.S. Chamber of Commerce. 2016. *Immigration: Myths and Facts.* Washington, DC: U.S. Chamber of Commerce. 2016. Retrieved on November

9, 2020, athttps://www.uschamber.com/sites/default/files/documents
/files/022851_mythsfacts_2016_report_final.pdf.
Zallman, Leah, Fernando A. Wilson, James P. Stimpson, Adriana Bearse,
Lisa Arsenault, Blessing Dube, David Himmelstein, and Steffie Woold-
handler. 2016. "Unauthorized Immigrants Prolong the Life of Medicare's Trust Fund." *Journal of General Internal Medicine* 31(1):122–127.
https://doi.org/10.1007/s11606-015-3418-z.

Q32. DO IMMIGRANTS TAKE JOBS AWAY
FROM OR LOWER THE WAGES OF
NATIVE-BORN AMERICANS?

Answer: Generally, no. Although research findings are somewhat mixed,
research to date generally shows little negative effect of immigration on
employment and the wages of most native-born American workers. Studies that indicate adverse effects of immigration on employment suggest
that such impact primarily affects the lowest segment of the labor market:
that is, new immigrants tend to compete for jobs with (1) prior immigrants
and (2) native-born high school dropouts—whose skill sets are similar to
new immigrants. The bulk of research, however, shows that immigrant
workers typically complement native-born workers, as the former tend
to work in different sectors of the labor market. Skilled immigrants also
create jobs by starting new businesses at rates higher than the native-born
population.

   The Facts: In 2019, immigrants made up 17.4 percent of the civilian
labor force in the United States (a 5.4 percent rise from 1995), although
they are overrepresented in certain industries (Bureau of Labor Statistics
2020). Immigrants are a significant presence in industries that demand
highly skilled workers, such as information technology and high-tech
manufacturing; in these sectors, immigrants made up 27 percent of all
workers in 2014 (DeSilver 2017). Immigrants also supplied a large number of workers (approximately one-fifth of the workforce) in industries
with a more mixed or primarily low-skilled workforce, including construction, food services, and agriculture. The greatest concentrations of immigrant workers are found in private households (45 percent) and in textile,
apparel, and leather manufacturing (36 percent) (DeSilver 2017).
   Given the rapid increase of immigrants into the United States
(13.6 percent of the national population in 2017), many Americans, not
surprisingly, view immigration as a major policy issue facing the nation.

One question raised in the media and by politicians concerns the impact of immigration on the economy, specifically on the jobs and wages of native-born Americans. Many Americans believe that immigration has adverse effects on American workers. Such a belief, however, wrongly assumes that the U.S. economy is static, with little growth, and does not account for the varying impact of immigration on different sectors and industries, with both short- and long-term effects.

According to *The Economic and Fiscal Consequences of Immigration* (National Academies of Sciences, Engineering, and Medicine [hereafter NASEM] 2017)—a comprehensive report by 14 leading economists, demographers, sociologists, and other scholars—immigration, in general, has little impact on the overall employment level of U.S.-born workers. Further, when measured over a period of more than 10 years, the overall impact of immigration on both wages and the employment rates of the native-born population is limited.

Economists acknowledge the difficulties of empirical estimation and the complexities of measuring the impact on wages and employment resulting from the entry of foreign-born workers into the labor market (see Borjas, Grogger, and Hanson 2006; Friedberg and Hunt 1999; Martin 2015; NASEM 2017). The U.S. economy and labor market are flexible, making it challenging to measure the fluctuations in the numbers of migrants, U.S.-born workers, and the employers hiring immigrants (Martin 2015). The net impact of immigration on the labor market in an immigrant-receiving country over a specific short-term period is particularly difficult to measure due to effects not directly related to immigration. The effects of immigration must be isolated from other influences that shape local and national economies and relative wages among different groups of workers—including changes in technology, global supply chains, international trade, and foreign investment. The impact of immigration on labor markets varies with time and place, reflecting the size of the immigrant inflow, the skill sets of native-born Americans and incoming immigrants, the local industrial mix, the mobility of capital and other inputs, and the overall health of the economy (NASEM 2017).

While research generally indicates the limited effect of immigration on native employment and wages (Card 2001, 2005; Friedberg and Hunt 1999; Peri 2010a, 2010b), some studies have found negative effects on those occupying the lowest segment of the labor market. Prior immigrants are most likely to experience the impact, followed by native-born high school dropouts (NASEM 2017). For example, a study in 2016 found a negative impact of immigration on low-skilled native workers, especially African Americans (Borjas, Grogger, and Hanson 2006). In other words, the groups that are most likely to be affected by incoming immigrant workers are those that share job qualifications with new immigrants and those that typically compete for low-skilled jobs (NASEM 2017). Nonetheless, other studies emphasize that over the long run (10 years), immigrants do not reduce native employment rates, but they do increase productivity and hence average income for both immigrants and native-born workers (Peri 2010a, 2010b). In the short run, immigration may at first reduce native employment and average income slightly, though this changes with time as the economy makes adjustments.

Furthermore, both legal and undocumented immigrants continue to fill essential jobs that native-born American workers tend to shun (Cohen 2019; Pais 2013; Peri 2010a). Demand for workers at the bottom of the occupational hierarchy—lower-paying, manual, dirty, dangerous, and menial jobs—has remained strong. Because these jobs are typically avoided by native-born Americans, employers predominantly depend on immigrants for these forms of labor (Pais 2013). In fact, immigrants are critical in sustaining industries such as construction, food, health care, and hospitality, as well as seasonal industries, including agriculture and leisure resorts (Cohen 2019). Undocumented workers, in particular, tend to gravitate to the unpleasant, backbreaking jobs that native-born workers are unwilling to do—here, contrary to popular perception, undocumented immigrants rarely compete with U.S.-born workers (Becerra et al. 2012).

Until recently, the impact of highly skilled immigrants on native wages and employment has received less attention than that of their low-skilled counterparts. Several studies have found a positive impact from the inflow of skilled immigrants (especially in technology and science) on the wages and employment of both college-educated and non-college-educated natives. This is consistent with theories of economic complementarity, which suggests that high-skilled immigrant and U.S.-born workers have skills that typically complement rather than compete with each other. For example, high-skilled immigrant workers fill positions in STEM fields (science, technology, engineering, and math), where native-born labor is relatively scarce. Skilled immigrants have also spurred business and technology innovation, thereby helping to create jobs, including those for native-born American workers (NASEM 2017; Preston 2016).

Immigrants also create jobs by starting new businesses; approximately 18 percent of all U.S. businesses are founded by immigrants. In fact, immigrants are more entrepreneurial than their native-born counterparts, with 34 percent being business owners, compared to just 19 percent of the native born. Further, more than half of all U.S. startup companies valued at $1 billion or more were founded by immigrants (Anderson

2016; Hoban 2017), and a quarter of Silicon Valley high-tech firms in the late 1990s had at least one immigrant cofounder (Martin 2015). Companies such as Google and Intel (among others) were founded by skilled immigrants and are cited as businesses that benefit the founding immigrants as well as native-born workers, who gain increased job opportunities (Bahar 2017).

Immigration is integral to national economic growth. In the long run, it has a net positive effect on the U.S. economy by expanding the labor market (Peri 2010b). Immigrants also contribute through the consumption of goods and services—which in turn increases aggregate demand and employment growth (Bahar 2017). With the rapidly aging native population (as the Baby Boom cohort enters old age and retirement) and low native fertility, many analysts believe that the American economy will increasingly depend on immigrants and their children to fill jobs and create new ones as the century proceeds (Hoban 2017; Singer 2012).

FURTHER READING

Anderson, Stuart. 2016. *Immigrants and Billion Dollar Startups*. National Foundation for American Policy Brief. Arlington, VA: National Foundation for American Policy. Retrieved on November 9, 2020, at https://www.immigrationresearch.org/system/files/Immigrants-and -Billion-Dollar-Startups.NFAP-Policy-Brief.March-2016.pdf.

Bahar, Dany. 2017. "A Spicy Red Sauce and How Immigrants Generate Jobs and Growth in the U.S." *Up Front* (blog), February 7. Brookings. Retrieved on November 9, 2020, at https://www.brookings.edu/blog /up-front/2017/02/07/a-spicy-red-sauce-and-how-immigrants-generate -jobs-and-growth-in-the-us/.

Becerra, David, David K. Androff, Cecilia Ayón, and Jason T. Castillo. 2012. "Fear vs. Facts: Examining the Economic Impact of Undocumented Immigrants in the U.S." *Journal of Sociology & Social Welfare* 39(4): 111–135.

Borjas, George J., Jeffrey Grogger, and Gordon H. Hanson. 2006. "Immigration and African-American Employment Opportunities: The Response of Wages, Employment, and Incarceration to Labor Supply Shocks." NBER Working Paper No. 12518. Cambridge, MA: National Bureau of Economic Research.

Bureau of Labor Statistics. 2020. "Foreign-Born Workers: Labor Force Characteristics—2019." News Release, May 15. U.S. Department of Labor. Retrieved on November 9, 2020, at https://www.bls.gov/news .release/pdf/forbrn.pdf.

Card, David. 2001. "Immigrant Inflows, Native Outflows, and the Local Labor Market Impacts of Higher Immigration." *Journal of Labor Economics* 9(1): 22–64.

Card, David. 2005. "Is the New Immigration Really So Bad?" *Economic Journal* 115: 300–323.

Cohen, Patricia. 2019. "Is Immigration at Its Limit? Not for Employers." *New York Times*, August 22. Retrieved on November 9, 2020, at https://www.nytimes.com/2019/08/22/business/economy/trump-immigration-employers.html.

DeSilver, Drew. 2017. "Immigrants Don't Make Up a Majority of Workers in Any U.S. Industry." Pew Research Center, March 16. Retrieved on November 9, 2020, at https://www.pewresearch.org/fact-tank/2017/03/16/immigrants-dont-make-up-a-majority-of-workers-in-any-u-s-industry/.

Friedberg, Rachel M., and Jennifer Hunt. 1999. "Immigration and the Receiving Economy." Pp. 342–359 in *The Handbook of International Migration: The American Experience*, edited by Charles Hirschman, Philip Kasinitz, and Josh DeWind. New York: Russell Sage.

Hoban, Brennan. 2017. "Do Immigrants 'Steal' Jobs from American Workers?" *Brookings Now* (blog), August 24. Brookings. Retrieved on November 9, 2020, at https://www.brookings.edu/blog/brookings-now/2017/08/24/do-immigrants-steal-jobs-from-american-workers/.

Martin, Philip. 2015. "Economic Aspects of Migration." Pp. 90–114 in *Migration Theory: Talking across Disciplines*, edited by Caroline B. Brettell and James H. Hollifield. New York and London: Routledge.

National Academies of Sciences, Engineering, and Medicine (NASEM). 2017. *The Economic and Fiscal Consequences of Immigration*. Washington, DC: National Academies Press. https://doi.org/10.17226/23550.

Pais, Jeremy. 2013. "The Effects of U.S. Immigration on the Career Trajectories of Native Workers, 1979–2004." *American Journal of Sociology* 119(1): 35–74.

Passel, Jeffrey S., and D'Vera Cohn. 2017. "Immigration Projected to Drive Growth in U.S. Working-Age Population through at Least 2035." Pew Research Center, March 8. Retrieved on November 9, 2020, at https://www.pewresearch.org/fact-tank/2017/03/08/immigration-projected-to-drive-growth-in-u-s-working-age-population-through-at-least-2035/.

Peri, Giovanni. 2010a. "The Effects of Immigrants on U.S. Employment and Productivity." FRBSF Economic Letter. 2010-26. August 30. Federal Reserve Bank of San Francisco. Retrieved on November 9, 2020, at https://www.frbsf.org/economic-research/publications/economic-letter/2010/august/effect-immigrants-us-employment-productivity/.

Peri, Giovanni. 2010b. *The Impact of Immigrants in Recession and Economic Expansion.* Washington, DC: Migration Policy Institute.

Preston, Julia. 2016. "Immigrants Aren't Taking Americans' Jobs, New Study Finds." *New York Times*, September 21.

Singer, Audrey. 2012. "Report: Immigrant Workers in the U.S. Labor Force." Brookings Institution, March 15. Retrieved on December 5, 2020, at https://www.brookings.edu/research/immigrant-workers-in-the-u-s-labor-force/.

7

❖❖❖

A Post-Racial America?

Christian Cooper, a New York City resident and avid bird-watcher, woke up early one May morning in 2020 and headed to Central Park. As usual, he entered the Ramble, a heavily wooded region of the park popular among birders because it is known to attract hundreds of bird species. When Cooper saw an unleashed dog darting through the thick vegetation, the 57-year-old science editor and NYC Audubon Society board member told the dog's owner, a white woman by the name of Amy Cooper (no relation), that her dog needed to be leashed in accordance with the law. After an unsuccessful back-and-forth (she declined to leash the dog), a seemingly frustrated Christian Cooper began recording their interaction on his cell phone.

AMY: "Would you please stop [recording]. Sir, I'm asking you to stop."

CHRISTIAN: "Please don't come close to me." He repeats this several times.

She again asks him to stop recording and then threatens to call police.

CHRISTIAN: "Please call the cops. Please call the cops."

AMY: "I'm going to tell them there's an African American man threatening my life."

CHRISTIAN: "Please tell them whatever you like."

Amy (now on the phone to police): "I'm sorry, I'm in the Ramble, and there's a man, African American, he has a bicycle helmet. He is recording me and threatening me and my dog."

She repeats that he's African American and that he's threatening her and her dog.

Amy (now screaming into the phone): "I'm being threatened by a man in the Ramble. Please send the cops *immediately*."

When the video of the encounter went viral, many viewers accused Amy Cooper of putting Christian Cooper in needless danger when she falsely reported to 911 operators that he was "threatening" her. She had also repeatedly invoked his race, and in doing so, had perhaps intentionally appealed to societal stereotypes about Black men as aggressors. The recording was important because it allowed police to see what actually transpired in their confrontation, but even more so, it showcased how African Americans and other people of color are confronted with racism even when engaging in activities as mundane as bird-watching. A second 911 call by Amy Cooper was disclosed in court later that same year that revealed that she had also falsely accused him of trying to assault her.

Though some may see the aforementioned incident as an aberration, a 2020 *Washington Post* interview with Walter Kitundu suggests that Christian Cooper's experience was no anomaly. Kitundu is a recipient of a MacArthur genius grant, a Carnegie Hall performer, an inventor, a photographer, and, like Christian Cooper, an African American bird-watching enthusiast. He told the *Washington Post* that when out photographing birds, white people have called police on him so many times that he finally resorted to making a sign to explain his hobby. It is his way of keeping himself safe.

Though substantial progress has been made in the United States over the years, the experiences of Cooper and Kitundu suggest that much work remains. This final chapter examines where the United States is currently positioned in terms of race relations. Undoubtedly, America has come a long way from the flagrant and overt racism regularly observed during the slavery and Jim Crow eras and, for many Americans today, even the thought of holding personal biases is perceived as taboo and distressing. Nonetheless, every person likely possesses biases. Question 33, however, considers the question, "Can a person hold racial biases without even knowing it?" This entry draws on social experiments and empirical studies to look at whether biases can operate at the subconscious level—even in "good" people who pride themselves on their egalitarian attitudes. Finally, Question 34 asks, "Did the election of Barack Obama in 2008 mark the beginning of a new 'post-racial' America?"—in other words, is race mostly irrelevant and unimportant in American society today? The entire book essentially answers this final question, though this entry takes a more focused look at the current state of race relations in the United States and, in doing so, also discusses the differing perceptions of race relations by race—for instance, whites and Blacks see race relations in the United States quite differently. This entry also draws on empirical research to investigate the belief by some whites that they experience just as much, or perhaps even more, discrimination than do people of color in twenty-first-century United States.

Q33. CAN A PERSON HOLD RACIAL BIASES WITHOUT EVEN KNOWING IT?

Answer: Yes. Though many people possess explicit biases (biases that they are well aware they hold), they can also hold implicit biases (biases unknown to them that operate outside of their conscious control). People of all races can hold implicit biases, and this is important to know because these biases affect their judgments of and interactions with others—all without their even realizing it.

The Facts: Speaking on education at a town hall meeting in Des Moines, Iowa, in 2019, then presidential candidate Joe Biden told a crowd of mostly Asian and Latinx voters, "Poor kids are just as bright, and just as talented, as white kids." He paused momentarily and then quickly added, "[As] wealthy kids, Black kids, Asian kids," likely in an attempt to repair his initial comment, which implicitly (or perhaps not so implicitly) equated people of color with poverty; his original words also completely discounted white poverty. Some critics ridiculed his comments as racist, though his campaign manager said he merely "misspoke" and emphasized that Biden had a strong, decades-long record on civil rights (Stracqualursi 2019). But is it possible for a person who has supported civil rights and racial equality in his political career to also hold racial biases without even knowing it? According to more than two decades of research, yes.

All people (of all races) arguably hold biases. Some biases may be explicit—prejudicial attitudes that individuals knowingly hold about particular groups of people (such as those based on race, gender, sexuality, religion, nationality, and so on). For example, in 2005, Lawrence Summers, then president of Harvard University, came under fire for claiming that there were fewer women in science and math professions because of innate biological differences between genders (Dillon 2005). In other words, regarding STEM disciplines, he claimed that men are smarter than women. Because he knowingly held (and perhaps still holds) this attitude, this is an example of an explicit bias.

In addition to explicit biases, Mahzarin Banaji and Anthony Green-wald, authors of *Blindspot: Hidden Biases of Good People* (2013), argue that people can also hold implicit biases. *Implicit biases*, also termed *unconscious biases* or *subconscious biases*, refer to prejudices that are unknown to individuals; they are biases that exist outside of conscious awareness and control. These biases can even be found in "good people"—people who have the best of intentions—such as those who pride themselves on their egalitarian attitudes. Thus, while Joe Biden may or may not hold explicit biases about children of color, his subconscious racial biases arguably inadvertently surfaced in his unscripted comments.

A 2010 social experiment from the popular television show *What Would You Do?* illustrates implicit bias. With the help of hidden cameras, the show's producers set up a scene of a male teen (who was actually a paid actor) appearing to steal a bike in the middle of a public park in Portland, Oregon. They equipped him with bolt cutters, a chain saw, and a hammer, and they wanted to see how onlookers would react to seeing a "burglary" in broad daylight—would they simply pass by or intervene? Most notably, the show's producers wanted to see whether the public's response would differ depending on whether the teen actor was white or Black. It did.

When the actor was white, people often walked by without comment. A few stopped and stared or asked him whether the bike belonged to him; if he claimed the bike as his own (he said he "lost his key"), they generally took him at his word and continued on their way. In fact, of the hundred or so people who passed by, only two actually tried to stop him. By contrast, when the actor was Black, most onlookers stopped. People congregated in large groups around him, pulled out their cell phones and snapped his photo for evidence, removed his tools, yelled at him, and even called 911. Afterward, when stopped by the show's host and asked whether the teen's color had anything to do with their responses, most people said "no" and claimed that they would have stopped the teen even if he was white. However, this clearly was not the case. Some bystanders may have possessed explicit biases about Black teens that provoked their angry reactions, though others arguably held implicit biases that they did not realize they had: they may have sincerely believed that skin color had nothing to do with their responses, yet the widely different reactions to the Black and white actors indicated otherwise.

In 1998, psychologists Anthony Greenwald, Debbie McGhee, and Jordan Schwartz introduced the Implicit Association Test (IAT) to measure implicit bias. People can take the test online through Harvard University to find out whether they have a slight, moderate, or strong preference for white people or Black people. The test is useful because researchers cannot simply ask people whether they have implicit biases. Given that these biases operate at the subconscious level, people do not know. Thus, to uncover people's implicit biases, the IAT presents test takers with a seemingly simple computer task: they must associate concepts (such as "Black" or "white") with evaluations (such as "good" or "bad") or stereotypes (such as "smart" or "dangerous"). To determine whether people have implicit biases, the test measures how quickly people associate the concepts. According to the test's creators, if one is consistently quicker to link "white" with positive concepts than "Black" with positive concepts, for instance, then he or she has some degree of implicit bias in favor of white people. The IAT is not without criticism (Landy 2008), though it has been widely used by researchers to assess implicit bias for more than two decades.

If these biases are at the subconscious level, why does this matter? According to scientists, it matters because subconscious biases inadvertently affect verbal and nonverbal behavior toward others. Our implicit biases determine how we react to others and influence our body language, interactions, and judgments. Those with negative implicit biases toward Black people, for example, may unknowingly smile less, stiffen, avoid eye contact, keep a distance, move away, pull their purses closer, or even cross to the other side of the street when nearing a Black person. Implicit biases may also affect the shoot/don't shoot decisions of police officers, choices made by politicians regarding where and in what communities to make budget cuts, grades and awards given by teachers, recommendations to gifted programs by teachers, punishments by school administrators, hiring and promotion decisions by employers, medical treatment by physicians, and so on. The following are a few examples of studies utilizing the IAT that find that implicit bias clearly affects behavior (see Rudman's 2008 review):

- A 2001 study found that white college students who showed an implicit bias for whiteness were less friendly in their interactions with Black peers—they smiled less, made fewer positive comments, and showed greater discomfort.
- A 2003 study found that Black respondents who showed an implicit bias for whiteness were more likely to choose a white partner over a Black one when assigned an intellectually challenging task.
- A 2003 study found that whites who showed an implicit bias toward whiteness were quicker to judge Black faces as angry than white faces

when presented photographs of Black and white faces in sequential stages of the onset and dissolution of anger.

- A 2006 study showed that whites who had an implicit stereotype that Black people are more physical and less mentally engaged than whites rated Black essay writers lower than white essay writers—even though the essays were the same.
- A 2007 study found that doctors who showed an implicit bias for whiteness were more likely to recommend effective treatment for white rather than Black cardiac patients.
- A 2008 study observed that people who held an implicit bias that automatically linked Black people with weapons were more likely to shoot unarmed Blacks than unarmed whites in a video game simulation.

Our implicit biases, though subconscious, matter. They shape our judgments of others and affect the ways in which we interact with the people around us. Having implicit biases does not make you a bad person; rather, they make you human. Everyone has them. However, recognizing your implicit biases is an important first step to reducing their effects.

FURTHER READING

Banaji, Mahzarin, and Anthony Greenwald. 2013. *Blindspot: Hidden Biases of Good People*. New York: Bantam Books.

Boyes, Alice. 2015. "6 Ways to Overcome Your Biases for Good." *Psychology Today*, August 20.

Dillon, Sam. 2005. "Harvard Chief Defends His Talk on Women." *New York Times*, January 18.

Landy, F. J. 2008. "Stereotypes, Bias, and Personnel Decisions: Strange and Stranger." *Industrial and Organizational Psychology: Perspectives on Science and Practice* 1(4): 379–392.

Rudman, Laurie. 2008. "The Validity of the Implicit Association Test Is a Scientific Certainty." *Industrial and Organizational Psychology* 1: 426–429.

Stracqualursi, Veronica. 2019. "Joe Biden's Campaign Says He Misspoke When He Said 'Poor Kids' Are Just as Bright as 'White Kids.'" CNN, August 11.

Tropp, Linda, and Rachel D. Godsil. 2015. "Overcoming Implicit Bias and Racial Anxiety." *Psychology Today*, January 23.

What Would You Do? 2010. Retrieved on November 30, 2020, at https://www.youtube.com/watch?v=8ABRlWybBqM.

Q34. DID THE ELECTION OF BARACK OBAMA IN 2008 MARK THE BEGINNING OF A NEW "POST-RACIAL" AMERICA?

Answer: No. Though perhaps a noble ideal, America is not post-racial. The legacy of past racism continues to affect contemporary life, and research clearly shows that present-day racism persists. Opinion polls further reveal that most Americans recognize that race relations in the United States are a major problem, and many believe that race relations have become worse since January 2017, when Donald Trump succeeded Barack Obama as president. A spring 2019 Pew Research poll, for example, found that 56 percent of respondents felt that President Trump had made American race relations worse (15 percent felt that he had made progress in improving race relations) (Lopez 2019). One interesting caveat is that despite mounting empirical evidence to the contrary, many white Americans believe that they face more discrimination today than other racial groups. However, no known data support this belief.

The Facts: When Barack Obama was elected president in 2008, becoming the first Black president in American history, many hailed his victory as evidence of a new "post-racial America." The term *post-racial* refers to the belief that the United States has transcended race. It is the idea that we, as a nation, have finally moved into a new era—one in which race no longer has real relevance or meaning. In 2010, for example, author John McWhorter claimed that "America is post-racial," writing that "when it comes to race, Obama's first year [of presidency] has shown us again and again that race does not matter in America the way it used to. We've come more than a mere long way—we're almost there." But is the United States truly post-racial?

While many Americans believe that Obama's political victory was proof that the nation and its people had transcended race, others bristle at the idea. Author Ta-Nehisi Coates claims that there is no post-racial America, writing in 2015 that "the United States needs more than a good president to erase centuries of violence." Other observers emphasize that while Obama's 2008 victory and his reelection to a second term in 2012 were major landmarks in American history, significant socioeconomic disparities persist between racial and ethnic groups in the United States. In addition, opinion polls suggest that racial tensions may have actually risen across much of the United States during the Trump presidency, which critics contend was characterized by numerous instances in which

Trump had engaged in "race-baiting"—inciting racial hatred and hostility through the use of explicit stereotypes and coded language for political advantage (coded language used by politicians to their supporters are also called *dog whistles*). Trump has repeatedly denied these charges.

To understand race in the United States today, both past and present-day racism must be examined. Current inequalities observed between racial groups did not develop in a social vacuum and cannot be understood without fully understanding the country's deep-rooted history of racism— including that of enslavement, Jim Crow segregation, mass violence against people of color (including against African Americans, Native Americans, and Latinx Americans), the removal of Native Americans to reservations, the forced assimilation of Native children, the violent expulsion of people of color (e.g., Blacks, Mexicans, and Asians) from cities and towns across the nation, Depression-era repatriations of people of Mexican ancestry to Mexico (many of whom were American-born U.S. citizens), disenfranchisement of people of color, internment of Japanese Americans during World War II (most of whom were American-born U.S. citizens), racist federal housing policies, and so on. Moreover, though many Americans imagine this racist history as "so long ago," it was not. The United States is a relatively young nation, and these atrocities have plagued much of its short history. Regarding African Americans, some examples include the following: As a group, they were enslaved longer than they have lived free in the United States (200 years enslaved vs. 155 years free as of 2020); some living today have parents and grandparents who survived the total obliteration of their communities by white mobs (for more information, see Q12); some personally remember when they could not vote, serve on juries, or hold public office; and many remember growing up sitting in the backs of buses and trains, drinking from "colored only" water fountains, and being excluded from businesses, public spaces, and schools deemed "white only." Further, many American universities refused to admit Black students until the 1960s, and the last documented lynching of a Black man was as late as 1981. In short, the nation's cruel and violent history of systemic racism is held in the memories of Americans still living today.

Further, racism still exists. In addition to the residual effects of historical racism, there is *present-day* systemic racism across American institutions—including, for example, in health care (see Q16), housing (Q11 and Q12), education (Q13 and Q14), work (Q15), banking and lending (Q17), criminal justice (Q18, Q19, and Q20), and media (Q23). An extensive and expanding body of research reveals persistent disparities in the treatment of and outcomes for white Americans as compared to all other racial groups. Americans of color are disadvantaged in just about every aspect of American life—this is particularly true not only for African Americans and Native Americans but also for Latinx Americans and Asian Americans. Thus, while some people argue that we live in a "post-racial" society, the well-documented unequal treatment of Americans of color as compared to white Americans across most, if not all, institutions indicates otherwise.

Moreover, according to opinion polls, most Americans agree that race remains problematic in American society. A 2018 NBC News poll found that nearly all Americans (94 percent) agreed that racism exists in the United States (Arenge, Perry, and Clark 2018). The majority (64 percent) saw race relations as a "major problem," and almost half (45 percent) believed that race relations in the United States are getting worse (Scott 2018). Perceptions of worsening race relations have been attributed to several factors. For one, many Americans blame Donald Trump, asserting that, during his presidency, his rhetoric was particularly divisive and xenophobic. A 2017 poll, for example, found that most Americans, 6 in 10, believe that Trump has worsened race relations in the United States since his election. For example, he publicly referred to Mexican immigrants as rapists and criminals; Haitians as all having AIDS; undocumented immigrants as "animals"; immigrants from Haiti, El Salvador, and African nations as arriving from "shithole" countries; low-income Americans moving into suburban communities as "invaders"; kneeling professional athletes (who do so to protest police brutality against African Americans) as "very nasty" and sons of "B—"; and the COVID-19 virus as the "China virus" and the "Kung Flu," to name some examples.

A 2020 poll conducted by NPR/PBS NewsHour/Marist found that two-thirds of those surveyed believed that Trump had increased racial tensions since the murder of George Floyd by Minneapolis police (Montanaro 2020). Given that more than 60 percent of Americans viewed the protests as legitimate, his repeated negative characterizations of protestors was perceived by many as problematic and divisive.

Another possible factor in American perceptions that race relations are worsening is the ubiquity of cell phones with camera and video functions. These handheld devices have been used to capture everything from day-to-day slights and harassment faced by Americans of color to egregious instances of police brutality. Relatedly, the ease of sharing these videos and images on social media likely also contributes to worsening perceptions. Moreover, videos that "go viral" after being uploaded on popular social media platforms (e.g., YouTube, Twitter, and Facebook) are sometimes picked up by traditional media outlets, allowing for even greater viewership and public attention.

For instance, a CNN news story in 2018 titled "Living while Black" assembled a list of routine activities for which police were called that year on African Americans (Griggs 2018). The list included a white woman who called police on a 12-year-old Black boy who, when mowing a neighbor's lawn, accidently mowed a strip of her yard. In another example from that same year, a group of white men called 911 multiple times to report five Black women for allegedly golfing too slowly. In both incidents, the people involved or onlookers pulled out their cellphones to record the encounters; had they not done so, these incidents, like many others that happen daily across the United States, would have likely gone undocumented and unseen by anyone outside those directly involved. Other examples that year include police being called on Black people (including Black children) for: waiting for friends at Starbucks without ordering, operating a lemonade stand without a permit, barbequing at a park, working out a gym, campaigning door to door, moving into an apartment, shopping for prom clothes, napping in a university common room, asking for directions, leaving an Airbnb, redeeming a coupon, selling bottled water on a sidewalk, eating lunch on a college campus, riding in a car with a white grandmother, babysitting two white children, working as a home inspector, working as a firefighter, helping a homeless man, delivering newspapers, swimming in a pool, shopping while pregnant, driving with leaves on a car, and trying to cash a paycheck (for more details, see Griggs 2018). Most of these incidents were documented by cameras and shared online. Perhaps race relations have not worsened but, rather, camera phones and social media have made discrimination more visible.

Perceptions of Racial Bias and Race Relations Differ by Race

Even though most Americans say race relations are generally bad, beliefs about racial bias and race relations differ widely by race. According to a 2019 Pew Research Center opinion poll, more Blacks than whites believe that race relations are generally bad, that President Trump has worsened race relations, that our country has not done enough to give equal rights to Black people and that discrimination is a major issue for Black Americans. More Blacks than whites also believe that they are treated less fairly than whites in police interactions, the criminal justice system, employment, stores and restaurants, and health care (Horowitz, Brown, and Cox 2019). See table 34.1 for a breakdown of the different perceptions of Black and white Americans.

Furthermore, even with the substantial body of evidence to the contrary, many white Americans believe that bias against white people is

Table 34.1 Perceptions of Race Relations by Race

Percent Saying . . .	Whites	Blacks
Race relations in the United States are generally bad.	56	71
Trump has made race relations worse.	49	73
Our country has not gone far enough in giving Blacks equal rights with whites.	37	78
Discrimination is a major obstacle for Black people.	54	84
Blacks are treated less fairly than whites in dealing with police.	63	84
Blacks are treated less fairly than whites by the criminal justice system.	61	87
Blacks are treated less fairly than whites in hiring, pay, and promotions.	44	82
Blacks are treated less fairly than whites when applying for a loan or mortgage.	38	74
Blacks are treated less fairly than whites in stores or restaurants.	37	70
Blacks are treated less fairly than whites when seeking medical treatment.	26	59

Source: Pew Research Center (Horowitz, Brown, and Cox [2019]).

more of a problem than bias against Black people (Sommers and Norton 2016) and that it is they who experience the most discrimination in today's America. A 2017 poll found that more than half of whites (55 percent) believe there is discrimination against whites today, though notably a much smaller percentage reported that they had ever experienced it personally: 19 percent believed they had been discriminated against when applying for jobs, 13 percent regarding equal pay and promotions, and 11 percent when applying to or while at college (Gonyea 2017). Even more "jarring," according to journalist Jamelle Bouie, is that nearly half of white millennials (48 percent of those aged 14 to 24 at the time of survey) reported that discrimination against white people is "as big of a problem" as discrimination against racial minorities (2014).

Poll data in the wake of the murder of George Floyd and the subsequent nationwide protests of his death, however, suggest that attitudes may be changing and that more white Americans are "awakening to long-standing societal discrimination against black people in the United States" (Tesler 2020). White attitudes regarding race appear to be liberalizing, but more research is needed to determine whether recognition of anti-Black discrimination will persist once Floyd's death (and similar instances of police brutality) fade from news headlines and collective memory. For example, white attitudes regarding race temporarily shifted after the 1968 assassination of Dr. Martin Luther King Jr. (i.e., they became more sympathetic to discrimination faced by Black people), but the effect faded over time. It remains to be seen whether whites' increased awareness of systemic racism toward Black people in the United States immediately following Floyd's death will prove similarly short-lived (Jackson 2020).

Additionally, Keith Payne of *Scientific American* (2019) notes that there is a growing number of experimental studies that directly examine the issue of racial bias. He writes that polls generally treat the question of discrimination "as a matter of opinion. . . . But the question of whether discrimination disadvantages whites or blacks is not really a matter of opinion. It is a factual question that can be answered by science. In fact, it has been." Payne points to experimental data that clearly show that persistent and widespread discrimination exists against racial minorities in America. Some examples include the following:

- Researchers listed iPods for sale on Craigslist and found that buyers were less likely to respond to listings that showed an iPod held by a Black hand than one held by a white hand—they received 13 percent fewer responses and 17 percent fewer offers (Doleac and Stein 2013).
- Researchers measured e-mail responses of 6,500 professors at more than 250 American universities. The messages, all well written and with identical content, were sent by "students" (in actuality, the researchers), who expressed interest in attending graduate school and requested a meeting. Researchers only varied the names attached to the e-mails (they used "white" names like Brad Anderson and Meredith Roberts or "Black" names like Lamar Washington and LaToya Brown). Other names included those associated with Latinx, Indian, and Chinese students. They found that faculty were significantly more responsive to e-mails from white males than to all other categories of students, and this was especially true for professors in higher-paying disciplines and private institutions (Milkman, Akinola, and Chugh 2015).

- Researchers in a Harvard study altered their names on Airbnb accounts (to present either a "white" or "Black" name) and tried to book rooms at 6,400 Airbnb listings across five American cities. They found that Airbnb hosts were significantly more likely (16 percent) to tell prospective Black renters that the listing had already been rented as compared to prospective white renters (Edelman, Luca, and Svirsky 2017).

These studies and others repeatedly find bias against Black Americans and other people of color, demonstrating that race still matters in American society. Further, Payne writes that "not a single study" to date has found antiwhite bias. Not one. This is not to say that individual whites never experience instances of discrimination, but that they, as a group, do not experience it at higher rates than people of color.

In sum, racial bias is real, discrimination persists, and racism remains an unfortunate reality in the twenty-first-century United States. Though the election of Barack Obama, the first Black president, was undoubtedly a watershed moment for America, the nation has a long way to go to realize a truly "post-racial" society.

FURTHER READING

Arenge, Andrew, Stephanie Perry, and Dartunorro Clark. 2018. "Poll: 64 Percent of Americans Say Racism Remains a Major Problem." NBC News, May 29.

Bouie, Jamelle. 2014. "Why Do Millennials Not Understand Racism?" Slate, May 16.

Coates, Ta-Nehisi. 2015. "There Is No Post-Racial America." *The Atlantic*, July/August.

Doleac, Jennifer L., and Luke C. D. Stein. 2013. "The Visible Hand: Race and Online Market Outcomes." *Economic Journal* 123(572): F469–492.

Edelman, Benjamin, Michael Luca, and Dan Svirsky. 2017. "Racial Discrimination in the Sharing Economy: Evidence from a Field Experiment." *American Economics Journal: Applied Economics* 9(2): 1–22.

Gonyea, Don. 2017. "Majority of White Americans Say They Believe Whites Face Discrimination." NPR, October 24.

Griggs, Brandon. 2018. "Living While Black: Here Are All the Routine Activities for Which Police Were Called on African-Americans This Year." CNN, December 28.

Horowitz, Juliana Menasce, Anna Brown, and Kiana Cox. 2019. "Race in America 2019." Pew Research Center, April 9.

Jackson, Reggie. 2020. "The Inevitability of a White Backlash to the George Floyd Protests." *Milwaukee Independent*, June 12.

Lopez, German. 2019. "Most Americans Agree Trump Has Made Race Relations Worse." Vox, April 9. https://www.vox.com/policy-and-politics/2019/4/9/18302159/trump-racism-race-relations-pew-survey.

McWhorter, John H. 2010. "It's Official: America Is 'Post-Racial' in the Age of Obama." TheGrio, January 14.

Milkman, Katherine L., Modupe Akinola, and Dolly Chugh. 2015. "What Happens Before? A Field Experiment Exploring How Pay and Representation Differentially Shape Bias on the Pathway into Organizations." *Journal of Applied Psychology* 100(6), 1678–1712.

Montanaro, Dominico. 2020. "Two-Thirds Think Trump Made Racial Tensions Worse after Floyd Was Killed." NPR, June 5.

Payne, Keith. 2019. "The Truth about Anti-White Discrimination." *Scientific American*, July 18.

Schermerhorn, Calvin. 2019. "Why the Racial Wealth Gap Persists, More Than 150 Years after Emancipation." *Washington Post*, June 19.

Scott, Eugene. 2017. "Race Relations under Trump: Majority of Americans Say He's Made Them Worse." *Washington Post*, December 19.

Scott, Eugene. 2018. "Most Americans Say Race Relations Are a Major Problem, but Few Discuss It with Friends and Family." *Washington Post*, May 31.

Sommers, Samuel, and Michael Norton. 2016. "White People Think Racism Is Getting Worse. Against White People." *Washington Post*, July 21.

Tesler, Michael. 2020. "The Floyd Protests Have Changed Public Opinion about Race and Policing. Here's the Data." *Washington Post*, June 9.

Index

About the Authors

Nikki Khanna, PhD, is an associate professor of sociology at the University of Vermont, where she regularly teaches courses on race relations in the United States. She is the author of *Biracial in America: Forming and Performing Racial Identity* (2011) and the editor of *Whiter: Asian American Women on Skin Color and Colorism* (2020).

Noriko Matsumoto, PhD, is a senior lecturer in the Department of Sociology at the University of Vermont, where she also teaches in the Critical Race and Ethnic Studies program. She is the author of *Beyond the City and the Bridge: East Asian Immigration in a New Jersey Suburb* (2018).